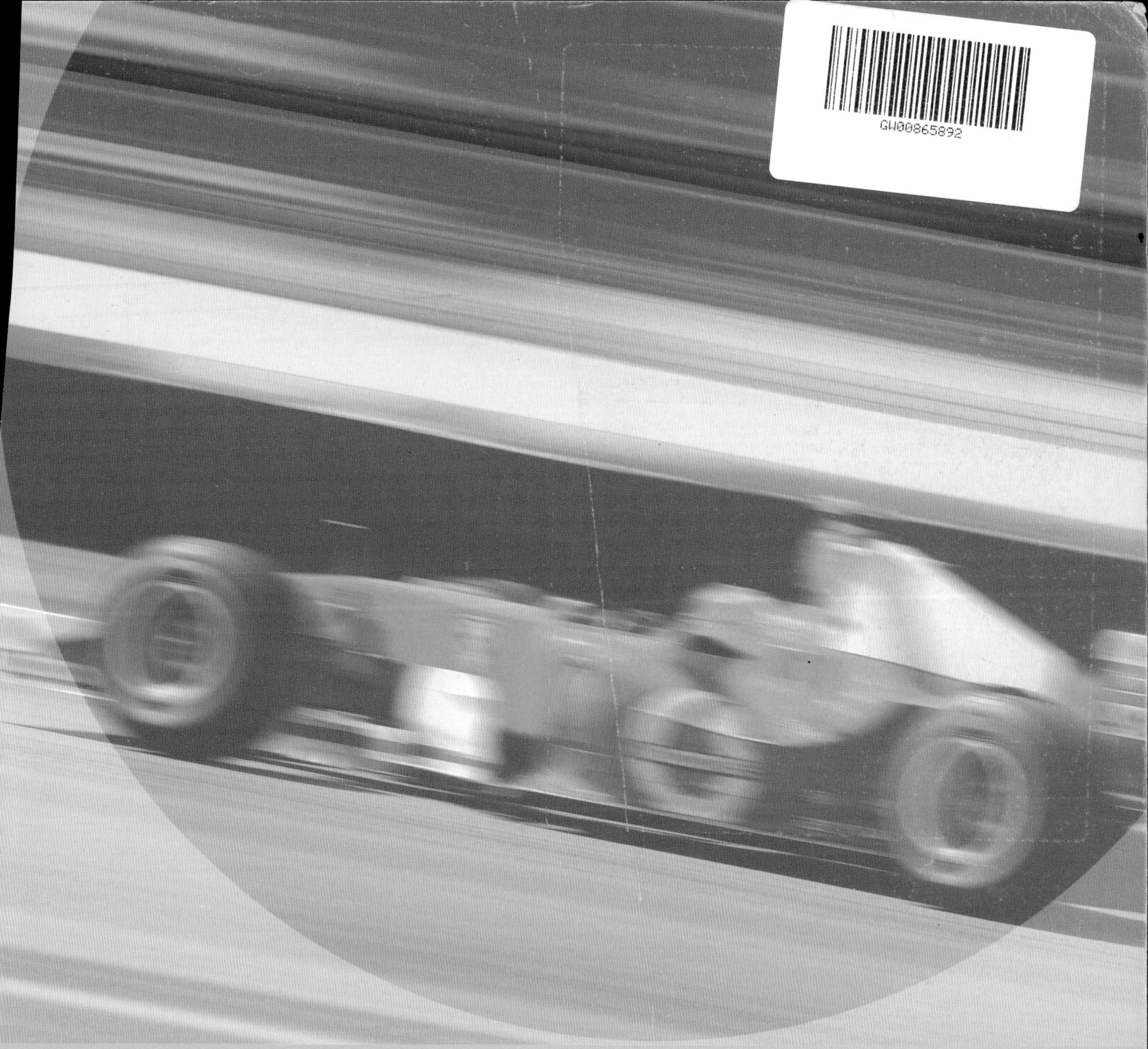

Na klar! 2

MICHAEL SPENCER AND ALAN WESSON
SERIES EDITOR: CLIVE BELL

Published in 2005 by:
Nelson Thornes Ltd
Delta Place
27 Bath Road
CHELTENHAM
GL53 7TH
United Kingdom

06 07 08 09 / 10 9 8 7 6 5 4 3 2

A catalogue record for this book is available from the British Library
ISBN 0 7487 9159 0

Illustrations by Gary Andrews, Mike Bastin, Mark Draisey, kja-artists.com, Angela Lumley, Mark Ruffle, Dave Russell, Mel Sharp (c/o Sylvie Poggio Artists Agency)

Page make-up by eMC Design, www.emcdesign.org.uk

Printed and bound in China by Midas Printing International

Welcome to Na klar! 2

- **Most pages have the following features to help you:**

Grammatik
Examples of how you put German words together to make sentences.

 **Lauter Laute:**
Practice of German sounds to improve your pronunciation and spelling.

A list of the key words and phrases you'll need to do the activities.

Strategie!
Tips to help you learn better and remember more.

Activities in which you'll listen to German.

Activities in which you'll practise speaking German with a partner.

Activities in which you'll practise reading and writing in German.

extra! **Activities which provide an extra challenge – have a go!**

- **The *Zusammenfassung* at the end of each unit lists the key words of the unit in German and English. Use it to look up any words you don't know!**

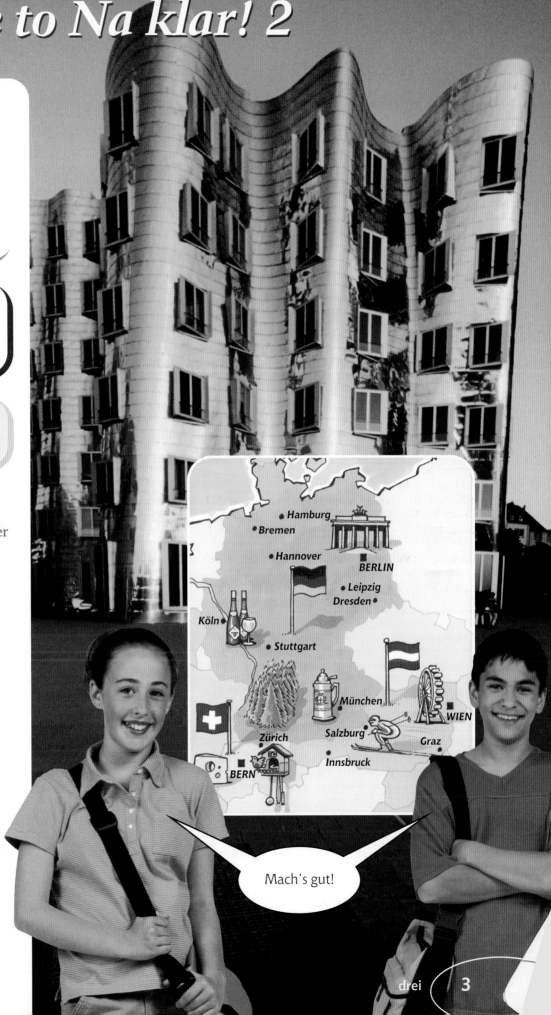

Hamburg
Bremen
Hannover
BERLIN
Leipzig
Dresden
Köln
Stuttgart
München
WIEN
Zürich
Salzburg
Graz
Innsbruck
BERN

Mach's gut!

Inhalt *Contents*

1 Ich über mich

1A Das mag ich!

- talk about what you like and prefer doing
- learn how to use the present tense of verbs
- learn the correct word order with *gern*, *lieber* and *am liebsten*

1 **Hör zu (1–4) und schreib Notizen!**

Beispiel: **1 Inge – fernsehen**

Ich gehe gern mit meinen Freundinnen Gabi und Frauke aus. Am liebsten gehen wir einkaufen, aber wir hören auch gern Popmusik. Meine Lieblingsband ist Red Hot Chili Peppers, aber Gabi und Frauke hören lieber Madonna. Ich mache nicht gern Hausaufgaben.

Bettina, 16, Augsburg

Jedes Wochenende gehe ich mit meiner Freundin Anneke aus. Wir segeln und kegeln gern und wir fahren noch lieber Rollschuh. Ich spiele am liebsten Fußball, aber ich schwimme nicht gern.

Matthias, 14, Dresden

Grammatik: present tense verbs

To make the present tense of a German verb, you use the following pronouns with these verb endings.

gehen – to go

*ich (geh)**e***	*wir (geh)**en***
*du (geh)**st***	*ihr (geh)**t***
*er/sie/es (geh)**t***	*sie/Sie (geh)**en***

Sometimes small changes are made to make the verbs easier to say, e.g. instead of *segelen* you say *segeln*, and some verbs have a vowel change in the second and third person singular forms. For example:

ich fahre	*ich sehe*	*ich lese*
du fährst	*du siehst*	*du liest*
er/sie/es fährt	*er/sie/es sieht*	*er/sie/es liest*

siehe Seite **143** >>

2 **Füll die Lücken mit der passenden Verbform aus!**

Beispiel: **1 Ich sehe gern fern.**

1. Ich (**sehen**) gern fern.
2. Ulf (**gehen**) mit seinen Freunden aus.
3. Wir (**spielen**) am Wochenende Fußball.
4. Wann (**gehen**) ihr einkaufen?
5. Renate (**lesen**) gern und (**spielen**) gern am Computer.
6. (**Fahren**) du am Wochenende Rollschuh?

3 a **Lies die Texte oben rechts!**

3 b **Beantworte die Fragen! Wer …?**

Beispiel: **1 Mika und Adrian**

1. … liest nicht gern?
2. … hört lieber Madonna?
3. … spielt am liebsten Fußball?
4. … geht gern aus?
5. … schwimmt nicht gern?

3 c **Beantworte jetzt folgende Fragen!**

Beispiel: **1 Sie gehen am liebsten einkaufen.**

1. Was machen Bettina und ihre Freundinnen am liebsten?
2. Was macht Bettina nicht gern?
3. Was machen Mika und Adrian nicht gern?
4. Was machen Mika und Adrian am liebsten?
5. Was machen Matthias und Anneke gern?

Wir sehen gern fern und wir gehen noch lieber ins Kino, aber wir lesen nicht gern. Am liebsten bleiben wir zu Hause und spielen am Computer. Manchmal gehen wir aus, oder wir reden über Computer.

Mika und Adrian (Brüder), 15 und 17, Frankfurt a. d. Oder

4 **Was macht ihr gern, nicht gern usw.? Macht Dialoge!**

Beispiel: **A** **Was machst du gern?**
B **Ich … gern …, aber ich … lieber/ am liebsten … .**
A **Und was machst du nicht gern?**
B **…**

Ich	sehe fern. kegele. gehe (mit Freunden) aus. segele. gehe ins Kino. fahre Rollschuh. lese. mache Hausaufgaben. spiele Fußball/ am Computer. schwimme. gehe einkaufen. höre Musik.

5 *extra!* **Stellt und beantwortet Fragen!**

Beispiel: **A** **Was macht Gisela am liebsten?**
B **Sie … .**
A **Und was macht sie nicht gern?**
B **…**
A **Was machen Harald und Kai …?**

1 Gisela  

2 Harald und Kai  

3 Ihr? Wir …  

Grammatik: *(nicht) gern, lieber, am liebsten*

When you want to say you like, don't like or prefer doing something, you use the words *gern*, *nicht gern*, *lieber* and *am liebsten*. They go **after** the verb.

*Was machst du **gern**?*
What do you like doing?

*Ich höre **gern** Musik.*
I like listening to music.

*Ich mache **nicht gern** Hausaufgaben.*
I don't like doing homework.

*Ich spiele **am liebsten** Fußball.*
I like playing football best of all.

If the verb is separable, the words for liking go after the main part of the verb and before the separable prefix.

*Ich sehe **lieber** fern.*
I prefer watching TV.

siehe Seite **146** >>

6 **Was machst du (nicht) gern usw.? Und deine Freunde/Freundinnen? Schreib etwa 30–40 Wörter! Benutze:**

manchmal | und | aber  | normalerweise | jedes Wochenende | oder

Beispiel: **Ich spiele gern Fußball, aber ich spiele lieber Tennis. Jedes Wochenende spiele ich Tischtennis, aber manchmal … . Meine Freundin Nicola … .**

7 *extra!* **Dein(e) Partner(in) überprüft. Wie ist die Wortstellung? Und wie sind die Verbendungen?**

Beispiel:

Am Wochenende **ich spiele** gern Fußball, aber meine zwei Brüder **kegelen** lieber. …

1B Das war so toll!

- talk about what you have done in the past
- say when you did it and what it was like
- learn to use the perfect tense with *haben*

1 **Hör zu und lies die Texte (1–4) rechts mit!**

2 **Hör noch einmal zu! Welches Bild passt zu welcher Person aus Übung 1?**

Beispiel: **a Ahmed**

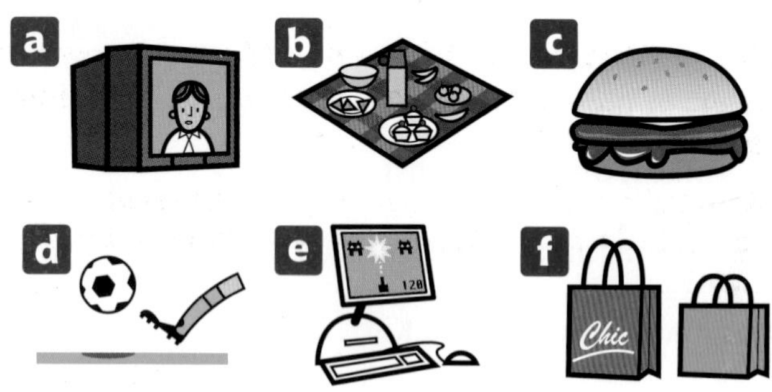

3 **Lies die Texte noch einmal! Richtig, falsch oder nicht im Text?**

Beispiel: **1 falsch**

1. Alex hat Fußball gespielt.
2. Trudi hat mit ihren Freundinnen im Park gegessen.
3. Das hat Trudi viel Spaß gemacht.
4. Bernd hat Probleme mit seinem Computer gehabt.
5. Er hat einen Chatroom besucht.

4 **A ist eine der Personen aus Übung 1 und sagt, was er/sie gemacht hat. B macht das Buch zu und sagt, wer das ist. Tauscht Rollen!**

Beispiel: **A Ich habe Fußball und Tennis gespielt.**
B Du bist Ahmed.
A Falsch. Ich bin Trudi.

5 **Füll die Lücken aus!**

Beispiel: **1 Was habt ihr gemacht?**

1. Was ________ ihr gemacht?
2. Wir ________ Musik gehört.
3. Hast du am Computer ________ ?
4. Das hat viel Spaß ________ .
5. Ich ________ nichts Interessantes ________ .

Was hast du am Wochenende gemacht?

1 Ich habe den Morgen in der Stadtmitte verbracht. Ich habe nichts Interessantes in den Läden gefunden. Danach habe ich in einem Hamburger-Restaurant gegessen, aber der Hamburger war ekelhaft.
Alex, 15

2 Ich habe den Nachmittag im Park verbracht und ich habe Fußball und Tennis gespielt. Ich habe ein Picknick mit meinen Freundinnen gemacht und wir haben Musik gehört.
Trudi, 16

3 Ich habe an meinem Computer gespielt. Es hat viel Spaß gemacht und ich habe einige neue Computerspiele heruntergeladen. Außerdem habe ich meinen Lieblingschatroom besucht.
Bernd, 14

4 Ich habe den ganzen Tag zu Hause verbracht und habe ferngesehen. Ich habe eine Lottosendung, eine Talkshow und zwei Reality-TV-Shows gesehen. Ich habe die Sendungen alle furchtbar gefunden!
Ahmed, 17

Grammatik: the perfect tense

For most verbs in German, you use the present tense of *haben* with the past participle of the verb you want to use to say what you have done – the perfect tense. The participle goes at the end of the sentence or clause.

Most past participles (but not verbs that start with **ver-** and **be-**) begin with **ge-**. Participles of weak verbs usually end in **-t**, but participles of strong verbs have a vowel change and end in **-en**.

Separable verb participles include **-ge-** between the separable prefix and the 'doing' part of the participle.

haben	**past participle**
ich habe	*gespielt*
du hast	*gemacht*
er/sie/es hat	*gehört*
wir haben	*gegessen*
ihr habt	*gefunden*
sie/Sie haben	*besucht*
	ferngesehen
	heruntergeladen
	verbracht

siehe Seite **144** >>

6 **Trag die Tabelle in dein Heft ein! Hör dann zu und füll die Tabelle aus!**

Beispiel:

	Samstagmorgen	Samstagnachmittag	Samstagabend
Bernd	Fußball		
Silke			
Rita			

Hamburger Hausaufgaben im Bett
im Park Einkäufe Computer Fußball fernsehen

7 **Was habt ihr gestern/letztes Wochenende (usw.) gemacht? Macht Dialoge – aber manchmal sagst du nicht die Wahrheit! Dein(e) Partner(in) muss sagen, ob du lügst!**

Beispiel: **A** Gestern habe ich den Morgen im Park verbracht.
B Du lügst! Du hast den Morgen in der Schule verbracht!
A Ja, richtig!

8 **Was hast du letztes Wochenende gemacht? Schreib 50 Wörter!**

Beispiel: Ich habe den Morgen im Bett verbracht, und dann habe ich … .

9 extra! **Schreib Sätze und benutze folgende Verben im Perfekt!**

Beispiel: Letztes Wochenende habe ich … .

fernsehen (*to watch TV*)
finden (*to find*)
kaufen (*to buy*)
kochen (*to cook*)
Karten spielen (*to play cards*)
Trompete spielen (*to play the trumpet*)
Klavier spielen (*to play the piano*)
tanzen (*to dance*)
verbringen (*to spend time*)

Strategie! ***Making your writing more interesting***

You can make your writing more interesting by adding connectives, opinions, extra information about when you did things, etc. If you do this, it will stop your writing reading like a shopping list and give it a bit of life! Below are some expressions you might want to use.

am Samstag (usw.)	*on Saturday (etc.)*
am Morgen (usw.)	*in the morning (etc.)*
gestern	*yesterday*
erstens	*first(ly)*
dann	*then*
danach	*after that*
Es war toll/prima.	*It was great.*
Es war furchtbar.	*It was awful.*
Es war langweilig.	*It was boring.*
Es hat viel Spaß gemacht.	*It was good fun.*

1C Ich bin zu Hause geblieben

- say where you went and what you did
- give opinions in the past tense
- learn to use the perfect tense with *sein*

Hallo, Lutz. Wie war das Wochenende?
Furchtbar! Ich bin mit meiner Mutter in den Supermarkt gegangen. Es war so langweilig. Und du, Martina?

1 a **Hör zu und lies die Bildgeschichte mit! Wer hat was gemacht?**

Beispiel: **Lutz – e**

a 

b 

c 

d 

e 

f 

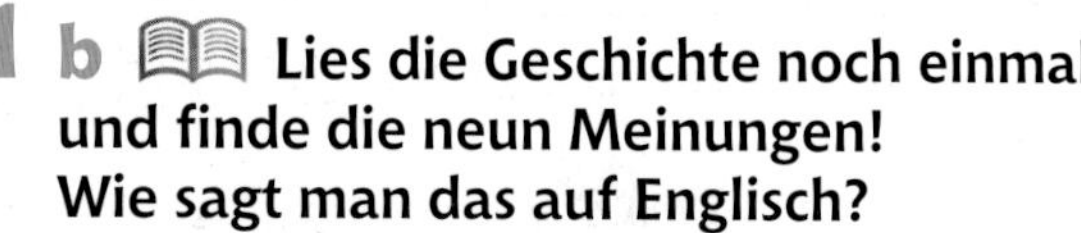

1 b **Lies die Geschichte noch einmal und finde die neun Meinungen! Wie sagt man das auf Englisch?**

Beispiel: **furchtbar – *terrible***

Strategie! ***How to say 'was' or 'wasn't'***

To say what something **was** (or **wasn't**) like, use *war*:

Es ***war*** *prima/(ziemlich/sehr/ganz/nicht) teuer usw.*

2 **Hör zu und füll die Lücken mit Wörtern aus den Kästchen aus!**

Beispiel: **1 Sabine ist Rad gefahren. Es war deprimierend.**

1. Sabine ist ________ . Es war ________ .
2. Werner ist ________ gegangen. Es war ________ .
3. Willem ist ________ . Es war sehr ________ .
4. Nuray ist ________ geblieben. Er war sehr ________ .
5. Lotte ist ________ gegangen. Der Film war ________ .
6. Sven ist ________ gegangen. Es war sehr ________ .

einkaufen	anstrengend
ins Kino	deprimierend
Rad gefahren	langweilig
schwimmen	müde
Ski gefahren	nicht schlecht
zu Hause	teuer

Grammatik: the perfect with *sein*

To make the perfect tense of some verbs (mostly verbs of movement like *gehen* or *fahren*), you use the verb *sein* instead of *haben* with the past participle. As before, some of the participles end in **-t** and some have a vowel change and end in **-en**. You will have to learn these individually.

sein		**past participle**
ich bin		*in den Supermarkt gegangen*
du bist		*ins Kino gegangen*
er/sie/es ist		*einkaufen gegangen*
wir sind	*(nicht)*	*schwimmen gegangen*
ihr seid		*Rad gefahren*
sie/Sie sind		*Ski gefahren*
		nach (Klosters) gefahren
		(zu Hause) geblieben

siehe Seite **144** >>

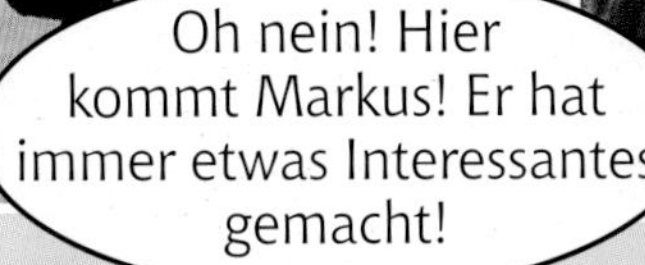

Ich bin zu Hause geblieben. Es war ganz deprimierend.
Oh nein! Hier kommt Markus! Er hat immer etwas Interessantes gemacht!
Hi Markus! Hast du ein gutes Wochenende gehabt?
Ja, sicher! Am Samstag bin ich Rad gefahren. Es war anstrengend, aber ziemlich interessant. Dann bin ich schwimmen gegangen. Es war toll! Und am Abend sind wir ins Kino gegangen. Der Film war nicht schlecht.
Und am Sonntag?
Wir sind nach Klosters gefahren und ich bin Ski gefahren. Es war sehr teuer, aber es war prima!
2005
Wir gehen ins Café. Kommst du mit?
Es tut mir Leid, ich habe kein Geld mehr.
Also, tschüs!

3 **Ihr seid jetzt die Jugendlichen aus Übung 2. Macht Dialoge!**

Beispiel: **A (Lotte), was hast du am Wochenende gemacht?**
B (Ich bin ins Kino gegangen.)
A Wie war es?
B (Der Film war langweilig.) Und du, (Sabine), was hast du gemacht?
A …

4 **Lies die E-Mail und beantworte die Fragen! Überprüfe dann die Antworten!**

Beispiel: **1 Manchmal isst er bei Pizzaman.**

1 Wo isst Alex manchmal am Wochenende?
2 Was macht er meistens?
3 Was gibt es jetzt beim Einkaufszentrum?
4 Was hat Alex letztes Wochenende gemacht?
5 Was hat es pro Person gekostet?

```
An: Peter Walker
Von: Alex Meißner
Betr.: letztes Wochenende

Hi, Peter!

Was machst du normalerweise am Wochenende? Manchmal essen wir bei Pizzaman, aber meistens bleiben wir zu Hause und sehen fern. Weil wir nur einen Fernseher im Hause haben, ist das oft langweilig.

Aber letztes Wochenende sind wir Ski gefahren! Beim Einkaufszentrum gibt es eine künstliche Outdoor-Skipiste. Es war toll – und es hat nur drei Euro pro Person gekostet!

Was hast du letztes Wochenende gemacht? Und wie war es?

Tschüs – bis bald!

Alex
```

Strategie! ***Meanings in context***

Some German words have more than one meaning! What are the two meanings of *Hause* and *bei* in the text above? And how many meanings does *fahren* have?

5 **A fragt B, was er/sie normalerweise am Wochenende macht und was er/sie letztes Wochenende gemacht hat. Wie war es? Macht Dialoge!**

6 **Schreib jetzt eine Antwort auf die E-Mail!**

7 **Lauter Laute: u, ü**

- Hör zu und sprich nach!

Gudrun, Susanna und Uschi sind im Jugendzentrum und es ist furchtbar! Rüdiger, Jürgen und Günter sind müde und lügen über ihre Ausflüge!

1D Ich bin in die Stadt gegangen

- understand a poem
- write new verses of a poem

1 a Hör zu und wiederhole das Gedicht!

1 b Lies das Gedicht noch einmal und sieh dir die Wörter unten an! Welches Wort passt jeweils nicht?

1 Strophe 1: Stadt – Kaffee – Toilette – Pommes frites
2 Strophe 2: Hamburger – Tee – riesiger Burger – nichts
3 Strophe 3: Einkaufen – Geschäft – Geld – Bank

1 c Kannst du das Gedicht weiterschreiben? Die Wörter im Kasten können dir helfen.

Beispiel: **Ich bin in den Park gegangen Das war so, so toll!**

in den Park
viel Sport treiben
Fußball hier, Tennis da
kleines/großes Spiel
sehr müde

in die Schule
sehr schlecht essen
kotzen hier/da
kleines/großes Kotzen
furchtbar

zum Zahnarzt
Zahnschmerzen haben
Schmerzen hier/da
kleines/großes Schmerzen
nach Hause

Ich bin in die Stadt gegangen
Das war so, so toll!
Dort hab' ich 'ne Tasse Kaffee getrunken
Das war so, so toll!
Kaffee hier, Kaffee da,
Kaffee überall!
Kleiner Kaffee, großer Kaffee,
riesiger Kaffee!
Dann auf die Toilette!

Ich bin in die Stadt gegangen
Das war so, so toll!
Dort hab' ich 'nen Hamburger gegessen
Das war so, so toll!
Hamburger hier, Hamburger da,
Hamburger überall!
Kleiner Burger, großer Burger,
riesiger Burger!
Jetzt kann ich nichts mehr tun!

Ich bin in die Stadt gegangen
Das war so, so toll!
Dort bin ich einkaufen gegangen
Das war so, so toll!
Einkaufen hier, Einkaufen da, Einkaufen überall!
Kleines Geschäft, großes Geschäft, riesiges Geschäft!
Jetzt muss ich auf die Bank!

Zusammenfassung

Freizeit	***Free time***
mit Freunden ausgehen	*to go out with friends*
ins Kino gehen	*to go to the cinema*
am Computer spielen	*to play on the computer*
einkaufen gehen	*to go shopping*
kegeln	*to bowl/go bowling*
segeln	*to sail/go sailing*
Rollschuh fahren	*to go roller-skating*
schwimmen	*to swim*
Musik hören	*to listen to music*
Hausaufgaben machen	*to do homework*

Wie oft? Wann?	***How often? When?***
am Wochenende	*at the weekend*
jedes Wochenende	*every weekend*
manchmal	*sometimes*
meistens	*usually*
normalerweise	*normally*
gestern	*yesterday*
am Samstag	*on Saturday*
am Morgen	*in the morning*
am Nachmittag	*in the afternoon*
am Abend	*in the evening*

Letztes Wochenende	***Last weekend***
Ich habe (Du hast usw.) …	*I (You, etc.) …*
(Fußball) gespielt.	*played (football).*
ferngesehen.	*watched TV.*
(den Morgen) in … verbracht.	*spent (the morning) in … .*
Einkäufe gemacht.	*went shopping.*
einen Hamburger gegessen.	*ate a hamburger.*
ein Picknick gemacht.	*had a picnic.*
Musik gehört.	*listened to music.*
am Computer gespielt.	*played on the computer.*
Computerspiele heruntergeladen.	*downloaded computer games.*
einen Chatroom besucht.	*visited a chatroom.*
(nichts) gefunden.	*found (nothing).*
eine Reality-TV-Show gesehen.	*watched a reality TV show.*
Es hat viel Spaß gemacht.	*It was a lot of fun.*

Ich bin (Du bist usw.) …	*I (You, etc.) …*
(zu Hause) geblieben.	*stayed (at home).*
ins Kino gegangen.	*went to the cinema.*
nach (Klosters) gefahren.	*went to (Klosters).*
einkaufen gegangen.	*went shopping.*
schwimmen gegangen.	*went swimming.*
Rad gefahren.	*went cycling.*
Ski gefahren.	*went skiing.*

Wie war es?	***How was it?***
Es war …	*It was …*
deprimierend.	*depressing.*
anstrengend.	*tiring.*
langweilig.	*boring.*
interessant.	*interesting.*
furchtbar.	*terrible.*
prima.	*great.*
toll.	*brilliant.*
nicht schlecht.	*not bad.*
teuer.	*dear, expensive.*

Grammatik:

★ *(nicht) gern, lieber, am liebsten*: to say what you like doing, prefer doing, or like doing best, you use *gern, lieber* or *am liebsten*.

*Ich spiele **gern** Fußball.*	I like playing football.
*Ich sehe **lieber** fern.*	I prefer watching TV.
*Ich lese **am liebsten**.*	I like reading best of all.

★ The perfect with *haben* or *sein*: to say what you have done in German, use the verb *haben* or *sein* with the past participle of the verb you wish to use. The past participle goes at the end of the clause or sentence.

ich habe … (gespielt)	*ich bin … (gegangen)*
du hast …	*du bist …*
er/sie/es hat …	*er/sie/es ist …*
wir haben …	*wir sind …*
ihr habt …	*ihr seid …*
sie/Sie haben …	*sie/Sie sind …*

siehe Seite **144, 146** ➤➤

Strategie!

★ Make your writing more interesting by adding connectives, opinions, etc.

★ Say something 'was' or 'wasn't' using *war*.

★ Watch out for expressions or words that mean different things in different contexts.

gern *like* • **lieber** *prefer* • **am liebsten** *best of all* • **zu** *too* • **sehr** *very* • **ganz** *completely* • **ziemlich** *quite, rather* • **erstens** *first of all* • **dann** *then* • **danach** *after that*

Lauter Laute: u, ü

2 Kleidung

2A Was trägt man?

- talk about clothes
- learn how to use *man*
- learn how to use subject pronouns

1 a Hör zu (1–6)! Welches Bild ist das?

Beispiel: **1 f**

1 b Richtig oder falsch?

Beispiel: **1 falsch**

1. Thomas trägt eine Jeans und ein T-Shirt. Er geht einkaufen.
2. Martha geht einkaufen. Sie sucht ein Kleid und einen Mantel.
3. Das Pferd trägt einen Hut. Es spielt Theater!
4. Dani und Türkan spielen Basketball. Sie tragen bunte Kleidung!
5. Der Lehrer sieht nicht cool aus! Er trägt einen Trainingsanzug.
6. Was trägt man zur Karnevalszeit? Man trägt Shorts und ein Sweatshirt.

1 c Hör noch einmal zu! Hast du Recht? Dein(e) Partner(in) überprüft deine Antworten.

2 Schreibt vier Kleidungsstücke auf! A stellt Fragen. B antwortet mit *ja* (A darf noch einmal fragen) oder *nein* (B ist dran). Wer hat am schnellsten alle vier?

Beispiel:
A Trägst du einen Hut?
B Nein. Ich trage keinen Hut. Trägst du ein Kleid?
A Ja, ich trage ein Kleid.
B Trägst du ein Kleid und einen Mantel?

Ich trage … Man trägt …	einen Hut. einen Mantel. einen Trainingsanzug. eine Jeans. ein Sweatshirt. ein Kleid. Shorts.

3 a Übersetze folgende Sätze ins Deutsche mit ***man***!

Beispiel: **1 In Deutschland spielt man Fußball.**

1. In Germany they play football.
2. You wear bright clothes at carnival time.
3. At the weekend people often go to the cinema.
4. We wear t-shirts in summer.
5. In the evening, people like watching television.

Grammatik: *man*

Use the pronoun *man* with third person singular verbs to say that people in general do something. It can mean 'one', but it is mostly used for 'you', 'we' or 'they'.

Im Sommer trägt man Shorts.	You wear shorts in summer.
In der Schule spielt man Fußball.	We play football at school.
In Amerika isst man Hamburger.	They eat hamburgers in America.

siehe Seite **142** >>

3 b Schreib zwei oder drei weitere Sätze mit ***man***!

Philipp

4 a Sieh dir die Bilder an und lies die Sätze unten! Welche Sätze passen zusammen?

Beispiel: **Philipp 1 c**

Hannah

1 Ich trage eine Jacke.	**a** Es ist grün, rosa und rot.
2 Das ist mein Rock.	**b** Es ist klein und schwarz.
3 Mein Hemd ist sehr cool!	**c** Sie ist schwarz und aus Leder.
4 Siehst du meine Schuhe?	**d** Sie sind gelb!
5 Das ist mein Lieblingskleid.	**e** Er ist lang und dunkelblau.
6 Heute trage ich einen Mantel.	**f** Er ist kurz und blau.

Grammatik: *er, sie, es*

Er, ***sie*** and ***es*** are **subject pronouns**. They replace nouns in the nominative case and save you having to repeat the nouns. They are used with the third person of the verb.

Notice that ***er*** and ***sie*** can be used to refer to objects as well as people. Why do you think this is?

	noun		pronoun
m	*der/ein Hut*	→	*er* (he, it)
f	*die/eine Jeans*	→	*sie* (she, it)
n	*das/ein Kleid*	→	*es* (it)
pl	*die/meine Shorts*	→	*sie* (they)

siehe Seite **142** >>

4 b Was tragen die jungen Leute? Wie sind ihre Kleider? A stellt Fragen. B macht das Buch zu und beantwortet die Fragen. Tauscht Rollen!

Beispiel:
A Was trägt Philipp?
B Er trägt eine Jacke.
A Wie ist die Jacke?
B Sie ist schwarz und aus Leder.

4 c Was tragen sie sonst noch? Wähl zwei Personen und beschreib sie! Dann beschreib dich selbst!

Beispiel: **Philipp trägt einen Pullover. Er ist rot. Ich trage ...**

2B Schuluniform

- talk about school uniform
- learn how to use adjectives
- give opinions

Grammatik: adjectives (indefinite article)

When you use an adjective before a noun, it needs certain endings. These depend on the noun's **case** (nominative, accusative), its **gender** (masculine, feminine, neuter) and the **determiner** (*der, ein, kein, mein*, etc.).

Here are the endings you would use with *ein, kein, mein* in the accusative case (usually the object of the sentence).

	masc	fem	neut	pl
accusative	meinen blau**en** Pulli	meine rot**e** Hose	mein grün**es** Hemd	meine gelb**en** Socken

In the plural, you sometimes don't have a determiner at all and the adjective just ends in *-e*: gelb**e** Socken

siehe Seite **141** >>

1 a Hör zu und lies die E-Mail mit!

An: Jens-Peter Löffler
Von: Kieran McNally
Betr.: Schuluniform

Hallo, Jens-Peter!

Was trägst du in der Schule? Wir müssen eine Schuluniform tragen. Normalerweise trage ich ein weißes Hemd, eine blau-weiß gestreifte Krawatte, einen dunkelblauen Pulli, eine schwarze Hose und schwarze Schuhe.

Die Mädchen tragen eine weiße Bluse, eine Krawatte, einen Pulli oder ein Sweatshirt, einen dunkelblauen Rock, eine dunkle Strumpfhose oder weiße Socken und schwarze Schuhe. Sie können auch eine dunkelblaue Hose tragen.

Für Sport trägt man ein weißes Polohemd, ein graues Sweatshirt, dunkelblaue Shorts, weiße Socken und Sportschuhe.

Wie ist es bei dir in der Schule? Was trägst du?

Schreib bald!

Dein Kieran

eine Strumpfhose – *pair of tights*

1 b Lies den Text noch einmal und sieh dir die Bilder an! Welche Bilder passen zu Kierans Schule?

a b c d e

2 Hör zu (1–4)! Was tragen diese vier Schüler? Mach Notizen auf Englisch!

Beispiel: **1 black trousers, grey jumper, ...**

3 a Hör zu und lies mit!

3 b ***Look at the adjectival endings in the speech bubbles. Can you see any differences from those on page 16? Some adjectives (e.g. praktisch, cool, ...) have no endings added at all. Can you explain why this is?***

Ich finde die schwarze Hose und den blauen Pulli praktisch, aber ein bisschen langweilig.

Ich trage das weiße Hemd nicht so gern. Es sieht altmodisch aus.

Ich mag die grauen Sweatshirts. Sie sehen cool aus, finde ich.

Ich mag die gestreifte Krawatte überhaupt nicht. Sie ist total blöd!

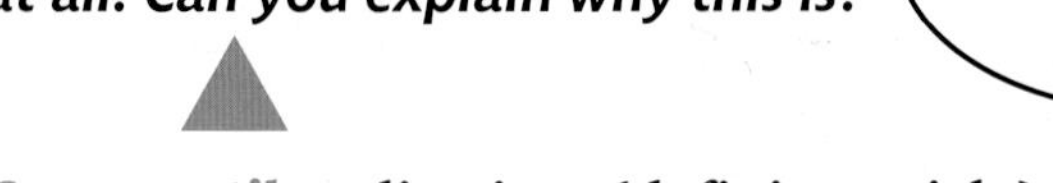

Grammatik: adjectives (definite article)

With the words for 'the' you use the adjective endings *-e* or *-en*, so the only difference from the endings with the indefinite article is in the neuter words:

	masc	fem	neut	pl
accusative	den blau**en** Pulli	die rot**e** Hose	das grün**e** Hemd	die gelb**en** Socken

siehe Seite **142** >>

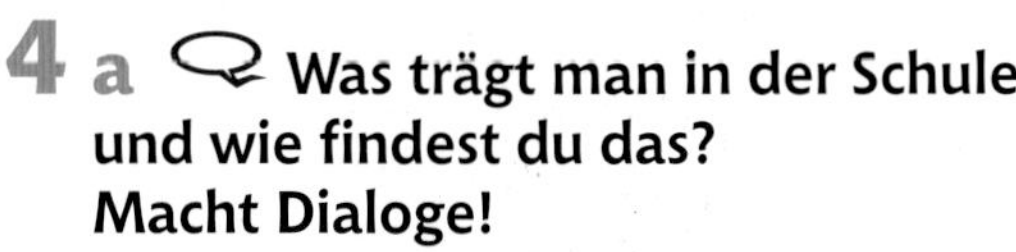

4 a **Was trägt man in der Schule und wie findest du das? Macht Dialoge!**

Beispiel: **A** **Wie findest du die Schuluniform?**
B **Ich mag die rot-gelb gestreifte Krawatte nicht!**
A **Ich auch nicht. Sie sieht doof aus!**
B **Aber ich finde die gelben Sweatshirts sehr cool!**
A **Was?! Igitt! Sie sind furchtbar!**

4 b **Was trägt man in einer anderen Schule und wie findest du das? Macht Dialoge!**

Beispiel: **A** **Was trägt man in der (Nelson High) Schule?**
B **Die Mädchen tragen ein rotes Kleid, ...**
A **Ich mag das rote Kleid überhaupt nicht. ...**

Wie findest du ...? Was trägst du (nicht) gern? Was magst du (nicht)?	Ich finde ... Ich trage ... (nicht) gern. Ich mag ... (überhaupt) nicht.
Er/Sie/Es sieht ... Sie sehen ...	(nicht) gut aus.
Er/Sie/Es ist ... Sie sind ...	praktisch/(total) blöd. langweilig/furchtbar. altmodisch/(nicht) cool.

5 a **Was trägst du in der Schule? Wie findest du das? Schreib einen Bericht!**

Beispiel: **In der Schule trage ich eine dunkle Hose, ...**
Ich finde die gelbe Krawatte sehr schön, aber ... .

Strategie! ***Improving your writing***

Vary the word order and use connectives to improve the quality of your writing.

5 b extra! **Was hast du in der Grundschule getragen?**

Beispiel: **In der Grundschule habe ich graue Shorts (usw.) ... getragen.**
Das war cool!

2C Suchst du was?

- give opinions about clothes and other things
- learn how to use object pronouns
- learn how to use negatives

Steffi, magst du den blauen Rock?
Hmm … nicht schlecht, aber ich finde ihn zu kurz.
Und das grüne Kleid?
Nein, Karla, bestimmt nicht! Ich mag es überhaupt nicht.

Ich mag die karierte Jacke.
Ja, ich mag sie auch, aber ich suche keine Jacke! Wie gefällt dir der Mantel?
Ich mag ihn sehr, aber ich trage nie einen Mantel.

1 a Hör zu und lies die Bildgeschichte mit!

1 b Richtig oder falsch?

1. Steffi findet den blauen Rock zu lang.
2. Karla mag die karierte Jacke.
3. Steffi mag das hübsche Oberteil.
4. Die Jungen suchen einen Freund.
5. Die Mädchen gehen nicht zur Party.

das Oberteil – *top*

1 c Lies die Geschichte noch einmal! Was passt zusammen?

Beispiel: **1 b**

1	Steffi findet ihn zu kurz.	**a**	den Mantel
2	Steffi trägt ihn nie.	**b**	den blauen Rock
3	Karla mag ihn sehr.	**c**	die karierte Jacke
4	Karla mag sie.	**d**	Thomas
5	Steffi mag es nicht.	**e**	das grüne Kleid

2 Macht Dialoge! Magst du das oder nicht?

Beispiel: **A Magst du die weiße Jacke?**
B Ja, ich mag sie (sehr)./
Nein, ich mag sie nicht.
Ich finde sie toll/doof usw.

ELVIS

Grammatik: object pronouns

In the accusative, the pronoun *er* changes to *ihn* (like the article *der* changes to *den*).

	nominative (subject)		accusative (object)	
masc	er	*he, it*	ihn	*him, it*
fem	sie	*she, it*	sie	*her, it*
neut	es	*it*	es	*it*
pl	sie	*they*	sie	*them*

siehe Seite **142** >>

3 Hör zu (1–8)! Ist das positiv oder negativ?

Beispiel: **1 negativ**

Grammatik: negatives

There are different ways of making sentences negative:

- use *kein* (not a, not any) instead of *ein*;
- add *nicht* (not);
- use *nichts* (nothing), *niemand* (nobody), *nie* (never).

siehe Seite **145** >>

4 a **Sieh dir die Bildgeschichte (Übung 1a) an! Wie viele negative Ausdrücke findest du? Mach eine Liste!**

4 b **Füll die Lücken aus! Welches Wort passt am besten? Dein(e) Partner(in) überprüft deine Antworten.**

1 Heute gehe ich _________ zur Schule. Ich mache überhaupt _________ .
2 Ich habe _________ gekauft, weil ich _________ Geld habe.
3 Ich habe _________ hübschen Klamotten und _________ kommt zur Party!
4 Martin hat _________ Hund, weil er Haustiere _________ mag.
5 _________ hat mich gesehen oder gehört.

kein
nichts
keine
nichts
keinen
nicht
niemand
nicht
niemand

5 a **Lauter Laute:** ***reactions***

- Hör zu und sprich nach!

Nein, bestimmt nicht!	Hmm … nicht schlecht.	Doch!
Furchtbar!	Och, das geht.	Oh ja! Cool!
		Gute Idee!
		Ja, sicher!

Grammatik: ***doch***

Use *doch* to mean 'yes' in answer to a **negative** question.

*Kommst du **nicht** zur Party?*	Aren't you coming to the party?
Doch!	Oh yes, I am!

5 b *extra!* **Macht kurze Dialoge mit den Ausdrücken aus Übung 5a!**

Beispiel:
A **Ich gehe heute Abend ins Kino. Kommst du mit?**
B **Ja, sicher! Ich bringe Chips und Saft mit.**
A **Gute Idee!**

2D Na und?

- build up complicated sentences
- use connectives, phrases and clauses

1 Mach einen Satz aus vielen Sätzen!

Beispiel: 1 Mein neuer Pulli ist rot und ich mag ihn, weil er gut aussieht.

1 Mein Pulli ist neu. Der Pulli ist rot. Ich mag den Pulli. Der Pulli sieht gut aus.

2 Meine Freundin kommt. Wir gehen in die Stadt. Ich gehe auf eine Party. Ich möchte Klamotten kaufen. Ich habe kein Geld.

3 Es ist Montag. Ich gehe um 19 Uhr ins Kino. Mein Freund kommt auch. Mein Freund heißt Jonas. Ich mag Jonas. Wir sehen einen Film an. Der Film ist alt.

4 Ich habe letzten Dienstag Geburtstag gehabt. Ich habe viel Geld bekommen. Ich habe einen CD-Spieler gekauft. Ich habe CDs gekauft.

2 a Am Samstagabend gibt es eine Party ... Erzählt weiter! Wo? Wann? Warum? Was tragt ihr? Was kauft ihr für ...? Tauscht Rollen!

Beispiel:
A Am Samstagabend gibt es eine tolle Party bei Svenja, weil sie Geburtstag hat.
B Was trägst du?
A Ich würde gern meine Jeans und ein weißes T-Shirt tragen, aber eigentlich sind sie zu alt. Also kaufe ich am Freitag ein neues T-Shirt und eine schwarze Hose.
B Was kaufst du für Svenja?
A Ich habe gestern eine tolle Mütze gekauft, weil Svenja Mützen sehr gern trägt und ... .

2 b Schreib die Sätze als Bericht auf!

Beispiel: Am Samstagabend gibt es eine tolle Party bei Svenja, weil sie Geburtstag hat. Ich wollte meine Jeans und ein weißes T-Shirt tragen, aber ... .

Strategie! *Building complicated sentences*

Make your written and spoken German much more interesting by using and adapting language you have learnt. You can soon build up complicated sentences.

Join sentences and clauses using connectives:

- *und* (and), *oder* (or), *aber* (but) — just include these without changing the word order
- *weil* (because) send the verb to the end
- *dann* (then), *also* (so) — put the verb second

Add extra words:

- use adjectives (*groß, neu, blau, interessant, teuer …*)

Avoid repetition:

- use pronouns (*er, ihn, sie, es …*)
- use a range of different verbs
- use different word order (for emphasis, for variety …) (e.g. *Am Wochenende fahre ich …*)

Give opinions:

- *… finde ich toll/nicht so gut/furchtbar*
- *ich mag … (nicht)*
- *… gefällt/gefallen mir (nicht)*
- *… sieht/sehen gut/schlecht aus*

Zusammenfassung

Kleidung	***Clothes***
der Hut	*hat*
der Mantel	*coat*
der Trainingsanzug	*tracksuit*
die Jeans	*(pair of) jeans*
die Strumpfhose	*(pair of) tights*
die Schuluniform	*school uniform*
das Sweatshirt	*sweatshirt*
das Kleid	*dress*
das Oberteil	*top*
die Shorts (*pl*)	*shorts*
gestreift	*striped*
kariert	*checked*
lang	*long*
kurz	*short*

Wie findest du ...?	***What do you think of ...?***
Ich finde Krawatten toll.	*I think ties are great.*
Was trägst du (nicht) gern?	*What do you (not) like wearing?*
Ich trage ... (nicht) gern.	*I do (not) like wearing ... .*
Was magst du (nicht)?	*What do(n't) you like?*
Ich mag ... (überhaupt nicht).	*I (don't at all) like ... .*
Er/Sie/Es sieht gut aus.	*He/She/It looks good.*
Sie sehen (nicht) schlecht aus.	*They (don't) look bad.*
Er/Sie/Es ist .../Sie sind ...	*He/She/It is .../They are ...*
praktisch.	*practical.*
(total) blöd.	*(absolutely) stupid.*
furchtbar.	*terrible.*
altmodisch.	*old-fashioned.*
(nicht) cool.	*(not) cool.*

Positiv und negativ	***Positive and negative***
nicht	*not*
jemand	*somebody*
niemand	*nobody*
alles	*everything*
nichts	*nothing*
oft	*often*
nie	*never*

Grammatik: 

★ *man*: use the pronoun *man* with third person singular verbs to say that people in general do something. It can mean 'one', but it is mostly used for 'you', 'we' or 'they'.

★ Subject and object pronouns (third person):

	nominative (subject)		**accusative (object)**	
masc	er	*he, it*	ihn	*him, it*
fem	sie	*she, it*	sie	*her, it*
neut	es	*it*	es	*it*
pl	sie	*they*	sie	*them*

★ Adjectival endings:

determiner = *der:*

	masc	**fem**	**neut**	**pl**
accusative	den blau**en** Pulli	die rot**e** Hose	das grün**e** Hemd	die gelb**en** Socken

determiner = *ein, kein, mein, dein, sein, ihr:*

	masc	**fem**	**neut**	**pl**
accusative	meinen blau**en** Pulli	meine rot**e** Hose	mein grün**es** Hemd	meine gelb**en** Socken

no determiner:

	pl
nominative/accusative	gelb**e** Socken

★ Negatives: there are different ways of making sentences negative:

- use *kein* (not a, not any) instead of *ein;*
- add *nicht* (not);
- use *nichts* (nothing), *niemand* (nobody), *nie* (never).

★ *doch:* use *doch* to mean 'yes' in answer to a **negative** question.

*Kommst du **nicht** zur Party?* — Aren't you coming to the party?
Doch! — Oh yes, I am!

siehe Seite **141, 142, 145** ➤➤

Strategie!

★ Improve your writing by varying the word order and using connectives.

★ Build complex sentences using connectives, adjectives, pronouns, etc.

ihn, sie, es *he, she, it* • **und** *and* • **oder** *or* • **aber** *but* • **weil** *because* • **dann** *then* • **also** *so, therefore* • **kein** *not any* • **nicht** *not* • **nichts** *nothing* • **nie** *never* • **niemand** *nobody*

Lauter Laute: *actions*

Wiederholung

Kapitel 1 (Probleme? Siehe Seite 6–11!)

1 Was machen sie (nicht) gern/lieber/am liebsten?

Beispiel: **Max geht am liebsten mit Freunden aus, aber er liest nicht gern.**

Max								
Linda								
Mario								
Natascha								

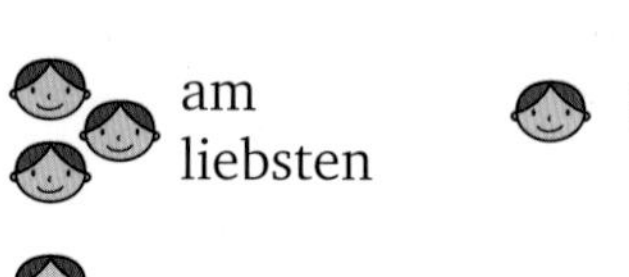

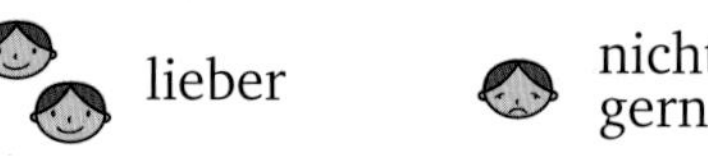

2 Lies die Satzteile! Was passt zusammen?

Beispiel: **1 e**

1 Letztes Wochenende bin ich
2 Am Samstag habe ich
3 Ich bin im Juli nach
4 Am Sonntag haben
5 Hast du am Samstagnachmittag
6 Bist du am Wochenende
7 Letztes Wochenende hat
8 Am Samstagabend ist

a Pizza gekauft?
b Maria zu Hause geblieben.
c wir meine Großmutter besucht.
d am Computer gespielt.
e einkaufen gegangen.
f Jens Fußball gespielt.
g Köln gefahren.
h ins Kino gegangen?

Kapitel 2 (Probleme? Siehe Seite 14–15, 18–19!)

3 Susi geht auf eine Party. Was trägt sie? Schreib die richtigen Buchstaben auf!

Beispiel: **e, …**

Was trage ich denn? Ich mag das weiße Kleid nicht mehr und ich möchte keine Hose tragen. Also, eine Jeans oder einen Rock? Ich trage lieber den blauen Rock und dazu nehme ich das gestreifte T-Shirt und eine Jacke … oder ein Sweatshirt … nein, ich trage die graue Jacke. So, und jetzt nehme ich meine roten Schuhe. Fertig!

4 Anke und Boris machen immer das Gegenteil. Vervollständige die Sätze! Benutze *ihn*, *sie* oder *es*!

Beispiel: **1 Anja mag die rote Hose, aber Boris mag sie nicht.**

1 Anja mag die rote Hose, aber Boris …
2 Boris mag den neuen Lehrer, aber …
3 Anja kauft das blaue T-Shirt, aber …
4 Boris sammelt Radiergummis, aber …
5 Anja deckt immer den Tisch, aber …
6 Boris macht immer seine Hausaufgaben, aber …

Uniform in Deutschland?

In Hamburg und Berlin haben es einige Schüler schon ausprobiert. Die Fünftklässler einer Schule in Hamburg haben sich grüne Sweatshirts gekauft. Damit kommen sie jetzt jeden Tag zur Schule. Einen Spitznamen haben sie auch schon: „Grüne Frösche".

Die Klasse 8a einer Berliner Schule trägt eine dunkelblaue, sportliche Freizeithose, ein weißes Polohemd oder langärmliges weißes T-Shirt und dunkelblaues Sweatshirt, dazu ein Wappen. Berit hat das Wappen ziemlich schnell abgerissen, wie andere Mitschüler auch: „Die lila Farbe hat uns nicht gefallen, außerdem war es zu groß", sagt sie.

Ob mit oder ohne Wappen: In den ersten Wochen war die Schuluniform die große Attraktion, zuerst einmal bei den Mitschülern. Denn von jeder Schule hat nur eine Klasse die Uniform getragen. In der Pause haben die anderen sich lustig über die neuen Uniformträger gemacht.

„Am Anfang war es ziemlich spannend, am Ende aber waren die meisten Schüler eher genervt", sagt Max von der 8a. „Am Nachmittag war ich froh, wieder meine eigenen Klamotten anziehen zu dürfen", sagt auch Berit.

Aus: *JUMA* 2/2002, www.juma.de

Berit

1 ***Use a dictionary to find the meaning of these words (and any others you don't remember):***
dunkel, das Wappen, abreißen, nur, spannend, genervt, anziehen.

2 ***Who has earned the nickname 'green frogs', and why?***

3 ***What was wrong with the logo on the Berlin uniform?***

4 ***Did the Berlin class find the experiment positive? Explain why (not).***

5 ***Describe the uniform worn by class 8a.***

Cool oder uncool?

Die Wörter „cool" und „uncool" sind cool! Aber man kann sie durch viele andere Wörter ersetzen!

Was ist eine Alternative zu „cool"?

Marieke, 17: Der Winter ist klasse, fantastisch, weil man da Ski fahren und snowboarden kann.

Thorsten, 16: Originell, erfinderisch ist für mich jemand, der nicht mit der Mode geht …

Simon, 17: Für mich ist amüsant, intelligent, wenn man nicht dauernd sagt, dass etwas cool ist …

Ariane, 15: Schule ist eigentlich ganz angenehm, nett, weil man dort jeden Tag seine Freunde trifft.

Was ist eine Alternative zu „uncool"?

Martin, 19: Überholt, altmodisch, unmodern sind die Klamotten aus dem letzten Jahr.

Klaus, 17: Ich finde es geistlos, anstrengend, wenn man die ganze Zeit krampfhaft versucht cool zu sein.

Tobias, 15: Schule finde ich total mühsam, blöd, weil man dort nicht machen kann, was man will.

Markus, 16: Lehrer sind grausam, unfair, weil die meisten so streng sind.

Aus: *JUMA* 2/2004, www.juma.de

1 ***Use a dictionary to find the meanings of these 'cool' and 'uncool' adjectives.***

2 ***Which of the statements do you agree with?***

3 Einkaufen und Essen

3A Wo bekomme ich das?

- discuss shopping trips
- say what you need to buy
- learn how to use some prepositions

A

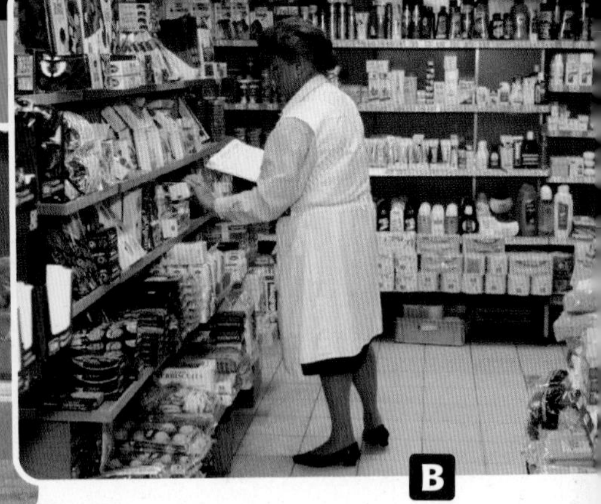
B

1 a Hör zu und sieh dir die Geschäfte an! Wie ist die richtige Reihenfolge?

Beispiel: **H, ...**

Strategie! *Using clues*

When listening, use visual clues to predict or anticipate what words you might hear.

1 b Sieh dir die Einkaufsliste an! Wo kauft man das?

Beispiel: **Tomaten – H**

8 Tomaten	1 Apfeltorte
6 Orangen	Shampoo
10 Brötchen	Kuli (schwarz)
1 Landbrot	Schreibblock
100 Gramm Wurst	1 Tischtennisschläger

1 c Hör noch einmal zu und überprüfe deine Antworten!

die Bäckerei	die Metzgerei
die Drogerie	der Schreibwarenladen
das Kaufhaus	das Sportgeschäft
die Konditorei	der Supermarkt

2 Macht Dialoge! Was brauchst du? Was hast du nicht? Wo kaufst du das?

Beispiel:
A Ich brauche einen Bleistift.
B Du kaufst ihn im Schreibwarenladen. Ich habe keine Wurst.
A Du kaufst sie in der Metzgerei.

Grammatik: *in* + dative

To say in which shop you buy something, use *in* with the **dative** case.

Remember, *der* and *das* change to *dem*; *die* changes to *der*.

And *in dem* is usually shortened to *im*.

der Supermarkt	*im (= in dem) Supermarkt*	in the supermarket
die Bäckerei	*in der Bäckerei*	at the baker's
das Kaufhaus	*im (= in dem) Kaufhaus*	in the department store

siehe Seite **141** >>

Ich brauche	einen .../eine .../ein ...	Bleistift/Lampe/Shampoo.
Ich habe	keinen .../keine .../kein ...	
Du kaufst	ihn/sie/es	im Supermarkt/Kaufhaus.
		in der Bäckerei/Drogerie.

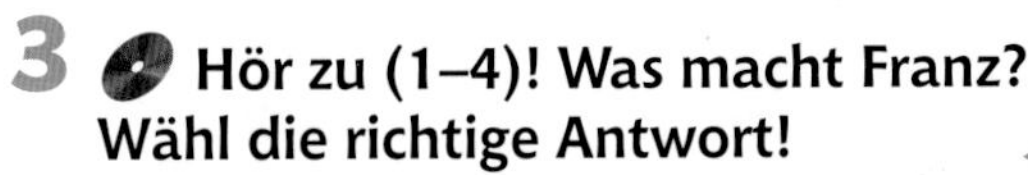

3 **Hör zu (1–4)! Was macht Franz? Wähl die richtige Antwort!**

1 **a** Er geht in den Supermarkt.
  b Er geht in die Bäckerei.

2 **a** Er geht in die Konditorei.
  b Er geht in die Metzgerei.

3 **a** Er geht ins Kino.
  b Er geht in die Imbissstube.

4 **a** Er geht ins Sportgeschäft.
  b Er geht in den Schreibwarenladen.

Grammatik: ***in*** **+ accusative or dative**

- To say which shop you are going **into**, use *in* with the **accusative** case.
  Remember, *der* → *den*; *in das* is usually shortened to *ins*.
- Use *in* with the **dative** case to say which shop you are **in**.
  Remember, *der/das* → *dem*, *die* → *der*; *in dem* is usually shortened to *im*.

der Supermarkt	*Ich gehe **in den** Supermarkt.*
	*Ich kaufe **im** (= in dem) Supermarkt ein.*
die Bäckerei	*Ich gehe **in die** Bäckerei.*
	*Ich kaufe **in der** Bäckerei ein.*
das Kaufhaus	*Ich gehe **ins** (= in das) Kaufhaus.*
	*Ich kaufe **im** (= in dem) Kaufhaus ein.*

siehe Seite **141** >>

4 a **Kettenspiel. Seht euch den Stadtplan an! Wohin gehst du?**

Beispiel: **A** **Wohin gehst du?**
B **Ich gehe in den Supermarkt. Und du, wohin gehst du?**
A **Zuerst gehe ich in den Supermarkt, dann in den Schreibwarenladen ...**

4 b **Wo bist du?**

Beispiel: **A** **Nummer 10: Wo bist du?**
B **Ich bin im Kino.**

5 **Du bist in Unsinn-Stadt, wo nichts im richtigen Geschäft ist. Beschreib, wohin du gehst und was du dort kaufst! Kauf mindestens fünf Sachen!**

Beispiel: **Zuerst gehe ich ins Sportgeschäft. Ich muss Schinken und Brot im Sportgeschäft kaufen. Dann ...**

3B Im Einkaufszentrum

- make arrangements to meet
- learn how to use some more prepositions
- learn how to use some more pronouns

1 Hör zu (1–6)! Welche Uhr zeigt die richtige Uhrzeit?

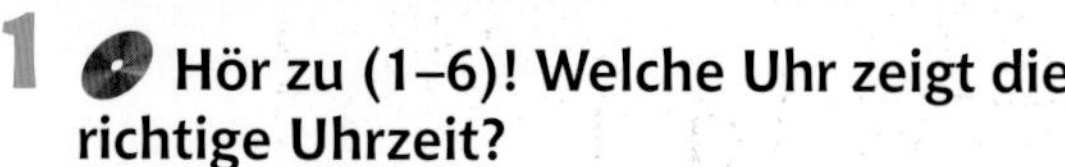

Beispiel: **1 c**

2 a Hör zu (1–8)! Welches Bild ist das?

Beispiel: **1 e**

a

b

c

d

e

f

g

h

2 b Welcher Text passt zu welchem Bild?

Beispiel: **1 b**

1 gegenüber dem Reisebüro
2 neben dem Geldautomaten
3 zwischen dem Modegeschäft und der Buchhandlung
4 im Restaurant
5 im Eiscafé über dem Schuhgeschäft
6 hinter der Telefonzelle
7 an der Bushaltestelle
8 vor der Apotheke

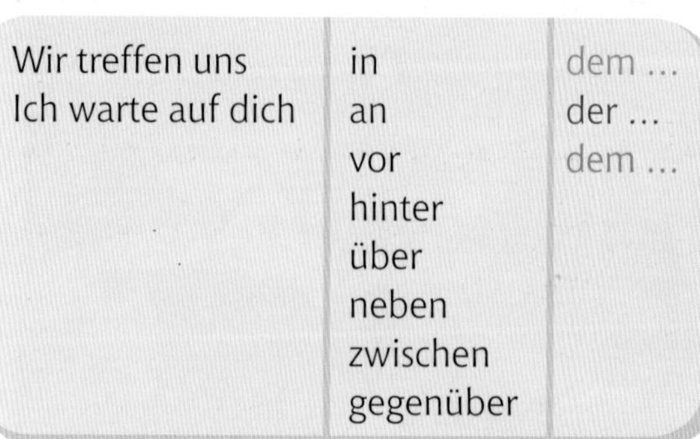

Wir treffen uns Ich warte auf dich	in an vor hinter über neben zwischen gegenüber	dem … der … dem …

3 Lest den Dialog und macht weitere Dialoge!

A **Hast du Lust ins Einkaufszentrum zu gehen?**
B **Ja, sicher. Um wie viel Uhr?**
A **Um halb elf.**
B **Wo treffen wir uns?**
A **Ich warte auf dich vor der Apotheke.**
B **O.K. Bis bald!**

Grammatik: more object pronouns

nom	acc	examples
ich	*mich*	*Holst du **mich** ab?*
du	*dich*	*Ich hole **dich** um zwei Uhr ab.*
wir	*uns*	*Wir treffen **uns** gegen drei Uhr.*
ihr	*euch*	*Ich warte auf **euch** im Eiscafé.*

siehe Seite **142** ➤➤

4 a **Hör zu (1–5) und sieh dir das Einkaufszentrum an! Wer ist wo?**

Beispiel: **1 A, D**

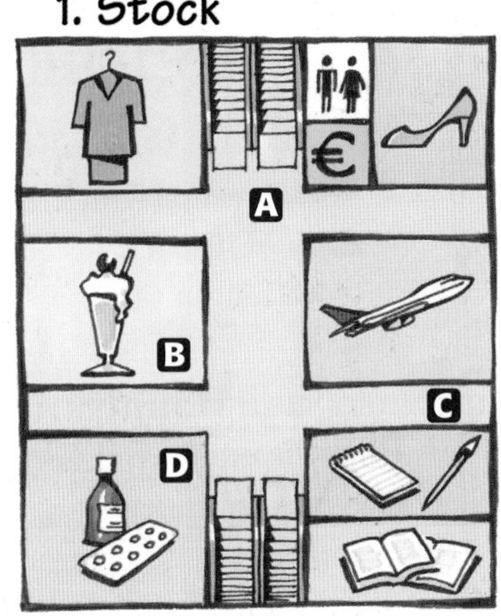

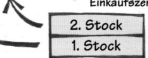

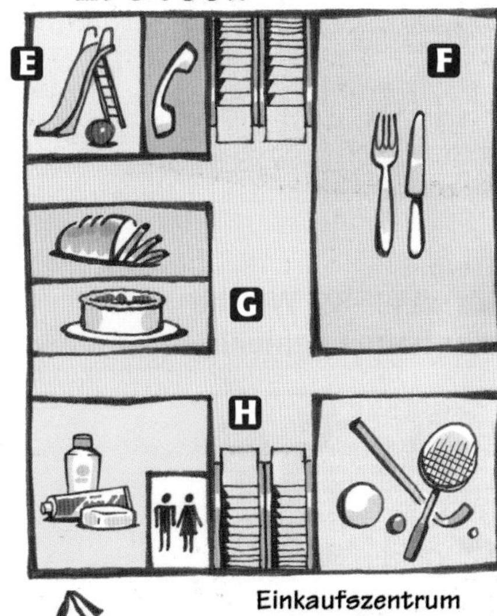

Einkaufszentrum
2. Stock
1. Stock
P
J
I

Grammatik: more prepositions

The preposition *gegenüber* means 'opposite' and it **always** takes the **dative** case.

Ich warte gegenüber dem Geldautomaten.

The following prepositions work like *in*: they take the **dative** case when indicating **position**.

an, auf, hinter, neben, über, unter, vor, zwischen

Wir treffen uns zwischen dem Reisebüro und der Apotheke.

They take the **accusative** case when there is **movement** from one place to another.

Ich gehe auf die Toilette.
Bist du an die Bushaltestelle gegangen?

Can you come up with ideas to help you remember which prepositions can take the accusative or dative?

siehe Seite **141** ➤➤

der Kinderspielplatz – *playground, play area*
die Rolltreppe – *escalator*
das Parkhaus – *(indoor) car park*

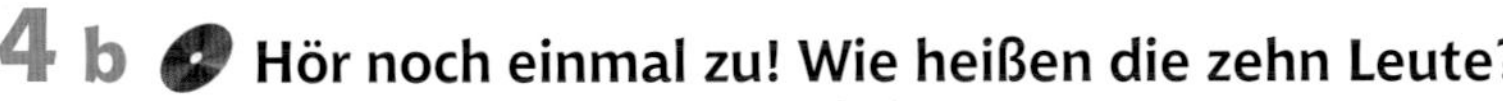

4 b **Hör noch einmal zu! Wie heißen die zehn Leute?**

Beispiel: **A = Annika**

4 c **Ratespiel. Wer bin ich?**

Beispiel:
A Bist du im Eiscafé?
B Nein.
A Bist du auf dem Kinderspielplatz?
B Nein.
A Bist du vor der Konditorei?
B Ja, richtig.
A Also, du bist Gerd.

Wo ist Ich suche	der/die/das ...? den/die/das	
Er/Sie/Es ist	neben vor hinter usw.	dem ... . der ... .
Ich habe ...	gemacht. besucht. gefunden. gegessen. gesehen.	
Ich bin ...	gegangen. geblieben. gefahren.	

5 **Du hast am Wochenende einen Einkaufsbummel gemacht. Beschreib ihn!**

Beispiel: **Zuerst bin ich ins Modegeschäft gegangen und habe ein rotes Kleid gekauft. Dann habe ich ein Eis mit meiner Freundin Elsa im Eiscafé gegessen und wir haben ...**

3C Ich hätte gern ...

- learn how to book a table in a restaurant
- learn how to order a meal
- revise how to use correct word order

Speisekarte

Vorspeise:

1 Tomatensuppe mit Brötchen
2 Aufschnittteller
3 Salatteller mit Ei

Hauptgericht:

4 Forelle mit Kartoffeln und Erbsen
5 Gulasch mit Reis
6 Spagetti mit Tomatensoße, Oliven und Mozzarella (vegetarisch)

Nachtisch:

7 Gemischtes Eis (nach Wahl)
8 Apfelstrudel
9 Rote Grütze

1 a Hör zu (1–3)! Welche zwei Bilder haben Fehler?

1

2

3

1 b Macht Dialoge! Die Bilder aus Übung 1a und die Wörter im Kasten unten helfen euch.

Beispiel: **A** **Ich möchte einen Tisch für heute Abend reservieren.**
B **Für wie viele Personen?**
A ...

Ich möchte einen Tisch für (heute Abend) reservieren.	
Für wie viele Personen? Um wie viel Uhr?	Für (zwei) Personen. Um/Gegen (sieben Uhr).
am Fenster/auf der Terrasse Raucher/Nichtraucher Auf welchen Namen, bitte?	

2 Was reservieren diese vier Personen? Hör zu und mach Notizen!

Beispiel: **1** **1 Tisch für 3 Personen, Sonntag, ...**

3 Lies die Speisekarte und sieh dir die Bilder (a–i) an! Was passt zusammen?

Beispiel: **1 e**

Strategie! ***Using cognates***

Look for cognates and familiar words or parts of words when trying to understand the menu.

4 a  **Hör zu und lies mit! Was bestellen sie? Wähl die richtigen Buchstaben aus Übung 3!**

Beispiel: **c, …**

Im Restaurant

- Die Speisekarte, bitte.
- Bitte.

…

- Haben Sie schon gewählt?
- Ja, als Vorspeise nehme ich den Aufschnittteller.
- Ja, den Aufschnittteller.
- Und als Hauptgericht nehme ich die Forelle mit Kartoffeln und Erbsen.
- So, danke. Und was nehmen Sie als Nachtisch?
- Hmm … was können Sie empfehlen?
- Der Apfelstrudel ist sehr gut.
- O.K. Ich nehme den Apfelstrudel.
- Und zu trinken?
- Ich hätte gern ein Mineralwasser.
- In Ordnung. Es kommt sofort.

Strategie! *Using* du *and* Sie

Note that the waiter addresses adults and older children as *Sie*, but younger children are addressed as *du* (singular) and *ihr* (plural).

Was nimmst ***du****? Was nehmt* ***ihr****?*
Was nehmen ***Sie****?*

4 b **Lest den Dialog in Übung 4a!**

4 c **Macht weitere Dialoge im Restaurant!**

Grammatik: verb second

Remember to put the verb as the second idea in a sentence.

Ich ***nehme*** *ein gemischtes Eis.*

Als Nachtisch ***nehme*** *ich Schokoladenkuchen.*

Ich ***hätte*** *gern einen Saft.*

Zu trinken ***hätte*** *ich gern eine Cola.*

siehe Seite **146** >>

5 **Du hast in einem Restaurant in Unsinn-Stadt gegessen, wo alles verkehrt ist. Beschreib den Abend!**

Beispiel: **Am Samstagabend bin ich mit meiner Familie in ein Restaurant gegangen. Als Vorspeise habe ich Tomateneis mit Ei gegessen/genommen. Meine Mutter hat …**

6 **Dein(e) Partner(in) überprüft. Ist die Wortstellung richtig? Sind die Verbendungen richtig?**

7 extra! **Macht Dialoge im Unsinn-Restaurant! Nehmt die Dialoge auf Kassette oder auf Video auf!**

3D Haben Sie gewählt?

- learn how to understand a menu
- learn how to understand what a dish consists of

Speisekarte

Vorspeisen und Suppen

- Knoblauchcremesuppe
- Gulaschsuppe
- Gebackener Camembert mit Preiselbeersahne und Toast
- Artischockenherzen in Olivenöl mit Knoblauchröstbrot

Hauptgerichte

- Gegrilltes Hühnerfilet auf Toast serviert mit Cocktailsoße und Salat
- „Pute Hawaii": Steak von der Pute mit frischer gegrillter Ananasscheibe und gemischtem Salat
- Jägerschnitzel, dazu Backkartoffel und saure Sahne
- Lachsroulade mit Scampimousse gefüllt auf Nudeln mit Nordseekrabbensoße
- Rumpsteak 180g mit Kräuterbutter, Bohnen und Kroketten
- Würstchen mit Pommes frites und Salat

Zum Nachtisch

- Vanilleeis mit heißen Himbeeren
- Hausgemachte Torte
- Rote Grütze mit Vanillesoße
- Milchreis mit Apfelmus

Strategie! **Understanding a menu**

- Look for familiar words and cognates.
- Remember that foreign words are often used in cookery, so look out for ones you recognise.
- Break up longer words (such as compound nouns) into more manageable chunks.
- Use your dictionary skills to look up words or parts of words.
- Look at which category a dish is in (*Vorspeisen*, etc.), as this can help narrow down the meaning.
- Don't be afraid to ask the waiter/waitress if you don't know what something is.

– Was ist Jägerschnitzel?
– Das ist eine Scheibe Fleisch mit Champignons in einer pikanten Soße.

1 a ***Work out as many items as you can from this menu. Use a dictionary for some of them.***

1 b ***Think of the shortest possible list of words you need to look up in order to understand the menu.***

2 ***Listen to the dialogues (1–3) and use your listening skills to understand and make notes. Then explain in English what you think the dishes are.***

3 **Lauter Laute:** a, ä, e

- Hör zu und sprich nach!

Ergun hätte gern Jägerschnitzel mit Äpfeln und Erbsen, aber Anna hat Lachs und Ananas gewählt.

Zusammenfassung

Einkaufen	***Shopping***
der Eingang	*entrance*
der Geldautomat	*cash machine*
der Kinderspielplatz	*play area, playground*
der Supermarkt	*supermarket*
der Schreibwarenladen	*stationer's*
die Apotheke	*chemist's, pharmacy*
die Bäckerei	*baker's*
die Buchhandlung	*bookshop*
die Bushaltestelle	*bus stop*
die Drogerie	*drugstore*
die Konditorei	*cake shop*
die Metzgerei	*butcher's*
die Rolltreppe	*escalator*
die Telefonzelle	*telephone kiosk*
das Eiscafé	*ice-cream parlour*
das Kaufhaus	*department store*
das Modegeschäft	*fashion store, boutique*
das Parkhaus	*multi-storey car park*
das Reisebüro	*travel agent's*
das Restaurant	*restaurant*
das Schuhgeschäft	*shoe shop*
das Sportgeschäft	*sports shop*
Ich brauche einen/eine/ein ….	*I need a ….*
Ich habe keinen/keine/ kein/keine ….	*I haven't any ….*
Du kaufst ihn/sie/es/sie im Supermarkt/Kaufhaus.	*You can buy it/them in the supermarket/ department store.*
in der Bäckerei.	*at the baker's.*

Wo?	***Where?***
Wo ist der/die/das …?	*Where is the …?*
Ich suche den/die/das ….	*I'm looking for the ….*
Wir treffen uns …	*We'll meet …*
Ich warte auf dich …	*I'll wait for you …*
an	*at/to*
auf	*on/onto*
hinter	*behind*
in	*in/into*
neben	*next to, near*
über	*above/over*
unter	*below/beneath*
vor	*in front of*
zwischen	*between*
gegenüber	*opposite*

Im Restaurant	***In the restaurant***
Ich möchte einen Tisch für (heute Abend) reservieren.	*I'd like to reserve a table for (this evening).*
Für wie viele Personen?	*For how many?*
Für (zwei) Personen.	*For (two) people.*
Um wie viel Uhr?	*What time?*
Um/Gegen (sieben Uhr).	*At/About (7 p.m.).*
am Fenster	*by the window*
auf der Terrasse	*on the terrace*
Raucher	*smoking*
Nichtraucher	*non-smoking*
Auf welchen Namen, bitte?	*What name, please?*
Die Speisekarte, bitte.	*The menu, please.*
Haben Sie schon gewählt?	*Have you chosen?*
Ich hätte gern …	*I'd like …*
Ich nehme …	*I'll have …*
als Vorspeise	*as a starter*
als Hauptgericht	*for the main course*
als Nachtisch	*for dessert*
Was können Sie empfehlen?	*What can you recommend?*
Zu trinken?	*What would you like to drink?*
Was ist …?	*What is …?*

Grammatik:

- Prepositions + accusative or dative case: the prepositions *an, auf, hinter, in, neben, über, unter, vor, zwischen*
  - take the **accusative** case when there is **movement** from one place to another;
  - take the **dative** case when indicating **position**.

  *ich gehe **in den** Supermarkt; ich kaufe **im** (= in dem) Supermarkt ein*
  *ich gehe **in die** Bäckerei; ich kaufe **in der** Bäckerei ein*
  *ich gehe **ins** (= in das) Kaufhaus; ich kaufe **im** (= in dem) Kaufhaus ein*
- *gegenüber*: the preposition *gegenüber* means 'opposite' and it **always** takes the **dative** case.
  Ich warte gegenüber dem Eiscafé.
- More object pronouns:

nom	**acc**
ich (I)	*mich* (me)
du (you)	*dich* (you)
wir (we)	*uns* (us)
ihr (you)	*euch* (you)

- Verb second: remember to put the verb as the second idea in a sentence.
  *Als Nachtisch **nehme** ich ein gemischtes Eis.*

siehe Seite **141, 142, 146** >>

Strategie!

- Use visual clues to predict or anticipate what words you might hear.
- Use cognates and familiar words or parts of words to understand texts.
- Use *du* for younger children and *Sie* for older children and adults.

Lauter Laute: a, ä, e

mich • dich • uns • euch • an • auf • hinter • in • neben • über • unter • vor • zwischen

4 Medien

4A Das mag ich!

- talk about going to the cinema
- learn how to make excuses
- learn to use modal verbs

Wollen wir Willst du mit mir Möchtest du mit mir	ins Kino gehen?
Kommst du mit ins Kino? Was läuft?	

ein Science-Fiction-Film/ Science-Fiction-Filme

ein Actionfilm/ Actionfilme

ein Horrorfilm/ Horrorfilme

ein Zeichentrickfilm/ Zeichentrickfilme

ein Martial-Arts-Film/ Martial-Arts-Filme

ein Kriegsfilm/ Kriegsfilme

ein Fantasyfilm/ Fantasyfilme

eine Komödie/ Komödien

1 a Hör zu (1–8) und ordne die Filme ein!

Beispiel: **1 Horrorfilm, …**

1 b Hör noch einmal zu und vervollständige die Meinungen!

Beispiel: **1 Ich mag keine Science-Fiction-Filme.**

1 Ich ____ keine Science-Fiction-Filme.
2 Martial-Arts-Filme mag ich ____ .
3 Kriegsfilme ____ ich gar ____ .
4 Ich ____ Komödien total ____ !
5 Ich ____ ____ gern Actionfilme.
6 ____ kann ich nicht leiden.

2 Wählt Filme und macht Dialoge!

Beispiel: **A Wollen wir ins Kino gehen?**
B Was läuft?
A Ein Horrorfilm.

3 Wie findest du die verschiedenen Filmtypen? Schreib mindestens vier Meinungen!

Beispiel: **Ich mag sehr gern Actionfilme, aber Science-Fiction-Filme kann ich nicht leiden.**

4 Hör zu (1–8)! Welche Ausrede (a–h) passt zu welchem Film?

Beispiel: **1 f**

1 Das Imperium schlägt zurück
2 Hennen Rennen
3 Fluch der Karibik
4 Spiderman
5 Die Monster-AG
6 Der Herr der Ringe
7 Das Medaillon
8 Der Weiße Hai

a

Ich darf nicht ausgehen. Ich muss zu Hause bleiben.

b

Ich muss Staub saugen.

c

Actionfilme mag ich nicht.

d

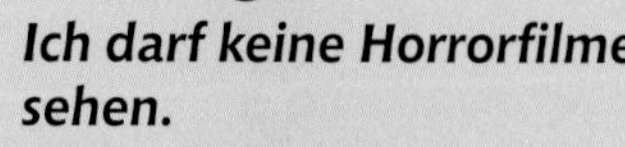

Ich darf keine Horrorfilme sehen.

e

Ich muss meinen Eltern helfen.

f

Ich kann nicht. Ich muss meine Hausaufgaben machen.

g

Ich muss mir die Haare waschen.

h

Das habe ich schon gesehen.

Grammatik: modal verbs

You have met some of these verbs before – they are all **modal** verbs. Most of them have to be used with **another** verb. They are all **irregular** in the **singular** but **regular** in the **plural** forms. When used with another verb, the second verb goes at the **end** of the sentence or clause. Here they are in full:

	können (to be able to: I can, etc.)	***dürfen*** (to be allowed to: I may/can, etc.)	***müssen*** (to have to: I must, etc.)	***wollen*** (to want to)	***mögen*** (to like)
ich	*kann*	*darf*	*muss*	*will*	*mag*
du	*kannst*	*darfst*	*musst*	*willst*	*magst*
er/sie/es	*kann*	*darf*	*muss*	*will*	*mag*
wir	*können*	*dürfen*	*müssen*	*wollen*	*mögen*
ihr	*könnt*	*dürft*	*müsst*	*wollt*	*mögt*
sie/Sie	*können*	*dürfen*	*müssen*	*wollen*	*mögen*

*Ich **kann** nicht ins Kino kommen.*
*Er **darf** keine Horrorfilme sehen.*
***Müsst** ihr eure Hausaufgaben machen?*
***Wollen** wir ins Kino gehen?*
*Sie **mögen** keine Kriegsfilme.*

siehe Seite **143** >>

5 Füll die Lücken mit der passenden Verbform aus!

Beispiel: **1 Er muss seiner Mutter helfen.**

1. Er (**müssen**) seiner Mutter helfen.
2. Sie (*She*) (**können**) nicht mit uns kommen.
3. Was (**wollen**) er machen?
4. (**dürfen**) ich diesen Film sehen?
5. (**mögen**) du gern Horrorfilme?

6 Macht jetzt einen Dialog! A schlägt einen Film vor und B akzeptiert oder gibt eine Ausrede! Tauscht Rollen!

Beispiel:
A Möchest du eine DVD bei mir sehen?
B Was hast du für eine DVD?
A „Der Herr der Ringe".
B Nein danke, ich darf nicht ausgehen. Ich muss meinen Eltern helfen.

7 extra! Erfindet neue Ausreden!

Beispiel: **Ich muss den Hund waschen.**

8 Welche Filme magst du und welche magst du nicht? Was sind deine Lieblingsfilme? Welche Filme möchtest du sehen? Schreib ungefähr 50 Wörter! Und überprüfe!

Strategie! *Using connectives*

Try to write longer sentences linked with connectives, and try to recombine the language you have learnt so that it expresses different opinions.

Example: *Ich kann „Der Herr der Ringe" nicht leiden, weil das ein Fantasyfilm ist, und Fantasyfilme mag ich gar nicht. Mein Lieblingsfilm ist … . Normalerweise mag ich keine … , aber … ist supertoll! Ich möchte gern „Scream" sehen, aber ich darf keine Horrorfilme sehen.*

9 Lauter Laute: o, ö

- Hör zu und wiederhole!

Wir mögen tolle Komödien im Kino, aber wir möchten keine total blöden Horrorfilme sehen!

4B Film- und Buchkritik!

- understand summaries of films and books
- give opinions about books and films
- learn to use *dieser* and understand relative clauses

1 Hör zu und lies (A–C) mit! Richtig, falsch oder nicht im Text?

Beispiel: 1 richtig

1. In „Vier Stunden in Paris“ müssen ein Mann und seine Frau ein Paket finden.
2. Die Polizei muss nach Berlin fahren.
3. In „Wo ist Lumpi?“ hat ein Junge eine alte Dame verloren.
4. Der Junge, der in dem Park ist, heißt Peter.
5. In „5.000.000 Jahre in die Zukunft“ finden zwei Kinder einen Roboter.
6. Die Kinder fahren in einem Raumschiff zu einem anderen Planeten.

2 Füll die Lücken mit der passenden Form von *dieser*, *diese*, *dieses* aus!

Beispiel: 1 Dieser Film handelt von einem Roboter.

1. _________ Film handelt von einem Roboter.
2. Ich kann _________ Film nicht leiden.
3. _________ Bücher sind sehr interessant.
4. _________ Haus ist in einem alten Film.
5. Ich habe _________ Buch sehr gern gelesen.
6. _________ Frau ist Schauspielerin.

Grammatik: *dieser, diese, dieses* (this)

The words *dieser, diese, dieses* mean 'this' and change their ending according to whether they are **masculine**, **feminine** or **neuter**, or **singular** or **plural**. The masculine also changes in the **singular** form in the **accusative** (when it is the **object** of a sentence or clause).

	masc	fem	neut	pl
nominative	dieser	diese	dieses	diese
accusative	diesen	diese	dieses	diese

siehe Seite **140** >>

A

Dieser Film ist ein Actionfilm, der „Vier Stunden in Paris“ heißt. Der Film handelt von einem Mann und seiner Frau, die ein Paket in Paris suchen. Sie müssen dieses Paket finden und mit dem Zug nach Berlin fahren, bevor die Polizei sie findet. Sie haben nicht viel Zeit und müssen das Paket in vier Stunden finden!

B

Dieses Buch ist eine Komödie und heißt „Wo ist Lumpi?“ Es handelt von einem Jungen, der seinen Hund in einem Park verloren hat. Der Hund, den er sucht, heißt Lumpi. Eine alte Dame hilft dem Jungen. Diese Dame, die sehr reich ist, hat auch ein Problem. Aber wer ist sie? Und hat sie den Hund wirklich gesehen?

C

Das letzte Buch, das ich gelesen habe, heißt „5.000.000 Jahre in die Zukunft“. Die Geschichte findet in der Zukunft statt und handelt von zwei Kindern. Diese Kinder, die in einem alten Haus wohnen, haben einen kleinen Roboter gefunden. Der Roboter, der die Kinder nach einem anderen Planeten in seinem Raumschiff fährt, heißt T2D. Was ist danach passiert? Viel Spaß beim Lesen!

Grammatik: ***der, die, das*** **(which, that, who) in relative clauses**

The words for 'which', 'that' or 'who' are the same as the words for 'the' (**der** – **den** in the accusative – ***die***, ***das***). They **agree** with the **gender** and **number** of the **noun** they refer to.

They also change the **word order**. You have to put a comma immediately before the **der/die/das** and move the **verb** to the end of that clause.

masc	*Der Film,* ***der*** *eine Komödie ist …*	The film **which/that** is a comedy …
fem	*Die junge Frau,* ***die*** *in Berlin wohnt …*	The young lady **who** lives in Berlin …
neut	*Das Buch,* ***das*** *ich gelesen habe …*	The book (**which/that**) I read …
pl	*Die Kinder,* ***die*** *einen Roboter finden …*	The children **who** find a robot …

Sometimes in English (but **never** in German!) you can miss out the word for 'that' or 'which' completely (as in the neuter example above).

siehe Seite **147** ➤➤

3 **Lies die Texte noch einmal! Welche Satzhälften passen zusammen?**

Beispiel: 1 a

1 Ein Mann und seine Frau müssen ein Paket finden,	**a** das in Paris ist.
2 Der Mann und die Frau,	**b** das von zwei Kindern handelt.
3 Ein Junge sucht einen Hund,	**c** der irgendwo in einem Park ist.
4 Der Hund,	**d** die die Polizei sucht, müssen nach Berlin fahren.
5 „5.000.000 Jahre in der Zukunft" ist ein Buch,	**e** den er sucht, heißt Lumpi.

4 **Lies die Sätze! Was passt zusammen?**

Beispiel: 1 e

1 Der Film/Das Buch war zu lang.	**a** *The film/book had a silly/great ending.*
2 Die Geschichte war interessant.	**b** *The story was interesting.*
3 Die Handlung war spannend/langweilig.	**c** *The characters were (un)believable.*
4 Der Film/Das Buch hatte ein blödes/tolles Ende.	**d** *The plot was exciting/boring.*
5 Die Darsteller waren überzeugend/unglaubhaft.	**e** *The film/book was too long.*

5 **Hör zu (1–5)! Welche Meinungen aus Übung 4 erkennst du wieder?**

Beispiel: 1 „Das Geheimnis des Rings": 3, 5

6 **Schreib eine Kritik von einem Film, den du gesehen hast, oder einem Buch, das du gelesen hast! Dein(e) Partner(in) überprüft deinen Text.**

Strategie! ***Writing continuous text***

Make your writing more interesting by using time expressions like *gestern, letzte Woche, letztes Wochenende* and connectives like *und, aber* and *weil*, as well as building relative clauses using *der, die, das*.

Don't forget that *weil* and *der, die, das* send the verb to the end of the clause.

And if you use expressions like *Meiner Meinung nach* (in my opinion) and *für mich* (for me), the verb must come immediately afterwards.

Example: *Für mich war die Handlung sehr komisch und die Darsteller waren toll.*

Try also changing the adjectives in the sentences above. Use a dictionary if necessary.

Example: *Die Darsteller waren lustig. Die Handlung war zu kompliziert.*

4C Berühmte deutschsprachige Leute – damals!

- find out about famous German-speaking people
- learn different question types
- understand complex texts

Paul Klee: Künstler

Paul Klee ist am 18. Dezember 1879 in der Schweiz geboren. Schon in der Schule hat er sich für Zeichnen interessiert und nach seinem Abitur hat er sich entschieden, Künstler zu werden. Er hat den Künstlerklub „Blauer Reiter" gegründet und er ist Lehrer an der Kunstschule „Bauhaus" geworden. Seine Bilder haben Fantasie gezeigt und haben viele Leute verwirrt. Er ist 1940 gestorben.

Strategie! *Understanding complex, longer texts*

When you are reading a complex, longer text, you don't usually need to understand every word, so first of all look quickly through the text and try to get the gist.

Then read the text again and try to understand more detail. Use the following ideas to help you.

- Look for cognates or near-cognates (words which are the same as or similar to English words). For example: *Autor, Konzert.*
- Use logic and context to help you work out meanings. For example, all of these texts about famous people start with a date plus the words *ist geboren* and finish with another date and the words *ist gestorben*. What do you think the dates refer to?
- Don't look up every unknown word, as this will slow you down. Use the glossary or dictionary to look up only key words, which will help you to understand a sentence. For example, in the sentence *Seine Bilder haben Fantasie gezeigt und haben viele Leute verwirrt*, you probably only need to look up *Fantasie gezeigt* and *verwirrt*.
- When you are looking up verbs, remember that they will be listed in the infinitive (ending in *-en*) and you will need to remove the *ge-* from the beginning of past participles. For example, you need to look up *gezeigt* under ***zeigen***.

Fritz Lang: Filmregisseur

Fritz Lang, Filmregisseur, ist am 5. Dezember 1890 in Wien geboren. Zwischen 1919 und 1929 hat er einige wichtige Stummfilme gemacht, wie zum Beispiel „Metropolis", einer der ersten Science-Fiction-Filme. Die Nazis haben seine Filme verboten, deshalb ist er nach Hollywood gegangen, wo er insgesamt 22 Filme gemacht hat. Er ist am 2. August 1976 in Los Angeles gestorben.

Michael Ende: Autor

Michael Ende ist am 12. November 1929 in Garmisch-Partenkirchen geboren. Er ist als Autor von Kinderbücher berühmt (zum Beispiel „Die unendliche Geschichte", „Die Niemalsgasse" und „Momo", ein Buch über einen Jungen, der Zeit stiehlt). Michael Ende ist am 28. August 1995 in Stuttgart gestorben.

1  **Lies die Texte rechts!**

2 **Richtig oder falsch?**

Beispiel: **1 falsch**

1. Paul Klee ist aus Deutschland gekommen.
2. Fritz Lang ist in Österreich geboren.
3. Michael Ende hat Kinderbücher geschrieben.
4. Mozart hat Klavier gespielt.
5. Fritz Lang hat Zeichentrickfilme gemacht.
6. Michael Ende ist in Amerika gestorben.

Wolfgang Amadeus Mozart: Komponist

Wolfgang Amadeus Mozart ist am 27. Januar 1756 in Salzburg in Österreich geboren. Als Kind hat er mit drei Jahren Klavier gespielt, mit vier Jahren hat er sein erstes Musikstück komponiert und mit fünf Jahren hat er sein erstes Konzert gespielt! Mit seinem Vater hat er überall in Europa viele Konzerte gegeben. Er ist am 5. Dezember 1791 gestorben, hat aber über 620 Werke komponiert.

3 Füll die Lücken aus!

Beispiel: 1 Wien

1 Fritz Lang ist in ________ geboren.
2 Michael Ende ist in ________ gestorben.
3 Mit fünf Jahren hat Mozart sein erstes ________ gespielt.
4 Die Bilder von Paul Klee haben viele ________ verwirrt.
5 Michael Ende hat das ________ „Die unendliche Geschichte“ geschrieben.
6 Fritz Lang hat den Science-Fiction-________ „Metropolis“ gemacht.
7 Mozart hat viele Konzerte mit seinem ________ gegeben.
8 Paul Klee hat sich für ________ in der Schule interessiert.

Grammatik: *W-Fragen*

- Most German question words begin with *w*: *wo* (where?), *wann* (when?), *was* (what?), *wie viel(e)* (how much/how many?).
- Be careful with *wer*. It does not mean 'where?' It means 'who?'
- When you are asking a question, the verb comes immediately afterwards: *Wann **ist** Mozart gestorben?*
- When you answer, you can often use the same verb as in the question: *Er **ist** 1791 **gestorben**.*

Wo ist Fritz Lang geboren? Er ist in Wien geboren.

Wer hat Kinderbücher geschrieben? Michael Ende hat Kinderbücher geschrieben.

Wann ist Mozart gestorben? Er ist 1791 gestorben.

Was hat Paul Klee gegründet? Er hat einen Künstlerklub gegründet.

Wie viele Werke hat Mozart komponiert? Er hat über 620 Werke komponiert.

siehe Seite **147** >>

4 Lies die Texte noch einmal und beantworte die Fragen!

Beispiel: 1 Er ist in der Schweiz geboren.

1 Wo ist Paul Klee geboren?
2 Was hat Fritz Lang gemacht?
3 Wer hat mit drei Jahren Klavier gespielt?
4 Wann ist Michael Ende gestorben?
5 Wie viele Filme hat Fritz Lang in Hollywood gemacht?
6 Wer hat Fantasiebilder gemalt?
7 Wo und wann ist Mozart geboren?
8 Was hat Michael Ende geschrieben?

5 Was kannst du über diese berühmten Leute herausfinden? Finde Texte in der Schulbibliothek oder im Internet!

4D www.webseitenkritik!

- give opinions about websites
- learn about the imperfect tense of *sein* and *haben*

1 Lies die Meinungen über Webseiten! Was heißt das auf Englisch? Schlag im Wörterbuch nach!

a Die Ladezeit war kurz.

b Der Inhalt der Seite war langweilig.

c Das Navigationsmenü war schwer zu verstehen.

d Die Struktur der Seite war benutzerfreundlich.

e Diese Seite hatte zu viel Text.

f Die Links auf dieser Seite waren gut.

g Die Seite war aktuell.

h Die Seite war gut designt und attraktiv.

i Die Seite war schlecht designt und hässlich.

j Die Seite war veraltet.

Grammatik: the imperfect tense of *sein* and *haben*

The imperfect tense is another past tense. It is mostly used in writing, although the imperfect of *sein* (e.g. *er/sie/es war, sie waren*) and *haben* (e.g. *er/sie/es hatte*) is also used in speech. You will learn more about this tense later on.

*Die Seite **war** gut designt.*	The site was well designed.
*Die Seite **hatte** zu viel Text.*	The site had too much text.

siehe Seite **145** >>

2 Hör gut zu (1–5) und sieh dir die Meinungen oben an! Wer hat was gemeint?

Beispiel: **1 Helmut – d, ...**

Helmut · Magda · Silke · Torsten · Gabi

3 Jetzt bist du dran! Schreib Kritiken von einer Webseite, die du besucht hast! Du kannst die Adjektive ändern, wenn du willst (z.B. Die Ladezeit war zu lang).

Beispiel: Ich habe *www.ebay.co.uk* sehr gut gefunden. Die Struktur der Seite war benutzerfreundlich ...

Zusammenfassung

Einen Film sehen	***Watching a film***
Wollen wir ins Kino gehen?	*Shall we go to the cinema?*
Möchtest du eine DVD bei mir sehen?	*Would you like to watch a DVD at my place?*
Was läuft?	*What's on?*
Was für DVDs hast du?	*What DVDs have you got?*
Ich mag … (sehr/unheimlich gern).	*I like … (very much/lots).*
der Science-Fiction-Film	*science fiction film*
der Horrorfilm	*horror film*
der Martial-Arts-Film	*martial arts film*
der Fantasyfilm	*fantasy film*
der Zeichentrickfilm	*cartoon film*
der Actionfilm	*action film*
der Kriegsfilm	*war film*
die Komödie	*comedy*

Ausreden machen	***Making excuses***
Ich kann nicht.	*I can't.*
Ich darf nicht ausgehen.	*I'm not allowed to go out.*
Ich darf keine Horrorfilme sehen.	*I'm not allowed to watch horror films.*
Ich muss zu Hause bleiben.	*I have to stay at home.*
Ich muss Staub saugen.	*I have to do the vacuuming.*
Ich muss meine Hausaufgaben machen.	*I have to do my homework.*
Ich muss meinen Eltern helfen.	*I have to help my parents.*
Ich muss mir die Haare waschen.	*I have to wash my hair.*
Das habe ich schon gesehen.	*I've already seen it.*

Film- und Buchkritiken machen	***Commenting on films and books***
Dieser Film/Dieses Buch handelt von …	*This film/book is about …*
Der Film/Das Buch hatte ein tolles/doofes Ende.	*The film/book had a great/silly ending.*
Die Handlung war zu kompliziert.	*The plot was too complicated.*
Die Geschichte war interessant.	*The story was interesting.*
Die Handlung war zu langweilig/sehr spannend.	*The plot was too boring/very exciting.*
Die Darsteller waren unglaubhaft/überzeugend.	*The characters/actors were unbelievable/convincing.*
die Zeichentrickfigur	*cartoon character*

Berühmte Leute	***Famous people***
… ist (in Wien/am 5. Dezember 1965) geboren.	*… was born (in Vienna/on 5 December 1965).*
… ist (in der Schweiz/am …) gestorben.	*… died (in Switzerland/on …).*

Webseiten beschreiben	***Describing websites***
der Inhalt	*content*
der Text	*text*
die Struktur	*structure*
die Ladezeit	*loading time*
das Navigationsmenü	*navigation bar/menu*
die Links	*links*
aktuell	*up-to-date*
attraktiv	*attractive*
benutzerfreundlich	*user-friendly*
gut/schlecht designt	*well/badly designed*
hässlich	*ugly*
schwer zu verstehen	*difficult to understand*
veraltet	*out-of-date*
zu viel	*too much*

Grammatik:

★ Modal verbs: **modal** verbs usually have to be used with **another** verb and are **irregular** in the **singular** but **regular** in the **plural**. They include *können* (to be able to – I can, etc.), *dürfen* (to be allowed to – I may/can, etc.), *müssen* (to have to – I must, etc.), *wollen* (to want to), *mögen* (to like).

★ Relative clauses: the words for 'which', 'that' or 'who' are the same as the words for 'the' (*der, die, das*). They change the **word order** in the clause after them:

masc	fem	neut	pl
Der Mann, ***der …***	*Die Frau,* ***die …***	*Das Haus,* ***das …***	*Die Tiere,* ***die …***

siehe Seite **143, 147** >>

dieser (diese, dieses usw.) *this* • **der, die, das, den** *as relative pronouns* • **dürfen** *to be allowed* • **können** *to be able, can* • **mögen** *to like* • **müssen** *to have to, must* • **wollen** *to want* • **wo** *where* • **wann** *when* • **wer** *who* • **was** *what* • **wie viel(e)** *how much, how many*

Strategie!

★ Write continuous text.

★ Understand complex, longer texts.

Lauter Laute: ö, o

Wiederholung

Kapitel 3 (Probleme? Siehe Seite 26–29!)

1 Sieh dir die Bilder an und schreib Sätze!

Beispiel: **1 Wir treffen uns neben dem Restaurant.**

2 Ordne die Wörter richtig ein! Ordne dann den Dialog richtig ein!

Beispiel: **5 Haben Sie schon gewählt?**

1 Ordnung In sofort kommt Es
2 trinken zu Und
3 als Tomatensuppe Ja, nehme Vorspeise ich
4 Glas hätte Ich Rotwein ein gern
5 schon Sie gewählt Haben
6 Gulasch nehme Als Reis Hauptgericht ich mit
7 Tomatensuppe So … Hauptgericht Und als

Kapitel 4 (Probleme? Siehe Seite 32–35!)

3 Lies die Meinungen und schreib + oder –!

Beispiel: **„Shrek" +**

Normalerweise mag ich keine Komödien, aber „Shrek" mag ich sehr gern. Die Handlung war interessant und der Film hatte ein tolles Ende. Ich mag auch gern „Hennen Rennen" – dieser Film ist auch eine Komödie, aber die Figuren waren trotzdem überzeugend. Im Gegenteil hatte „Der Herr der Ringe" ein doofes Ende und die Handlung von „Das Imperium schlägt zurück" war total blöd. Ich mag keine Science-Fiction-Filme und diese Filme waren viel zu lang. Meine Lieblingsfilme sind „Die Monster-AG" und „Toy Story".

4 Verbinde die Sätze mit *der*, *die* oder *das*!

Beispiel: **1 Das ist der Zug, der um neun Uhr ankommt.**

1 Das ist der Zug. Er kommt um neun Uhr an.
2 Das ist der Junge. Er spielt mit uns.
3 Das ist die Nachbarin. Sie besucht ihre Mutter.
4 Das ist die Frau. Sie hat keine Zeit für ihre Familie.
5 Das ist der Hund. Er sitzt auf meinem Bett.
6 Das ist der Bus. Er fährt um halb elf ab.

Berühmte deutschsprachige Leute – jetzt!

Claudia Schiffer: Modell

Claudia Schiffer ist am 25. August 1970 in Rheinbach, Deutschland, geboren. Ihre Modell-Karriere hat 1987 begonnen. Man hat sie als Studentin in einer Düsseldorfer Diskothek entdeckt. Sie hat auf mehr als 500 Titelblättern von Zeitschriften geglänzt und das „People Magazine" hat sie zu den „25 schönsten Menschen" der Welt gezählt. 1999 hat sie rund 1,8 Millionen Euro für die Opfer des Hurrikans „Mitch" gespendet.

Ute Lemper: Sängerin, Tänzerin und Schauspielerin

Ute Lemper ist 1963 in Münster geboren. Sie hat schon als Kleinkind Klavier und Gesang gelernt, ab dem neunten Lebensjahr Ballett. Mit 15 Jahren hat sie als Sängerin in Jazzklubs und Bars gearbeitet. 1987 hat Ute die Rolle der Sally Bowles in „Cabaret" gespielt und danach hat sie Velma Kelly in dem Musical „Chicago" gespielt. Sie wohnt mit ihren Kindern und ihrem Mann in New York.

1 ***Read the first text and answer the questions.***

1. Where was Claudia Schiffer born?
2. Where was she discovered?
3. According to 'People magazine', what group of people did Claudia Schiffer belong to?
4. What charity did Claudia Schiffer support?

2 **Lies den zweiten Text und wähl *a*, *b* oder *c*!**

1. Ute Lemper ist in **a)** Münster **b)** New York **c)** Chicago geboren.
2. Sie hat mit **a)** neun **b)** fünfzehn **c)** drei Jahren Ballett gelernt.
3. Mit 15 Jahren hat sie **a)** in einem Supermarkt **b)** in Jazzklubs **c)** an einer Tankstelle gearbeitet.
4. Heute wohnt sie in **a)** Münster **b)** London **c)** New York.

5 In der Gegend

5A Was wollen wir machen?

- describe what there is to see and do
- discuss where to go
- learn to use the present tense with a future meaning

1 **Was gibt es in jeder Stadt? Hör gut zu (1–4) und mach vier Listen!**

Beispiel: 1 Garmisch-Partenkirchen: d, ...

Garmisch-Partenkirchen **Luzern** **Salzburg** **Leipzig**

Grammatik: ***es gibt***

To say **what there is** in a town or region, use *es gibt*. Don't forget:

- to change it to *gibt es* if you put another word first;
- to change the **masculine** forms *der* and *ein* to *den* and *einen*;
- to use *keinen/keine/kein* to say what there **isn't**.

  ***Es gibt einen** Park in Leipzig.*
  *In Leipzig **gibt es einen** Park.*

  ***Es gibt keine** Kegelbahn in Altdorf.*
  *In Altdorf **gibt es kein** Freibad.*

Es gibt can't be translated literally into English. Its literal meaning is 'it gives', but that obviously doesn't make sense! What would we say in English?

siehe Seite **145** >>

2 **Was gibt es in deiner Stadt oder in deinem Dorf? Macht Dialoge!**

Beispiel: A Was gibt es in Nottingham?
B In Nottingham gibt es ein Freibad und eine Disko, aber kein italienisches Eiscafé ...

3 **Was gibt es in deiner Stadt oder in deinem Dorf? Wie findest du es dort? Und warum? Schreib einen Paragrafen!**

Beispiel: Hier in Reading gibt es viele Kinos, ein Jugendzentrum, ein Hallenbad, eine Kegelbahn und viele Geschäfte. Ich finde Reading prima!

Hier gibt es ...

a einen Park.

b eine Disko.

c eine Kegelbahn.

d ein italienisches Eiscafé.

e ein Kino.

f ein Sportzentrum.

g ein Jugendzentrum.

h ein Hamburger-Restaurant.

i ein Theater.

j ein Freibad.

k ein Hallenbad.

l viele Geschäfte.

4 Hör zu und lies die Dialoge! Was macht man? Was macht man **nicht**? Schreib für jedes Bild ✔ oder ✗!

a 

b 

c

d

Dialog 1
– Wohin gehen wir **heute Abend**?
– Willst du **ins Kino** gehen?
– Nein, was mich betrifft, ist das **langweilig**.
– Also, willst du **ins Schwimmbad** gehen?
– Tolle Idee! Bis dann – mach's gut.

Dialog 2
– Was machen wir **heute Abend**?
– **Wollt ihr** ins Eiscafé gehen?
– Nein – das mache ich nicht gern.
– Wollen wir denn **ins Sportzentrum** gehen?
– Toll!

5 Wie viele Vorschläge kannst du in den Dialogen oben finden? Schreib sie auf!

Beispiel: **Willst du ins Kino gehen?**

6 Ändert die fett gedruckten Wörter in den Dialogen oben und erfindet eure eigenen Dialoge!

Beispiel: **A** Wohin gehen wir **heute Morgen**?
B Willst du **einkaufen** gehen?
A Nein, was mich betrifft, ist das **zu teuer**.
B …

7 Schreib einen SMS! Benutze neue Vorschläge und Ausreden! Und überprüfe!

Beispiel: Hallo, Rudi/Rudi und Claudia.
Was machen wir (heute Abend)?
Willst du/Wollt ihr ins (Kino) gehen?
Oder willst du/wollt ihr ins (Freibad) gehen?
Ich will (nicht) ins (Freibad) gehen, weil ich das (langweilig) finde … (usw.)

Grammatik: the present tense with a future meaning

In these dialogues the **present tense** is used to talk about the **future** – usually with a time phrase like *heute Abend* or *morgen*. This happens in English too, e.g. 'I'm going shopping tomorrow' instead of 'I shall go shopping tomorrow'.

***Morgen gehe ich** einkaufen.*

***Ich fahre am Wochenende** Ski.*

***In den Ferien fahre ich** nach Paris.*

siehe Seite **145** ≫

5B Weißt du was?

- learn some colloquial expressions
- say where you are going, when and how
- use correct word order (time–manner–place)

1 ***On the previous spread you met* Was mich betrifft *and* Bis dann – mach's gut. *These are* colloquial *expressions. You don't usually see them written down, but you often hear them. Now listen to the six short dialogues and see if you can match up the meanings of the colloquial expressions below with the English meanings.***

1	Weißt du was?	**a**	*Bye, stay in touch.*
2	Du, ich muss dir was sagen!	**b**	*No, no – it's OK.*
3	Von mir aus.	**c**	*Have you got any plans?*
4	Ciao, meld' dich mal!	**d**	*Hey, I've got something to tell you!*
5	Bist du noch ganz dicht?!	**e**	*Brilliant!*
6	Nee, nee, ist O.K.	**f**	*It's all the same to me.*
7	Hast du was vor?	**g**	*Are you nuts?!*
8	Supertoll!	**h**	*Do you know what?*

Strategie! ***Using context clues when listening or reading***

A useful strategy to help you work out the meaning of new words or expressions is to use the **context** (what the text or conversation is about). Often, other words or expressions that you **do** know will help give you the meaning of the new vocabulary.

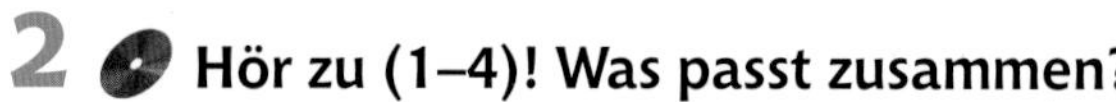

2 **Hör zu (1–4)! Was passt zusammen?**

Beispiel: 1 c

a

mit dem Auto

b

mit der Straßenbahn

c

mit dem Rad

d

mit dem Bus

masculine/neuter			***feminine***		
mit dem	Auto	*by car*	mit der	Fähre	*by ferry*
	Bus	*by bus*		Straßenbahn	*by tram*
	Rad	*by bike*		U-Bahn	*by underground*
Achtung! Zu Fuß = *on foot*					

3 Hör zu (1–3)! Wo fährt man hin? Wann und wie? Wähl für jeden Dialog **drei** Bilder!

Beispiel: **1 a, …**

a 
b 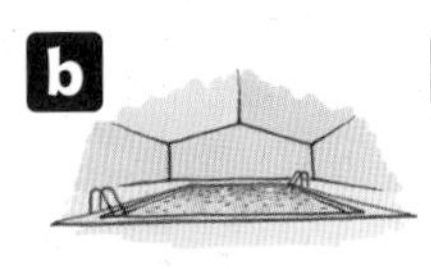
c 

d 
e 
f 

g 
h 
i 

Grammatik: word order with time phrases

In a sentence, time phrases like *normalerweise, am Wochenende, morgen, heute Abend, im Sommer*, etc., go **before** how you are going there and where you are going. This applies to all tenses, but in the perfect tense, remember that the **participle** goes at the **end** of the clause. So the word order rule is:

time – **manner** – **place**

or

when – **how** – **where (to)**

*Ich fahre **morgen mit dem Bus** ins Kino.*
*Fährst du **heute mit dem Rad** ins Jugendzentrum?*
*Ich bin **am Wochenende mit der Straßenbahn** in die Stadtmitte **gefahren**.*

siehe Seite **146** ≫

4 Lest den Dialog unten und macht ähnliche Dialoge!

Beispiel: **A** Weißt du was? Morgen gehen wir ins Sportzentrum.
B Supertoll! Wann und wie?
A Um achtzehn Uhr mit der Straßenbahn.

5 *extra!* Schreib deine eigene E-Mail! Benutze die Bilder unten! Ändere die fett gedruckten Wörter!

Beispiel: Hallo!
Wie geht's? Was machst du normalerweise in den Ferien?

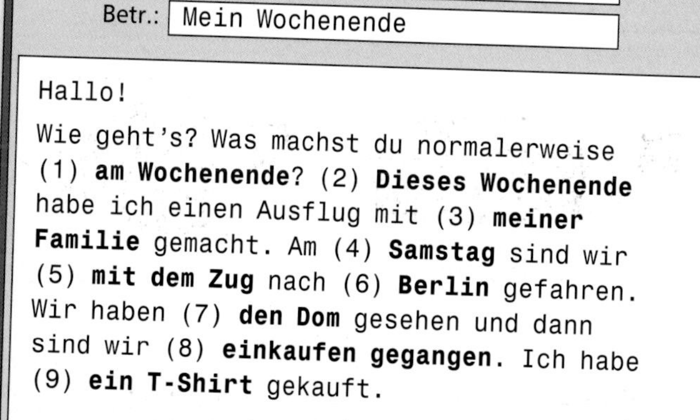
An: Anne Peters
Von: Käthe Jenne
Betr.: Mein Wochenende

Hallo!

Wie geht's? Was machst du normalerweise (1) **am Wochenende**? (2) **Dieses Wochenende** habe ich einen Ausflug mit (3) **meiner Familie** gemacht. Am (4) **Samstag** sind wir (5) **mit dem Zug** nach (6) **Berlin** gefahren. Wir haben (7) **den Dom** gesehen und dann sind wir (8) **einkaufen gegangen**. Ich habe (9) **ein T-Shirt** gekauft.

1 in den Ferien

2  in den Ferien

3 

4 

5 

6 

7 

8 

9 

5C Vorsicht bei der Abfahrt!

- ask for and give travel information
- understand times using the 24-hour clock
- use separable verbs in the present and perfect tenses

– **Einmal** nach **Bonn**, bitte.
– Einfach oder hin und zurück?
– **Hin und zurück**.
– Erster Klasse oder zweiter Klasse?
– **Zweiter Klasse**, bitte.
– Das macht **250 Euro**.
– Bitte schön.
– Danke schön.

1 Am Bahnhof. Hör zu und lies den Dialog!

2 Hör zu (1–5)! Kopiere die Tabelle und füll sie für jeden Dialog aus!

Beispiel:

Dialog	einfach/hin und zurück?	Klasse	Preis
1	h/z	2.	€250

3 Jetzt seht euch die Fahrkarten an und macht ähnliche Dialoge!

Beispiel: **A** Einmal nach Berlin, bitte.
B Einfach oder hin und zurück?
A …

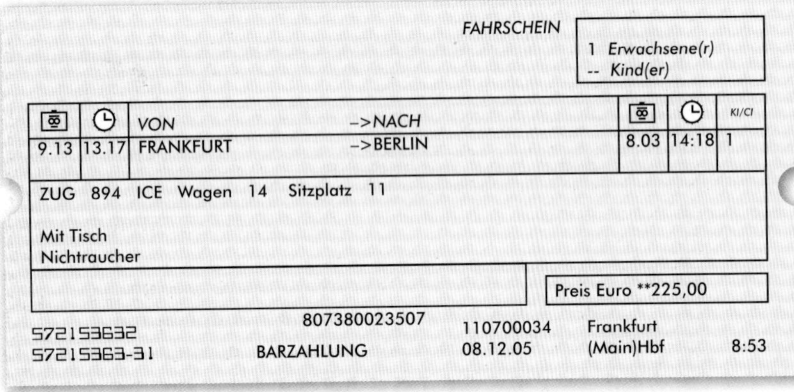

FAHRSCHEIN

1 Erwachsene(r)
-- Kind(er)

		VON	->NACH			Kl/Cl
9.13	13.17	FRANKFURT	->BERLIN	8.03	14:18	1

ZUG 894 ICE Wagen 14 Sitzplatz 11

Mit Tisch
Nichtraucher

Preis Euro **225,00

572153632
57215363-31
807380023507
BARZAHLUNG
110700034
08.12.05
Frankfurt
(Main)Hbf
8:53

ICE HIN– UND RÜCKFAHRT

FAHRSCHEIN

Gültig ab	Hinf.bis	Rückf.bis	Ruckf.ab
28.01.06	27.02.06	27.02.06	28.01.06

1 Erwachsene(r)
-- Kind(er)

		VON	->NACH			Kl/Cl
		Hannover Hbf Dresden Hbf	Dresden Hbf Hannover Hbf			2

über
(ICE: HH*S)

Fahrscheine mit einmonatiger Geltungsdauer gültig zu einer Hin– und Rückfahrt, längstens 4 Tage je Fahrtrichtung.

Preis Euro **175,00

187019895
18702989-84
BARZAHLUNG
010835576
27.01.06
Hannover Hbf
14
00
14:17

4 a Wie spät ist es? Schreib die Uhrzeiten auf! Zeichne die Uhren!

Beispiel: 1 23.25

1 Es ist dreiundzwanzig Uhr fünfundzwanzig.
2 Es ist sechzehn Uhr fünfundvierzig.
3 Es ist zweiundzwanzig Uhr fünfzehn.
4 Es ist neunzehn Uhr fünfzig.

Strategie! *The 24-hour clock*

For travel announcements German uses the **24-hour clock**. This is quite simple (add 12 to the normal time and follow it with a number between 1 and 59 to show the hours and minutes!) and it is also often used in Britain.

Es ist/Um …	It's/At …
dreizehn Uhr fünf.	13.05.
achtzehn Uhr dreißig.	18.30.

4 b Hör zu und ordne den Dialog richtig ein!

Beispiel: **6, ...**

1 Und wann kommt er in Aachen an?
2 Um 16.00 Uhr.
3 Ja, um 15.00 Uhr in Mönchengladbach.
4 Von Gleis 4.
5 Wann fährt er ab?
6 Von welchem Gleis fährt der Zug nach Aachen?
7 Um 14.22 Uhr.
8 Muss ich umsteigen?

Grammatik: *trennbare Verben* (separable verbs)

You have met some new **separable verbs** here. In the present tense, separable verbs split into two parts (the **verb** and a **prefix**). The verb goes in the usual place and the prefix goes at the end of the sentence:

*Wann **fährt** der Zug **ab**?*
*Der Zug **kommt** um 15.00 Uhr **an**.*

In the **perfect** tense, the two parts of the verb **join up** again, but they usually have ***-ge-*** in between them. Some separable verbs take *haben* and some take *sein* in the perfect tense.

*Der Zug ist spät **angekommen**.*
*Er ist um 15.00 Uhr **abgefahren**.*

siehe Seite **144** ➤➤

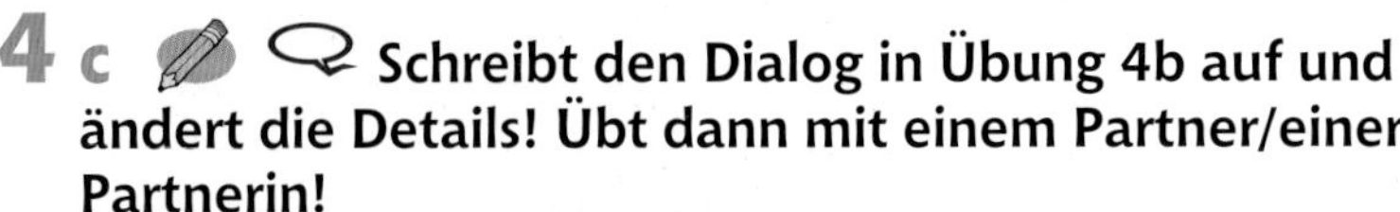

4 c **Schreibt den Dialog in Übung 4b auf und ändert die Details! Übt dann mit einem Partner/einer Partnerin!**

Beispiel: **Von welchem Gleis fährt der Zug nach München?**

5 **Hör zu (1–2) und mach Notizen! Und überprüfe!**

Beispiel: **1 Gleis 2, ab 22.15, umsteigen Bremen 23.00, an Hamburg 23.55**

6 **Lies den Text und wähl jeweils *a* oder *b*!**

Beispiel: **1 b**

1 Der Zug ist **a)** pünktlich **b)** spät in Bonn angekommen.
2 In Bonn sind sie zum **a)** falschen **b)** richtigen Gleis gegangen.
3 Nach **a)** drei **b)** zwei Stunden haben sie einen anderen Zug gefunden.
4 In Koblenz sind sie mit dem **a)** Auto **b)** Bus weitergefahren.
5 Dort ist der Bus am **a)** falschen **b)** richtigen Bahnhof angekommen.
6 In Mainz ist der Bus **a)** früh **b)** spät angekommen!

An: Erich
Von: Benno
Betr.: Reise nach Mainz

Meine Reise nach Mainz war „interessant"! Der Zug ist pünktlich von London abgefahren, aber er ist sehr spät in Bonn angekommen. (Ist das normal? Ich denke nicht!) In Bonn sind wir zum falschen Gleis gegangen und der Zug war nicht mehr da! Nach zwei Stunden haben wir einen anderen Zug gefunden, aber dieser Zug hat eine Panne in Koblenz gehabt und wir sind mit dem Bus weitergefahren! Der Bus ist am falschen Bahnhof angekommen(!) und wir sind zu spät am richtigen Bahnhof angekommen. Zum Schluss sind wir mit einer Verspätung von zwei Stunden in Mainz angekommen.

Lauter Laute: ü oder u?

- *Remember,* **ü** *and* **u** *are different sounds.*

In Leipzig, München und Düsseldorf gibt es fünfundfünfzig Büros.
In Luzern und Salzburg gibt es eine Rutschbahn und ein Jugendzentrum.
Über fünfzigtausend junge Leute führen Hunde über die Brücke.

5D Berlin

- learn about the history and size of Berlin
- use more reading strategies

Berlin hat eine lange und interessante Geschichte. Von 1806 bis 1808 wurde die Stadt von Napoleon besetzt. Zwischen 1925 und 1933 war sie die kulturelle Hauptstadt Europas, aber am 30. Januar 1933 wurde Adolf Hitler Reichskanzler.

Im Zweiten Weltkrieg wurde die Stadt weitgehend zerstört. Zwischen 1942 und 1945 haben insgesamt 23.407 Bomber mehr als 50.000 Tonnen Bomben auf die Stadt abgeworfen.

1948 sperrten die Sowjets die Land- und Wasserwege in die Stadt und zwischen Juni 1948 und Dezember 1949 gab es eine Luftbrücke zur Versorgung der Westsektoren Berlins.

Im August 1963 haben die Ostberliner eine Mauer durch die Stadtmitte gebaut. Westberlin wird gegen Ostberlin und die DDR durch einen „antifaschistischen Schutzwall“ abgeriegelt.

Am neunten November 1989 hat man die Übergänge der Mauer für Bürger der DDR geöffnet und bald danach hat man die Mauer abgerissen.

Berlin ist jetzt die größte Stadt Deutschlands, mit einer Bevölkerung von 3.396.300 (oder 2,4% der Gesamtbevölkerung von 81.852.744).

Seit 1989 findet die so genannte „Love Parade“ statt. Jedes Jahr kommen ungefähr 250 DJs, die ihre Botschaft von Frieden und Liebe mitbringen.

Strategie!

Using context clues when listening or reading

Look at this text about Berlin and see how much you can understand by looking for cognates and context clues to meaning (some of the questions will also give you clues as to what is in the text).

For instance, you might not know what *abgeworfen* means, but you can see from the rest of the sentence that it's something to do with bombs, and in one of the questions this word is paraphrased as *gefallen*. This should help you to work out the meaning.

1 Lies den Text! Richtig oder falsch?

Beispiel: 1 richtig

1 Napoleon hat die Stadt von 1806 bis 1808 besetzt.
2 Zwischen 1925 und 1933 war Adolf Hitler Reichskanzler.
3 Im Zweiten Weltkrieg sind nur wenige Bomben auf Berlin gefallen.
4 Im Juli 1949 konnte man mit dem Auto von Westdeutschland nach Berlin fahren.
5 Die Berliner Mauer wurde 1989 von den Sowjets gebaut.
6 Im November 1989 hat man die Grenzübergänge in Berlin geöffnet.
7 Die Bevölkerung Berlins ist jetzt 81.852.744.

Strategie! wurde/wurden …

Note that *wurde/wurden (besetzt/zerstört*, etc.) means was/were (occupied/destroyed, etc.) from the verb *werden*.

2 Lies den Text noch einmal und wähl *a*, *b* oder *c*!

Beispiel: 1 b

1 Zwischen 1925 und 1933 war Berlin die **a)** militärische **b)** kulturelle **c)** wirtschaftliche Hauptstadt Europas.
2 Im Zweiten Weltkrieg sind mehr als **a)** fünftausend Tonnen **b)** fünfzigtausend Tonnen **c)** fünfhunderttausend Tonnen Bomben auf Berlin gefallen.
3 1948 wurden die Wege in die Stadt von den **a)** Russen **b)** Deutschen **c)** Amerikanern gesperrt.
4 Die Berliner Mauer nannten die Ostberliner **a)** die antikommunistische Mauer **b)** die antiamerikanische Mauer **c)** den antifaschistischen Schutzwall.
5 Im November 1989 hat man **a)** die Übergänge nach Westdeutschland geöffnet **b)** viele Bomben auf Berlin abgeworfen **c)** einen „antifaschistischen Schutzwall“ gebaut.
6 Die „Love Parade“ handelt von **a)** Krieg **b)** Liebe und Frieden **c)** Einkaufen.
7 Berlin ist die **a)** zweitgrößte **b)** größte **c)** drittgrößte Stadt Deutschlands.

In der Gegend	***In the area***
Was gibt es in …?	*What is there in …?*
In … gibt es …	*In … there's/there are …*
Es gibt …	*There's/There are …*
Hier gibt es …	*Here there is/are …*
einen Park.	*a park.*
eine Disko.	*a disco.*
eine Kegelbahn.	*a bowling alley.*
ein Freibad.	*an open-air pool.*
ein Hallenbad.	*an indoor pool.*
ein Hamburger-Restaurant.	*a hamburger restaurant.*
ein italienisches Eiscafé.	*an Italian ice-cream parlour.*
ein Jugendzentrum.	*a youth centre.*
ein Kino.	*a cinema.*
ein Sportzentrum.	*a sports centre.*
ein Theater.	*a theatre.*
viele Geschäfte.	*lots of shops.*

Vorschläge	***Suggestions***
Wohin gehen wir heute Abend?	*Where shall we go this evening?*
(Also,) willst du … ?	*(OK,) do you want to …?*
Was wollt ihr machen?	*What do you want to do?*
Wollen wir (denn) … ?	*Shall we … (then)?*
Tolle Idee!/Supertoll!	*Great idea!/Brilliant!*
Nein, das finde ich langweilig.	*No, I think that's boring.*
Nein, das mache ich nicht gern.	*No, I don't like doing that.*

Umgangssprache	***Colloquialisms***
Weißt du was?	*Do you know what?*
Du, ich muss dir was sagen!	*Hey, I've got something to tell you!*
Von mir aus.	*It's all the same to me.*
Ciao, meld' dich mal!	*Bye, stay in touch.*
Bist du noch ganz dicht?!	*Are you nuts?*
Nee, nee, ist O.K.	*No, no – it's OK.*
Hast du was vor?	*Have you got any plans?*
Bis dann, mach's gut	*Till then, take care.*

Sagen, was du vor hast	***Say what you're planning***
Wir sind zum Essen eingeladen.	*We've been invited for a meal.*
Wir machen einen kleinen Spaziergang.	*We're going on a little walk.*
Ich gehe ins Schwimmbad.	*I'm going to the swimming pool.*

Zugfahrkarten kaufen	***Buying railway tickets***
Einmal nach … , bitte.	*A single to … , please.*
Einfach oder hin und zurück?	*Single or return?*
Erster oder zweiter Klasse?	*First or second class?*
Das macht insgesamt … Euro.	*That'll be … euros altogether.*
Bitte schön.	*Here you are/You're welcome.*
Danke schön.	*Thank you.*
Von welchem Gleis fährt der Zug nach …?	*Which platform does the train to … go from?*
Von Gleis … .	*From platform … .*
Wann fährt er ab?	*When does it leave?*
Wann kommt er in … an?	*When does it arrive in … ?*
Um … Uhr.	*At … o'clock.*
Muss ich umsteigen?	*Do I have to change?*
Ja, um … Uhr in … .	*Yes, at … o'clock in … .*

Transport	***Transport***
mit dem Auto	*by car*
mit der Fähre	*by ferry*
mit dem Bus	*by bus*
mit der Straßenbahn	*by tram*
mit dem Rad	*by bike*
mit der U-Bahn	*by underground*
zu Fuß	*on foot*

Grammatik:

- ★ *Trennbare Verben:*
  *Wann **fährt** der Zug **ab**?*
  *Der Zug **kommt** um 15.00 Uhr **an**.*
  *Der Zug ist spat **angekommen**.*
- ★ Word order with time phrases:
  *Ich fahre **morgen mit dem Bus** ins Kino.*
  *Fährst du **heute mit dem Rad** ins Jugendzentrum?*
- ★ *Die Uhrzeit sagen:*

Es ist/Um …	It's/At …
dreizehn Uhr fünfzehn.	13.15.
siebzehn Uhr fünfundfünfzig	17.55.
usw.	

siehe Seite **144, 146, 148** >>

Lauter Laute: ü, u

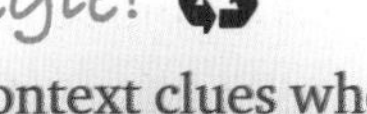

- ★ Use context clues when listening or reading.
- ★ Use the 24-hour clock for travel announcements in German.
- ★ Use *wurde/wurden (besetzt)* from *werden* to say 'was/were (occupied)', etc.

heute *today* • **morgen** *tomorrow* • **am Wochenende** *at the weekend* • **in den Ferien** *in the holidays*
Separable prefixes: **ab, an, um** • **es gibt + Akkusativ** *there is/there are*

6 Unsere Umwelt

6A Heiter bis wolkig

- talk about the weather and activities
- learn how to use *wenn*
- learn how to use the future tense

1 a Hör zu (1–10) und sieh dir die Bilder oben an! Wie ist das Wetter? Was passt zusammen?

Beispiel: **1 c**

1 b Sieh dir die Bilder aus Übung 1a an und lies die Sätze (1–10)! Was passt zusammen?

Beispiel: **1 e**

1	Es ist heiß.	**6**	Es ist neblig.
2	Es ist warm.	**7**	Es ist heiter bis wolkig.
3	Es ist kalt.	**8**	Es regnet.
4	Es ist windig.	**9**	Es schneit.
5	Es ist sonnig.	**10**	Es friert.

1 c Wie ist das Wetter? A wählt ein Bild aus Übung 1a. B sagt, wie das Wetter ist. A überprüft.

2 a Hör zu und mach Notizen! Was macht man bei welchem Wetter?

Name	Wetter	Aktivität
Siglinde	es regnet	einkaufen ...
Malik		

2 b Stellt und beantwortet Fragen!

Beispiel: **A** Was macht Siglinde, wenn es regnet?
B Wenn es regnet, geht sie schwimmen.

2 c extra! Sieh dir deine Notizen aus Übung 2a an und schreib einen Bericht!

Beispiel: **Wenn es regnet, geht Siglinde schwimmen, aber wenn es ...**

Grammatik: *wenn*

Use the connective *wenn* to say 'if', 'when' or 'whenever'.

*Ich gehe in den Park, **wenn** das Wetter gut **ist**.*

What has happened to the verb in the *wenn* part of the sentence (*wenn* clause)?

Which other connective do you know that sends the verb to the end of its clause?

Now see what happens if you put the *wenn* clause at the beginning of the sentence (which is a more common place for it to be).

***Wenn** das Wetter gut **ist**, **gehe** ich in den Park.*

Remember the 'verb second' rule? This time the whole *wenn* clause is the first part of the sentence, so the next word has to be a verb.

And don't forget the comma to separate the clauses. This gives the pattern 'verb – comma – verb'.

siehe Seite **146** ➤➤

3 a **Hör zu und sieh dir die Bilder an! Ist das Lotte oder Markus?**

Beispiel:

Lotte	Markus
	b

Grammatik: future tense

To say that something will happen in the **future**, use part of the irregular verb *werden* with an infinitive. Remember that infinitives go to the end of the sentence.

Ich	*werde*	*in den Park **gehen**.*
Du	***wirst***	*einen warmen Pulli **tragen**.*
Er/Sie/ Es/Man	***wird***	*das Auto **waschen**.*
Wir	*werden*	*nach Österreich **fahren**.*
Ihr	*werdet*	*zu Hause **bleiben**.*
Sie	*werden*	*Freunde **besuchen**.*

Don't forget that you can sometimes use the present tense for future meaning (see unit 5, page 43).

siehe Seite **145** ➤➤

3 b **Füll die Lücken aus!**

Beispiel: **1 wirst**

1. Was ______ du in den Ferien machen?
2. Ich ______ nach Österreich fahren.
3. Markus ______ einen warmen Pulli tragen.
4. Ihr ______ in den Park gehen.
5. Wo ______ es kalt sein?
6. Markus und seine Eltern ______ Freunde besuchen.

4 a **Macht Dialoge!**

Beispiel: **A Was wirst du am Wochenende machen, wenn es schneit?**
B Wenn es schneit, werde ich Ski fahren.
A Das wird toll sein!

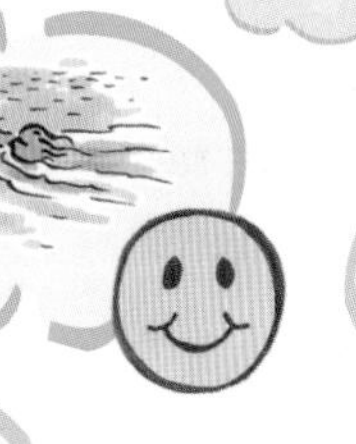

3 **dein Bruder**

5 **deine Eltern**

4 **Tania**

6 **Hella und Mehmet**

4 b *extra!* **Und du, was wirst du am Wochenende machen, wenn das Wetter gut/schlecht ist? Schreib etwa 50–60 Wörter!**

5 a **Lauter Laute: w, v, f**

- Hör zu und sprich nach!

Wenn das Wetter warm und windig ist, werden Waltraut und Wilhelm im Wald walzen.

Volkers freundlicher Vater hat vier verbrauchte Volkswagen für vierzehnhundertfünfzig Euro verkauft.

5 b *extra!* **Hör zu! Schreib den Satz mit *w*, *v* und *f* richtig auf!**

__enn __olkers __reund __alther im __inter mit der __amilie zum __ranken__ald __ährt, __ird er __ohl mit dem __olks__agen __ahren.

6B Die Umwelt stinkt!

- talk about the environment
- learn how to use some negatives
- work out the meaning of longer words

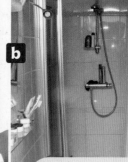

Ich bringe Flaschen zum Altglascontainer.

a

b

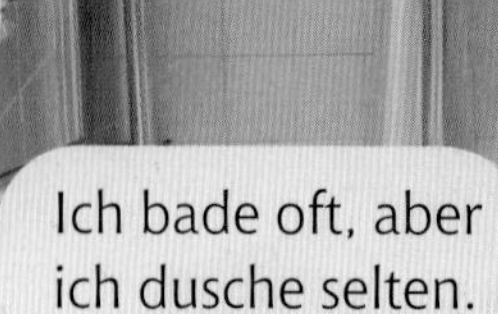

Ich bade oft, aber ich dusche selten.

c

Ich schalte das Licht aus.

Ich fahre mit dem Bus oder mit dem Rad.

d

e

Ich nehme Plastiktüten im Supermarkt.

1 a Hör zu (1–5)! Welche Bilder sind das?

Beispiel: **1 d, i**

1 b Ist das umweltfreundlich oder umweltfeindlich? Mach zwei Listen!

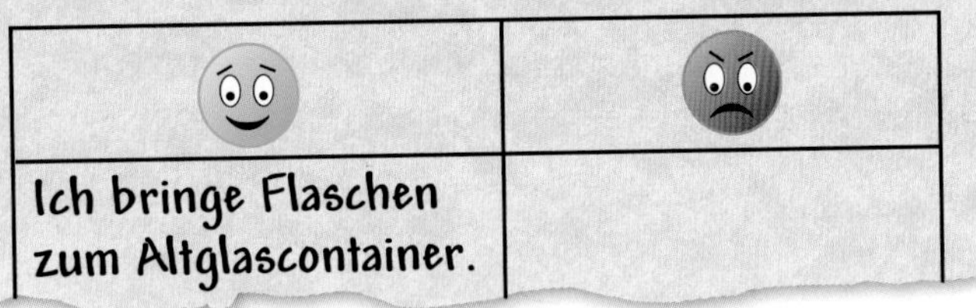

🙂	☹
Ich bringe Flaschen zum Altglascontainer.	

Strategie! *Working out meaning*

Not sure about the meaning of some words, especially long ones? Try to work out what they are by breaking them down and using clues in the text.

For example: *umweltfreundlich/umweltfeindlich.*

- *Welt* means 'world' and *um* means 'around', so *Umwelt* is the 'world around us' – the environment.
- You know the word *Freund* and we're looking at opposites here, so what might *Feind* mean?
- Putting *-lich* on the end of a word makes it into an adjective or adverb. This is similar to adding what in English?

2 a Mach eine Umfrage in der Klasse! Mach Notizen!

Beispiel: **A Was machst du für die Umwelt? Oder was machst du nicht?**
B Ich kaufe Recyclingpapier, aber ich fahre nicht oft mit dem Rad.

2 b Mach eine Grafik aus dem Resultat!

Beispiel:

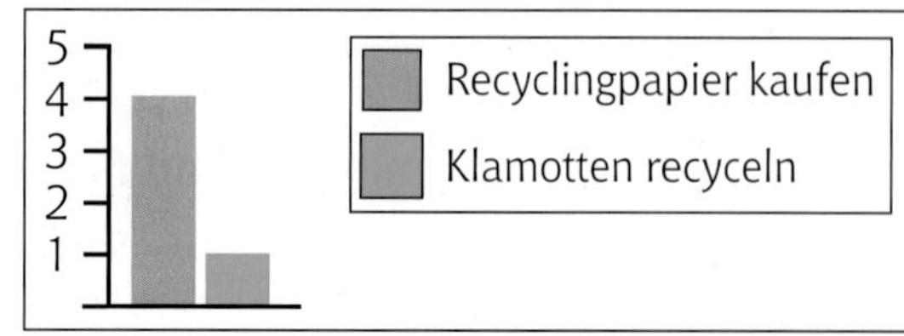

2 c extra! Schreib die Resultate auf! Wie findest du das?

Beispiel: **Vier Schüler kaufen Recyclingpapier, aber nur ein Schüler bringt alte Klamotten zum Recyclingcontainer. Das ist nicht sehr gut für die Umwelt.**

Ich recycle alte Klamotten.
f
g
Ich bringe alte Zeitungen zum Altpapiercontainer.
h
Ich kaufe oft Recyclingpapier.
Briefumschläge
50
i
Ich fahre immer mit dem Auto.
j
Altpapier
Ich trenne meinen Müll.

3 Hör zu! Ist das richtig oder falsch?

Beispiel: **1 falsch**

1. Altan macht überhaupt nichts für die Umwelt.
2. Daniela kauft kein Recyclingpapier, weil es nicht sehr billig ist.
3. Martina bringt weder Altpapier noch Glas zum Recyclingcontainer.
4. Kai ist nie mit dem Rad gefahren.
5. Tulai wird keine alte Kleidung recyceln.
6. Florian macht nicht immer das Licht aus, wenn er das Zimmer verlässt.

Grammatik: negatives

You've learnt *nicht* and *kein*. What other negative expressions can you find in the sentences in Exercise 3?

How is *nicht* different from *nichts*?

The expression *weder … noch …* is negative. It means 'neither … nor …'.

*Er recycelt **weder** Papier **noch** Glas.*	He recycles **neither** paper **nor** glass. He does**n't** recycle **either** paper **or** glass.

siehe Seite **145** ➤➤

4 Was heißt das auf Deutsch?

1. Diana has never travelled by bus.
2. I don't sort my rubbish.
3. They don't buy either recycled paper or old clothing.
4. Gregor doesn't take anything to the recycling bin.
5. At the supermarket I don't take any plastic bags.

5 Seht euch das Bild unten an! Was meint ihr, wie umweltfreundlich sind Frau Müller und Herr Grün? Was machen sie (nicht)?

Beispiel: **A Frau Müller bringt Glas zum Altglascontainer. Das finde ich umweltfreundlich.**

B Ja, aber sie bringt nur eine Flasche und sie fährt mit dem Auto! Das ist furchtbar!

Ich bin umweltfreundlich: Ich bringe diese Flasche zum Altglascontainer.

der Komposthaufen – *compost heap*
der Teich – *pond*
er/sie recycelt/ist … – *he/she recycles/is …*

6 Und du? Wie umweltfreundlich bist du? Was machst du für die Umwelt, oder was wirst du machen? Schreib einen Bericht mit etwa 60 Wörtern! Dein(e) Partner(in) überprüft.

6C Stadt oder Land?

- talk about town and country living
- learn to use the comparative and superlative
- learn to use present, past and future tenses

Lennard

Unsere Wohnung liegt in der Stadtmitte. Meine Straße ist ziemlich laut und gefährlich, weil es viel Verkehr gibt, aber Geschäfte und die Schule sind ganz in der Nähe. Das ist praktisch. Das größte Problem ist das Parken: Wir finden oft keinen Parkplatz in der Nähe.

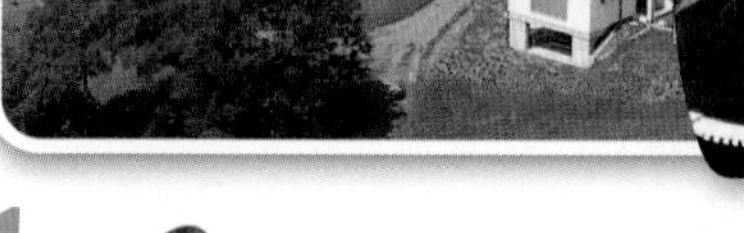

Meine Eltern finden das Leben auf dem Dorf sehr gut, aber meine Schwester und ich finden es total langweilig. Es ist zu ruhig, es gibt keine Geschäfte und wir müssen eine Stunde mit dem Bus zur Schule fahren. Am liebsten möchte ich in der Stadt wohnen.
Raphaela

Jonas
Das Stadtleben gefällt mir nicht: Es ist lauter, schmutziger und ungesünder als auf dem Land. Die Umweltverschmutzung ist am schlimmsten in der Stadt. Es gibt Lärm, Müll, Fabriken und Verkehr. Wenn ich älter bin, werde ich nicht in der Stadt wohnen.

1 a **Hör zu und lies mit!**

1 b **Lies die Texte! Was heißt das auf Deutsch?**

1. village life
2. It's too quiet.
3. because there's a lot of traffic
4. the biggest problem
5. I don't like town life.
6. Pollution is worst in town.
7. when I'm older
8. better than in the inner city
9. There's too much noise.
10. I'll live in the country.

1 c **Gruppenarbeit! Stadt oder Land? Was ist positiv und was ist negativ? Füllt die Tabelle aus! Beantwortet dann die Frage: Wo möchte die Gruppe wohnen – in der Stadt oder auf dem Land?**

Beispiel: **Gruppe A:** **Wir wohnen lieber in der Stadt, weil es viel für Junge Leute gibt, aber …**
Gruppe B: **Unsere Gruppe wohnt lieber auf dem Land, weil …**

Stadt		Land	
positiv	negativ	positiv	negativ
viel für junge Leute	zu viel Verkehr		

in der Stadt/Stadtmitte
am Stadtrand/auf dem Land
Das größte Problem ist … .
Die Umweltverschmutzung ist am schlimmsten.
besser als in der Stadtmitte
Ich wohne am liebsten auf dem Land.

Es gibt	(zu) viel	Verkehr/Lärm/Müll.	
	(zu) viele	Fabriken.	
Es ist (zu)		laut/ruhig/ungesund. schmutzig/gefährlich/ praktisch.	
Es ist		lauter/ruhiger (un)gesünder schmutziger	als …

Elena
Ich wohne am Stadtrand. Das ist schon besser als in der Stadtmitte und ich wohne ziemlich gern hier. Es gibt viel für junge Leute, aber es gibt auch zu viel Lärm und zu viel Verkehr. Ich liebe die Natur und später werde ich auf dem Land wohnen.

Grammatik: comparatives and superlatives

You have already used **comparative** adjectives to say that something is 'bigger', 'smaller', etc.: *groß – größer; klein – kleiner, gut – besser.*

To say something is 'the biggest', 'the smallest', etc. (the **superlative**) you usually add **-st** or **-est** to an adjective, very similar to English. And remember to add the normal adjective endings:
schlimm – das schlimmste Problem.

Short adjectives usually add an umlaut as well:
alt – mein ältester Bruder; groß – das größte Problem

And some superlatives are irregular:
*gut – meine **beste** Freundin.*

If you want to say something **is** the loudest or you **do** something the fastest, etc., use the pattern *am …(e)sten.*

laut/lauter	*Das Leben in der Stadt ist **am lautesten**.*
schnell/schneller	*Man fährt **am schnellsten** mit dem Zug.*
gern/lieber	*Ich wohne **am liebsten** auf dem Land.*

Listen for superlatives in Exercise 2.

siehe Seite **142** ➤➤

2 Hör zu und füll die Lücken aus!

Beispiel: **1 ältester**

Finn

1 Finns ____________ Bruder ist nach Berlin an die Uni gegangen.
2 Er kommt ____________ mit dem Zug dahin.
3 Das ____________ Problem für ihn ist der Lärm.

Miriam

4 Miriams ____________ Freundin wohnt gern in der Stadt.
5 In Lenas Straße ist der Verkehr morgens ____________ .
6 Radfahren ist in der Stadt ____________ , findet sie.

Bastian

7 Die ____________ Stadtbewohner machen nicht genug für die Umwelt.
8 Umweltverschmutzung ist heute das ____________ Problem, meint Bastian.
9 Auch die ____________ Tiere sind für Bastian wichtig.

3 Seht euch die Bilder und Ausdrücke unten an und macht Dialoge!

Beispiel: **1 A Wo wohnst du am liebsten?**
B Ich wohne am liebsten in der Stadtmitte.
A Warum?
B Weil die Geschäfte in der Nähe sind.
A Was ist das größte Problem?
B Es gibt zu viel Lärm.

4 Beschreib, wo du wohnst, wie es dir gefällt, was gut ist und was ein Problem ist! Wenn möglich, schreib im Perfekt, im Präsens und im Futur!

Beispiel:

```
Ich wohne am Stadtrand von … und
das finde ich gut, weil … .
Ich habe die Stadtmitte sehr
gefährlich gefunden. Ein Problem
in der Stadt ist … .
Wenn ich älter bin, werde ich auf
dem Land wohnen. Das wird cool
sein, weil … .
```

6D Umweltaktion

- understand an environmental poster
- learn about environmental issues

Umweltschutz und Umweltschmutz

Nichts machen ist keine Lösung! Was haben wir schon in der Heinrich-Heine-Schule gemacht?

Schüler, Lehrer und Eltern haben fleißig zusammengearbeitet und auf dem Schulgelände einen Teich gebaut. Dieser Teich und die in der Nähe liegenden Pflanzen sind jetzt die schönste Heimat für viele Tiere – Insekten, Vögel, Frösche usw.

Was werden wir jetzt machen?

Wir werden alte Handys sammeln! Warum? Rund 60 Millionen alte Handys liegen in deutschen Schreibtischschubladen und Schränken – die meisten landen im Hausmüll. Viele Wertstoffe stecken in den Handys, aber wir wollen sie recyceln. Die Deutsche Umwelthilfe (*www.duh.de*) bekommt fünf Euro pro Handy und gibt das Geld dann für Naturschutzprojekte aus. Super!

Wie kannst du helfen?

Du kannst mitmachen! Du kannst kaputte und nicht mehr benötigte Handys aussuchen!

Wir wollen eine bessere Zukunft. Du kannst helfen.

Wenn du nichts machst, gibt es keine Zukunft.

Strategie! ***Working out meaning***

Don't confuse *Umweltschmutz* and *Umweltschutz* – only one letter is different, but the meanings are very different.

You know that *schmutzig* means dirty, so the noun *Schmutz* means what?

The verb *schützen* means 'to protect', so what does *Schutz* mean?

When reading a text, remember to use a dictionary only as a last resort – look at (near-)cognates first, then use logic and grammatical knowledge to work things out.

1 Lies das Poster und beantworte die Fragen auf Englisch!

1. Who built a pond in the school grounds?
2. What creatures will benefit from this?
3. Where do old mobiles usually end up?
4. Why is the school collecting them?
5. What is the money used for?

2 Mach ein ähnliches Poster über eine Umweltaktion! Benutze Ideen aus dem obigen Poster oder erfinde deine eigenen Projekte!

Tipps:

- Benutze bekannte Wörter (besonders aus den Seiten 50–56)!
- Such nur ein paar neue Wörter im Wörterbuch, aber nicht viele!
- Schreib mindestens einen Satz im Perfekt, im Präsens und im Futur!

Beispiel: **Dieses Jahr haben wir jeden Tag Altpapier/Cola-Dosen/Kleidung gesammelt.**
Wir machen Teppiche aus Plastiktüten und verkaufen sie in der Stadt.
Im Sommer werden wir einen Umweltgarten in der Schule bauen.

Zusammenfassung

Das Wetter	***The weather***
Es ist heiß/warm/kalt.	*It's hot/warm/cold.*
Es ist sonnig/windig/neblig.	*It's sunny/windy/foggy.*
Es ist heiter bis wolkig.	*It's fair to cloudy.*
Es regnet.	*It's raining/It rains.*
Es schneit.	*It's snowing/It snows.*
Es friert.	*It's freezing/It freezes.*

Die Umwelt	***The environment***
Ich bringe Flaschen zum Altglascontainer.	*I take bottles to the glass recycling bin.*
Ich bade (selten).	*I (seldom) have a bath.*
Ich dusche (oft).	*I (often) shower.*
Ich schalte das Licht (nicht) aus.	*I (don't) turn off the light.*
Ich fahre mit dem Bus oder mit dem Rad.	*I go by bus or bike.*
Ich nehme (keine) Plastiktüten/Stofftüten.	*I (don't) take/use plastic bags/cloth bags.*
Ich recycle alte Klamotten.	*I recycle old clothes.*
Ich bringe alte Zeitungen zum Altpapiercontainer.	*I take old newspapers to the paper bank.*
Ich kaufe (oft) Recyclingpapier.	*I often buy recycled paper.*
Ich fahre (immer) mit dem Auto.	*I always go by car.*
Ich trenne meinen Müll.	*I sort my rubbish.*

Stadt und Land	***Town and country***
in der Stadt/in der Stadtmitte	*in town/in the town centre*
am Stadtrand	*in the suburbs*
auf dem Land	*in the country*
das größte Problem ist …	*the biggest problem is …*
die Umweltverschmutzung ist am schlimmsten	*pollution is worst*
besser als in der Stadtmitte	*better than in the inner city*
Ich wohne am liebsten auf dem Land.	*Most of all I like living in the country.*
der Verkehr	*traffic*
der Lärm	*noise*
der Müll	*rubbish*
die Fabrik (-en)	*factory*
(zu) laut/ruhig/ungesund	*(too) noisy/quiet/unhealthy*
schmutzig/gefährlich/praktisch	*dirty/dangerous/practical*
es ist lauter/ruhiger/(un)gesünder/schmutziger als …	*it's noisier/quieter/(un)healthier/dirtier than …*

Grammatik:

- *wenn:* means 'if', 'when' or 'whenever'.
  *Ich gehe in den Park, **wenn** das Wetter gut **ist**.*
  ***Wenn** das Wetter gut **ist**, **gehe** ich in den Park.*
- Future tense: to say that something will happen in the **future**, use *werden* + infinitive (at the end of the sentence).
  Du **wirst** *in den Park* **gehen**.
  Er **wird** *das Auto* **waschen**.
- Negatives:
  nicht – not; *nichts* – nothing; *kein, keine*, etc. – not a, no;
  nie – never; *weder … noch …* – neither … nor …
- Comparatives: to say 'bigger', 'smaller', etc. you usually add *-er* to an adjective: *klein – klein**er**; groß – gr**ö**ß**er**; gut – **besser**.*
- Superlatives: to say something is 'the biggest', 'the smallest', etc. you usually add *-(e)st* to an adjective (with the right endings).
  *schlimm – das schlimm**ste** Problem; alt – mein **ältester** Bruder; groß – das gr**ößte** Problem; gut – meine **beste** Freundin*
  To say something **is** the loudest or you **do** something the fastest, etc., use the pattern *am …(e)sten.*
  *Das Leben in der Stadt ist **am lautesten**.*

siehe Seite **142, 145, 146** ➤➤

Strategie!

- Work out the meaning of longer words.
- Use cognates, logic and grammatical knowledge when reading.

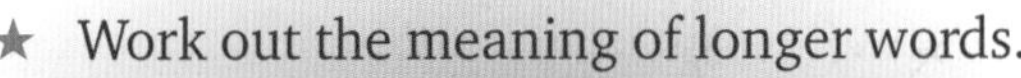

Lauter Laute: w, v, f

wenn *if* • **nicht** *not* • **nichts** *none* • **kein** *no* • **nie** *never* • **weder … noch …** *neither … nor …* • **oft** *often* • **immer** *always* • **selten** *rarely*

Wiederholung

Kapitel 5 (Probleme? Siehe Seite 42–45!)

1 a Welches Bild ist das?

Schinkenstadt ist schön!

a b c d e f g h i j

Beispiel: 1 a

1 Wollen wir heute Abend ins Kino gehen?
2 Ich will nicht ins Freibad gehen, weil es zu kalt ist!
3 Am Wochenende gehe ich ins Sportzentrum.
4 Willst du morgen in die Geschäfte gehen?
5 Morgen gehe ich nicht ins Eiscafé.

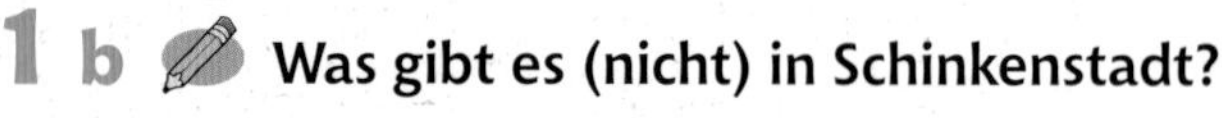

1 b Was gibt es (nicht) in Schinkenstadt?

Beispiel: In Schinkenstadt gibt es ein Kino, aber es gibt keine Disko …

2 Schreib die Sätze richtig auf!

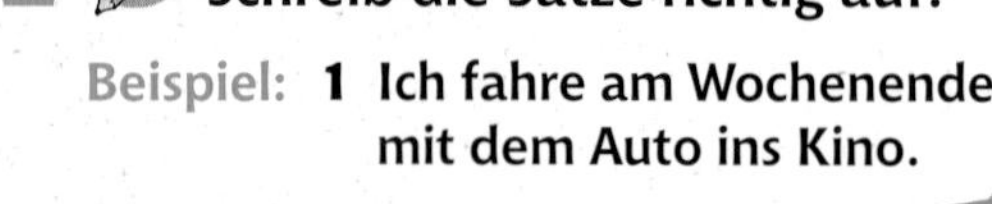

Beispiel: 1 Ich fahre am Wochenende mit dem Auto ins Kino.

1 Ich fahre
2 Wir fahren
3 Fährst du
4 Warum fahrt ihr
5 Meine Eltern und ich fahren
6 Benjamin fährt

Kapitel 6 (Probleme? Siehe Seite 50–53!)

3 Was wirst du am Wochenende machen? Schreib die Antworten auf!

Beispiel: 1 Wenn es schneit, werde ich Ski fahren. Das wird toll sein!

1

4

2

5

3

4 a Was passt zusammen?

Beispiel: 1 c

1 Ich werde Flaschen
2 Ich fahre mit dem Bus oder
3 Im Supermarkt nehme ich
4 Ich bringe alte Zeitungen
5 Für die Schule haben

a mit dem Rad in die Stadtmitte.
b wir oft Recyclingpapier gekauft.
c zum Altglascontainer bringen.
d nie zum Altpapiercontainer.
e viele Plastiktüten.

4 b Sieh dir Übung 4a an! Ist das umweltfreundlich 🙂 oder umweltfeindlich ☹?

Beispiel: 1 🙂

Schüleraustausch

Schüleraustausch nach England oder Frankreich, das macht fast jeder einmal. Aber innerhalb des eigenen Landes? Das gibt es eigentlich nicht. Und deswegen haben zwei Mädchen aus Bayern und Hamburg eine Woche lang getestet, wie es ist, am anderen Ende Deutschlands zu wohnen und in die Schule zu gehen.

Sonntag: Sophies Eltern haben mich in München am Bahnsteig gleich erkannt – ich habe vorher ein Foto von mir geschickt. Von München fahren wir mit dem Auto noch 'mal eine gute Stunde – die Landstraßen sind viel dunkler als in Hamburg. Das Haus von Sophies Familie in Riederau sieht hübsch aus, auch schön groß. Aber das ist kein Urlaub. In Sophies Zimmer liegt ihr Hausschlüssel und eine Nachricht: „Du musst um sechs aufstehen … . Eine Haltestelle nach dir steigt Heidi in den Bus, das ist eine Freundin von mir, die zeigt dir dann alles … . Schulbücher liegen im Fach in der Schule … . Und bitte schreib alles mit, was auf der Tafel steht …". Dann sehe ich den chaotischen Stundenplan – fast jeden Tag sechs verschiedene Fächer; in Hamburg haben wir viel mehr Doppelstunden. Ich gehe noch einmal ins Wohnzimmer, Sophies Vater und ihr Freund Richi unterhalten sich dort. Ich sage „Gute Nacht".

Martina, 17, kommt aus Hamburg und ist eine Woche lang in die 11. Klasse des Ignatz-Kögler-Gymnasiums in Landsberg am Lech gegangen.

Sophie, 17, kommt aus Riederau am Ammersee und ist eine Woche lang in die 11. Klasse der Wichern-Gesamtschule in Hamburg gegangen.

__Sonntag:__ Im Zug treffe ich einen älteren Mann, auch einen Bayern. Er findet es total gut, dass ich für eine Woche in Hamburg Schüleraustausch mache. Am Bahnhof stehen die Eltern von Martina; mit dem Auto brauchen wir 20 Minuten nach Hause – ein Hochhaus in Mümmelmannsberg: Aufzüge bin ich genauso wenig gewohnt wie den Ausblick auf so eine große Stadt von so einem hohen Balkon. Merkwürdiges Gefühl. Aber Martinas Zimmer ist ähnlich wie meins – sie hat auch Fotos von Fußballspielern an der Wand. Bayern München, glaube ich. Auf dem Tisch liegt auch die Nachricht: „Hallo, Sophie! Noch ein paar Tipps: Du triffst um 7.55 Uhr Mareike und Nicole am Kiosk vorm U-Bahnhof Bilstedt, Fotos von den beiden stehen im Regal …". Ja toll, aber wie komme ich denn zur U-Bahn?! Ich muss mit dem Bus erst 'mal eine Viertelstunde bis zur U-Bahn-Station fahren!

1 Lies das Tagebuch von Martina und Sophie und beantworte die Fragen auf Englisch!

1. How will Martina get to school?
2. What are the main differences between her timetable and Sophie's?
3. What two things about Martina's flat is Sophie not used to?
4. What aspect of their rooms do the girls have in common?
5. How will Sophie get to school?
6. How do you think they will each enjoy the week?

2 *Find out more about Bavaria (Bayern) and present your findings to the class.*

- Where is the region?
- What are its major cities, mountains and rivers?
- What are the regional specialities?
- What tourist attractions are there?

7 Gesundheit!

7A Das tut weh!

- report ailments
- explain how ailments happened
- use some exclamations in German

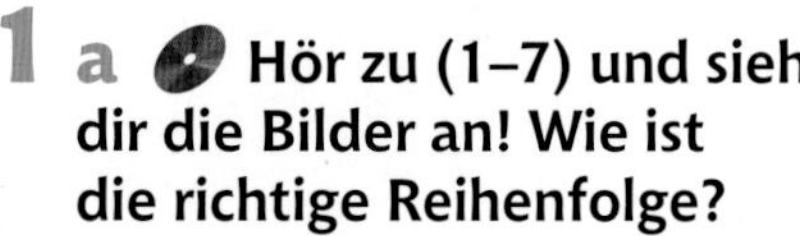

1 a Hör zu (1–7) und sieh dir die Bilder an! Wie ist die richtige Reihenfolge?

Beispiel: **1 c**

1 b Lies die Entschuldigungszettel! Wer ist das?

Beispiel: **1 d**

1 Ich habe Rückenschmerzen und meine Schultern tun mir weh.

2 *Das Bein und der Fuß tun ihm weh.*

3 Die Finger tun ihr weh.

4 *Die rechte Hand und der Arm tun weh.*

5 Ich habe Hals- und Magenschmerzen, meine Augen tun weh und ich habe Fieber.

6 Er hat Kopfschmerzen und Ohrenschmerzen und die Nase tut ihm weh.

1 c Du telefonierst mit der Schule. Wählt Bilder aus Übung 1a aus und macht Dialoge!

Beispiel:
A Guten Tag, hier ist Florian (aus der Klasse 9GW).
B Guten Tag. Wie kann ich helfen?
A Es tut mir Leid. Ich kann heute nicht zur Schule kommen.
B Oh, schade. Was ist mit dir los?
A Der rechte Arm und die Hand tun weh. Ich kann nicht schreiben.
B Danke. Ich notiere das.

1 d *extra!* **Was ist los? Such im Wörterbuch nach und telefoniere dann mit der Schule!**

Grammatik: dative pronouns

In certain phrases you need to use the **dative** form of pronouns.

Das Bein tut Die Arme tun	mir dir	weh.
Was ist mit	ihm ihr	los?
Es geht	uns euch	nicht gut.
Es tut	ihnen Ihnen	Leid.

siehe Seite **143** >>

Was ist (mit dir) los?

Es geht mir/ihm/ihr nicht gut.

Ich habe	Kopfschmerzen/Ohrenschmerzen/ Zahnschmerzen/Halsschmerzen/ Magenschmerzen/Rückenschmerzen.		
Der Fuß/Arm/Mund Die Hand/Nase Das Bein		tut	(mir) weh. (ihm) (ihr)
Die Augen/Schultern/Finger tun			
Ich habe Fieber.			

2 a Hör zu (1–4) und mach Notizen!

Wer?	Was ist los?	Seit wann?	Warum?
Hakan	Magenschmerzen	zwei Stunden	
Doris			vom Rad runtergefallen
Micki			
Julia			

Grammatik: *seit*

The preposition *seit* means 'since' or 'for'.

Seit gestern. Seit Montag. (since)
Seit einer Woche. Seit zwei Tagen. (for)

It always takes the **dative** case:

*seit ein**em** Tag/ein**er** Woche/ein**em** Jahr/zwei Tage**n***

It is used with the present tense, even though English uses the perfect.

Seit wann bist du krank? How long **have** you **been** ill?
(= Since when **are** you ill?)
Ich bin seit drei Tagen krank. I **have been** ill **for** three days.
(= I **am** ill **since** three days ago.)

siehe Seite **141** >>

2 b Macht Dialoge!

Beispiel:
A Was ist mit Hakan los?
B Er hat Magenschmerzen.
A Der Arme! Seit wann geht es ihm nicht gut?
B Seit zwei Stunden.
A Das ist schlimm. Weißt du, warum?
B Ja, er hat zu viel gegessen!
A Ach so!

2 c extra! Schreib einen Satz mit *weil* für jede Person!

Beispiel: **1** Hakan hat seit zwei Stunden Magenschmerzen, weil er zu viel gegessen hat.

3 Was heißt das wohl auf Englisch? Rate mal!

1 Drück die Daumen!
2 Aus den Augen, aus dem Sinn.
3 Hals- und Beinbruch!
4 Hände hoch!
5 Finger weg!

Fingers crossed.
Hands up!
Hands off!
Out of sight, out of mind.
Break a leg!

4 a Lauter Laute: Aua! Igitt! Ach nein! Mensch!

- Hör zu und sprich nach!

Frank ist krank,
Martina hat Fieber
Kerstin hat Schmerzen,
Und Uwe tut's weh.
Aua! schreit Frau Bauer.
AUA!
Ach nein! ruft Herr Klein.
ACH NEIN!
IGITT!
Igitt! sagt die Birgit.
MENSCH!
Mensch! denkt der Jens.

4 b Wie sagt man *Aua!*, *Igitt!*, *Ach nein!* und *Mensch!* auf Englisch?

7B Iss dich gesund!

- talk about healthy eating
- give opinions about food
- learn how to use *um ... zu ...*

Gesund essen hat nichts mit Hunger und Verzicht zu tun. Im Gegenteil: man kann sich richtig satt essen. Und zwar an den richtigen Lebensmitteln. Auch ganz wichtig: täglich zwei Liter Mineralwasser, ungesüßten Kräuter- oder Früchtetee trinken.

Die Ernährungs-Pyramide (Foto), aus Lebensmitteln aufgebaut, zeigt auf einen Blick, wie sich gesunde Ernährung zusammensetzt.

Die breite Basis bilden frisches Obst, Gemüse und Vollkornprodukte (so viel man mag!).

Im Mittelfeld sind Produkte, die gesunde Biostoffe (z.B. Eiweiß, Mineralien, Vitamine) liefern, aber auch viele Kalorien. Deshalb darf man sie nur in Maßen essen.

Und man soll sich selten von Süßem, Salzigem, Fettem, Weißmehlprodukten oder Alkohol verführen lassen.

Äpfel, Bananen, Avocado, Chips, Birnen, Cola, Eier, Fisch, Früchtetee, Hähnchen, Käse, Kekse, Kiwis, Landbrot, Limonade, Milch, Mineralwasser, Müsli, Nüsse, Oliven, Schwarzbrot, Orangen, Paprika, Salat, Süßigkeiten, Weintrauben, Weißbrot, Wurst, Reis, Rindfleisch, Schokolade, Schweinefleisch, Tomaten

1 a Hör zu und lies mit!

1 b Lies den Text noch einmal! Was heißt das auf Deutsch?

Beispiel: **1 Hunger und Verzicht**

1 hunger and going without
2 you can eat as much as you like
3 with the right foods
4 healthy nutrition
5 fresh fruit
6 wholemeal foods
7 protein, minerals, vitamins
8 eat in moderation
9 food made from white flour
10 you should only rarely allow yourself to be tempted by sweet things

1 c Lies die Wörter und mach drei Listen! Wie viel soll man davon essen? Was meinst du?

Beispiel:

oft/viel	in Maßen	selten/wenig
Äpfel	Eier	Chips

Strategie! ***Using a dictionary to find the correct German for a word***

Not sure what a particular food item is in German? Look it up in a dictionary, but remember to check carefully that you've got the right word, especially where several meanings are possible (e.g. mash, roll, pepper, ...). Check in both German-English and English-German sections of the dictionary!

2 a Was hast du gestern gegessen und getrunken? Schreib ein Tagebuch!

Beispiel:

	zum Frühstück	zu Mittag	zu Abend	dazwischen
Mo.	Ich habe Müsli und Toast mit Honig gegessen und Orangensaft getrunken.			Um 11 Uhr habe ich einen Marsriegel und eine Packung Chips gegessen. Ich habe 2 Glas Wasser getrunken.

2 b Hat das geschmeckt oder nicht? War das gesund oder ungesund? Was meint ihr?

Beispiel: **A** **Was hast du am Montagabend gegessen?**
B **Ich habe Fisch mit Erbsen und Reis gegessen, dann etwas Obst, und ich habe Tee mit Milch getrunken. Das hat nicht geschmeckt, aber es war ziemlich gesund! Was meinst du?**
A **Ich mag Fisch nicht, aber du hast Recht, es ist gesund.**

3 a Drei Teenager diskutieren gesundes Essen. Hör zu und lies die Texte! Finde den Fehler in jedem Satz!

Beispiel: **a Man soll wenigstens fünf *Portionen* Obst oder Gemüse essen.**

a Man soll wenigstens fünf Kilo Obst oder Gemüse essen.

Hannah

b Es ist wichtig, dass man von allem sehr viel isst, finde ich.

c Meine Eltern gehen immer zum Supermarkt, um frisches Obst und Gemüse zu kaufen.

Tina

d Ich habe dieses Jahr keine Eier gegessen.

Adem

f Wir müssen das essen, um fit zu bleiben; wir sollen das essen, um langweilig zu sein.

e Wenn man nicht zu viel isst, wird man dick bleiben!

Grammatik: *um … zu …*

To say 'in order to' (or usually just 'to'), use **um** at the beginning of a clause and **zu** with an infinitive at the end.

*Wir gehen auf den Markt, **um** frisches Obst **zu kaufen**.* We go to the market (in order) to buy fresh fruit.

If you start the sentence with *Um … zu …*, a verb must come next (verb – comma – verb).

*Um fit zu **bleiben, esse** ich gesund.*

Ich esse, um zu leben. *Ich lebe, um zu essen!*

siehe Seite **147** >>

3 b Hör noch einmal zu! Wer sagt oder glaubt das: Hannah, Tina oder Adem?

1. Chocolate gives you energy.
2. I'm fed up with 'healthy eating'!
3. You should eat a bit of everything.
4. We've hardly eaten any meat for two years.
5. You need to drink plenty of water.
6. Fish and eggs give us the right vitamins and minerals.

3 c A isst gesund, B isst nicht gesund. Was esst und trinkt ihr? Macht einen Dialog!

Beispiel: **A** **Isst du gesund?**
B **Ja, ich esse ziemlich gesund. Heute habe ich zum Frühstück Müsli gegessen und Orangensaft getrunken. Und du, was wirst du heute Abend essen?**
A **Ich werde zwei Hamburger mit Pommes essen. Das schmeckt super! …**

3 d extra! Was meinst du zum Thema *gesundes Essen*? Was machst du jetzt und was hast du gemacht, um fit zu sein? Was wirst du (nicht) machen, um gesund zu bleiben? Schreib einen Bericht!

Beispiel: **In der 8. Klasse *habe* ich viele Süßigkeiten *gegessen*, aber jetzt …**
Letztes Wochenende *bin* ich 15 km zu Fuß *gegangen*, dann habe ich … .
Um fit zu sein, esse ich …
Wenn ich älter bin, *werde* ich keinen Alkohol *trinken*, weil …

7C Trimm dich!

- discuss healthy living
- learn how to use infinitives
- learn how to use different forms of modal verbs

Was machst du, Henning?
Ich mache Yoga. Ich versuche innerlich und äußerlich fit zu sein.

Was wirst du noch machen, um fit zu werden?
Ich habe schon begonnen gesünder zu leben.

1 a **Hör zu und schau dir die Bilder an!**

1 b **Was heißt das auf Deutsch?**

1. I am trying to be fit.
2. I have begun to live more healthily.
3. I've decided to eat …
4. I hope to play tennis …
5. Do you want to come along?
6. I've forgotten to bring …

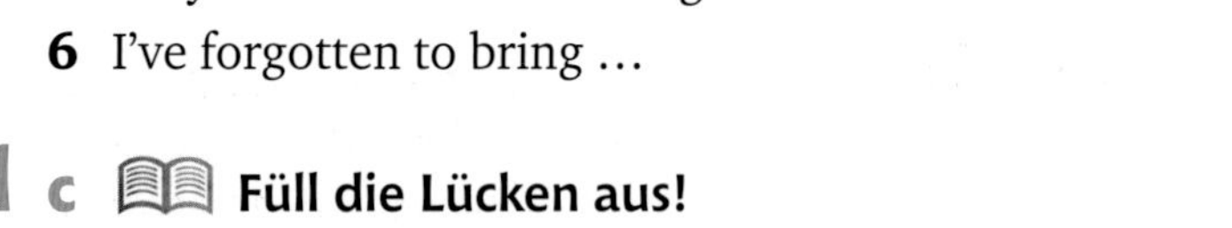

1 c **Füll die Lücken aus!**

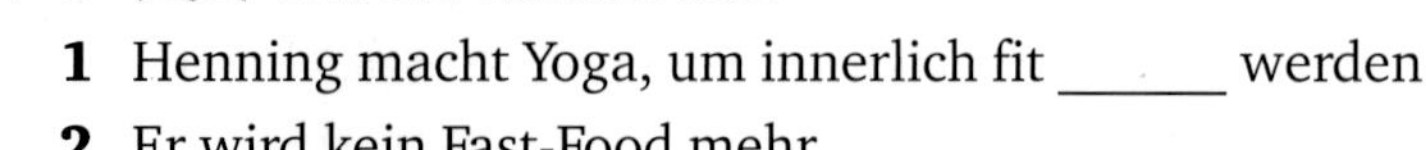

1. Henning macht Yoga, um innerlich fit ______ werden.
2. Er wird kein Fast-Food mehr ______ .
3. Er hofft regelmäßig Tennis zu ______ .
4. Er kann sich besser ______ , weil er gesünder ist.
5. Tina hat ______ schwimmen zu gehen.
6. Henning schwimmt nicht, weil er seine Badehose ______ hat.

Strategie! *Working out meaning*

Use a dictionary to try to find the infinitive and the meaning of the new verbs in the picture story. Watch out – some of them are in the perfect tense … and they are irregular, so some of the vowels might have changed from the infinitive!

2 **Vervollständige die Sätze mit den Verben unten!**

Beispiel: **1 Benno hat Lust Fußball zu spielen.**

mitbringen	spielen	nehmen
fahren	essen	gehen

1. Benno hat Lust …

2. Lena hat nicht vergessen …

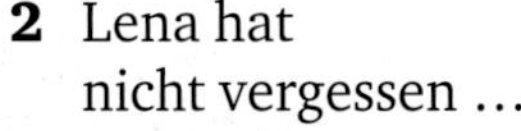

3. Um wie viel Uhr werden wir … ?

4. Mehmet und Pembe beschließen …

5. Möchtest du … ?

6. Wir haben versucht …

Grammatik: infinitives

When two verbs are used together, one of them is in the **infinitive** and, as you already know, it goes at the **end** of the clause.

Sometimes you need to add the extra word **zu** in front of the infinitive, as you did with *um … zu …*

- If the main verb is *gehen*, *werden* or a modal verb, you **don't need** *zu* before the infinitive.

  *Ich **gehe** heute **schwimmen**. Ich **werde** meine Badehose nicht **vergessen**.*
  *Tina **kann** auch **mitkommen**.*
  *Henning **möchte** kein Fast-Food **essen**.*

- Most other verbs do need *zu*.

  *Er **hat Lust** zu schwimmen. Er **hofft** Tennis zu spielen. Er **versucht** fit zu werden. Er **hat vergessen** seine Badehose mitzubringen.**

*Notice what happens with separable verbs like *mitkommen* and *mitbringen* – *zu* goes between the prefix and the infinitive.

siehe Seite **147** >>

Ich werde jeden Tag Rad fahren und ich hoffe zweimal pro Woche Tennis oder Basketball zu spielen.
Ich habe beschlossen kein Fast-Food mehr zu essen und keine süßen Getränke zu trinken.

Ich kann mich so viel besser konzentrieren, weil ich gesund bin. Ich gehe gleich schwimmen, Tina. Hast du Lust mitzukommen?
Ja, gerne.

Hast du denn keine Lust mehr zu schwimmen?

Doch … aber ich habe vergessen, meine Badehose mitzubringen!!

3 a Hör zu! Richtig oder falsch?

Beispiel: **1 richtig**

1. Boris joggt jeden Tag etwa zehn Kilometer.
2. Er hat keine Lust zu joggen, wenn es regnet.
3. Für seine Gesundheit sollte Deniz mehr Sport treiben.
4. Er hat viel Zeit Sport zu treiben.
5. Steffi darf nicht Rad fahren.
6. Deniz wird versuchen öfter mit dem Rad zu fahren.
7. Steffi findet Obst, Gemüse und Wasser wichtig, um gesund zu leben.
8. Man soll nicht rauchen und keinen Alkohol trinken, meint Boris.
9. Steffi findet Rauchen und Alkohol in Ordnung.
10. Es ist gesund mit Bier und Zigaretten vor dem Fernseher zu sitzen.

3 b Hör noch einmal zu und lies die Modalverben! Wie ist die richtige Reihenfolge? Und was heißt das auf Englisch?

Beispiel: **c 5, …**

a	ich **wollte**	**1**	*can you*
b	du **könntest**	**2**	*I have to*
c	ich **möchte**	**3**	*you ought to*
d	wir **sollen**	**4**	*you could*
e	wir **mussten**	**5**	*I would like to*
f	du **solltest**	**6**	*one (you/we) should*
g	**kannst** du	**7**	*we were not allowed to*
h	**durften** wir nicht	**8**	*we had to*
i	**muss** ich	**9**	*I wanted to*
j	man **soll**	**10**	*we should*

3 c Was soll man machen, um gesund zu leben? Was machst du (nicht)? Was hast du (nicht) gemacht? Was wirst du (nicht) machen? Was hoffst du (nicht) zu machen? Macht Interviews!

Beispiel:
A **Was soll man machen, um gesund zu leben?**
B **Ich meine, man soll viel Obst und Gemüse essen.**
A **Was machst du?**
B **Ich versuche ziemlich viel Sport zu treiben. (Zum Beispiel …)**
A **Was hast du letzte Woche gemacht?**
B **Letzte Woche habe ich zu viele Süßigkeiten gegessen.**
A **Was wirst du machen, oder was hoffst du zu machen?**
B **Ich werde nie rauchen – das finde ich schlimm.**

4 a Mach ein Poster über gesundes Leben! Benutze Ideen aus Übung 3!

Beispiel:

Wie viel Wasser hast du heute getrunken?

Man muss mehr Wasser trinken.

Was wirst du heute machen?

Ich habe Lust zu joggen! Kommst du mit?

4 b extra! Schreib eine Broschüre (60–80 Wörter) über gesundes Leben!

Beispiel: **Um fit zu bleiben, sollte man … .**
Du könntest … .

7D Rauchen? Nein, danke!

- learn how to follow a discussion
- learn how to understand opinions

A Ich finde es furchtbar, dass so viele Hauptschüler schon rauchen …
Ich meine … erstens sieht's ja echt doof aus, wenn so ein 12–13-Jähriger mit einer Tschick in der Hand herumläuft …
zweitens ist es in dem Alter (aber natürlich auch später) extrem schädlich …
und drittens kostet's sehr viel …
viertens: es macht abhängig …
fünftens: die Zähne werden gelb …
Tja … Was meint ihr zu dem Thema?

B Rauchen hat mich nie interessiert. Ich war manchmal mit Gruppen, wo ich der einzige Nichtraucher war, aber ich habe nicht angefangen. Warum soll es cool sein zu stinken, seine Lunge mit Teer vollzumüllen und dafür auch noch Geld zu bezahlen?! Das werde ich in meinem ganzen Leben nie verstehen.

C Genau! Aus diesem Grund finde ich die „RAUCHEN KANN TÖTEN"-Sticker auf Zigarettenpackerl so toll.

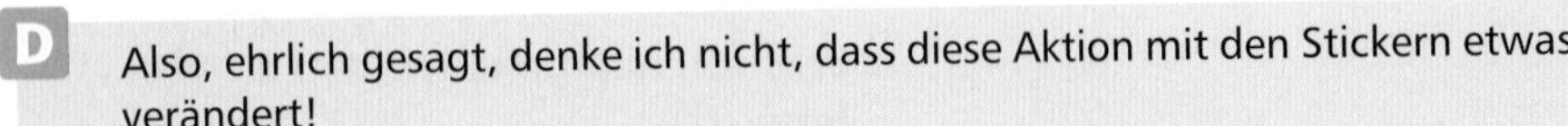

D Also, ehrlich gesagt, denke ich nicht, dass diese Aktion mit den Stickern etwas verändert!

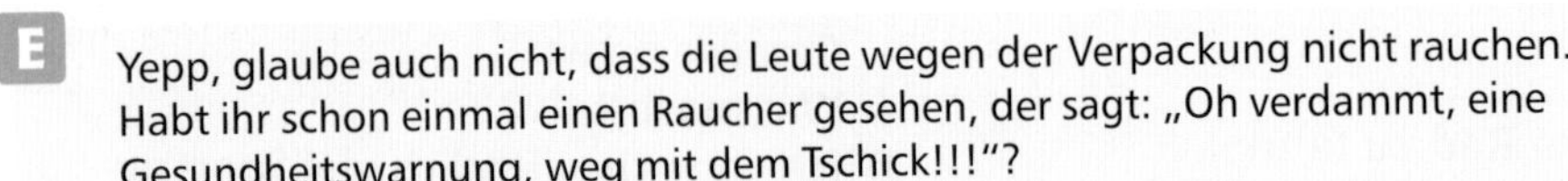

E Yepp, glaube auch nicht, dass die Leute wegen der Verpackung nicht rauchen. Habt ihr schon einmal einen Raucher gesehen, der sagt: „Oh verdammt, eine Gesundheitswarnung, weg mit dem Tschick!!!"?

F Ich bin selbst Raucher und die Sticker und Warnungen sind nutzlos. Nur der Preis könnte helfen: Zigaretten sind im Moment viel zu billig.

G Jeder kann rauchen, wenn er will. Das geht doch die anderen nichts an!

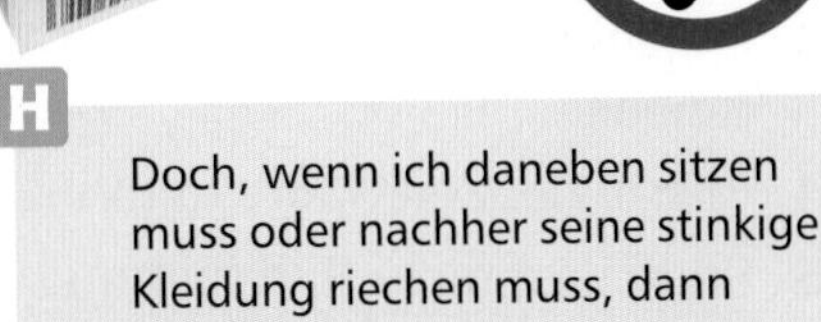

H Doch, wenn ich daneben sitzen muss oder nachher seine stinkige Kleidung riechen muss, dann schon.

I Fast alle an unserer Schule rauchen. Wer nicht raucht ist uncool, meinen sie, aber ich finde, wer nicht raucht ist cooler, weil der länger lebt.

Internet

1 Lies das österreichische Internet-Forum für Jugendliche und beantworte die Fragen!

1. Wer ist für Gesundheitswarnungen auf Zigarettenpackungen?
2. Wer meint, die Warnungen machen nichts?
3. Wer meint, Zigaretten sollten teurer sein?
4. „Packerl" und „Tschick" sind österreichische Wörter. Was könnte man dafür in Deutschland sagen?

2 Hör der Radiosendung zu! Wie viele Personen sind für das Rauchen und wie viele sind dagegen? Mach Notizen!

Beispiel:

für	gegen
?	?

3 Gruppenarbeit! Seht euch das Forum noch einmal an und findet drei gute Meinungen! Warum sind sie gut? Erklärt das in der Klasse!

Beispiel: **Wir finden Meinung H sehr gut. Es ist furchtbar, wenn man neben einem Raucher sitzt, weil das stinkt. Es ist ungesund und die Kleidung stinkt dann auch.**

Zusammenfassung

Krankheit	***Illness***
der Arm (-e)	*arm*
der Finger (-)	*finger*
der Fuß (¨-e)	*foot*
der Hals	*neck, throat*
der Kopf	*head*
der Magen	*stomach*
der Mund	*mouth*
der Rücken	*back*
die Hand (¨-e)	*hand*
die Nase	*nose*
die Schulter (-n)	*shoulder*
die Zahn (¨-e)	*tooth*
das Auge (-n)	*eye*
das Bein (-e)	*leg*
das Ohr (-en)	*ear*
Was ist (mit dir) los?	*What's wrong with you?*
Es geht mir/ihm/ihr nicht gut.	*I am/He/She is not well.*
Ich habe Kopf-/Ohren-/Magen-/Zahnschmerzen.	*I've got head-/ear-/stomach-/toothache.*
Er/Sie hat Hals-/Rückenschmerzen.	*He/She has a sore throat/back.*
Der Fuß/Arm tut (mir) weh.	*My foot/arm hurts.*
Die Hand/Das Bein tut (ihm/ihr) weh.	*His/Her hand/leg hurts.*
Die Augen/Schultern tun (mir) weh.	*My eyes/shoulders hurt.*
Ich habe Fieber.	*I've got a temperature.*

Gesundes Essen	***Healthy eating***
Es ist wichtig, dass man von allem ein bisschen isst.	*It's important that you eat a bit of everything.*
Man soll wenigstens fünf Portionen Obst oder Gemüse essen.	*You should eat at least five portions of fruit or vegetables.*
Wir müssen mehr Wasser trinken.	*We have to drink more water.*
Ich habe (kein Fleisch) gegessen, um fit zu bleiben.	*I've eaten (no meat) (in order) to stay fit.*

Gesundes Leben	***Healthy living***
Ich habe begonnen gesünder zu leben.	*I have begun to live more healthily.*
Ich habe beschlossen (gesünder) zu essen.	*I've decided to eat (more healthily).*
Ich hoffe Tennis zu spielen.	*I hope to play tennis.*
Ich habe vergessen … mitzu bringen.	*I've forgotten to bring … .*
Ich versuche fit zu sein.	*I am trying to be fit.*
Hast du Lust mitzukommen?	*Do you want to come along?*
Sport treiben	*to do sport*
joggen	*to jog*
Man soll nicht rauchen/keinen Alkohol trinken.	*You shouldn't smoke/drink alcohol.*

Grammatik: 

★ Dative pronouns: in certain phrases you need to use the **dative** form of pronouns.

	dative	
Das Bein tut Die Arme tun	mir dir	weh.
Was ist mit	ihm ihr	los?
Es geht	uns euch	nicht gut.
Es tut	ihnen Ihnen	Leid.

★ *seit:* the preposition *seit* means 'since' or 'for'. It always takes the **dative** case:
seit einem Tag/einer Woche/einem Jahr/zwei Tagen

★ *um … zu …:* to say 'in order to' (or usually just 'to'), use *um* at the beginning of a clause and *zu* with an infinitive at the end.

★ Infinitives: when two verbs are used together, one of them is in the **infinitive** and goes at the **end** of the clause.
Sometimes you need to add the extra word *zu* in front of the infinitive.

siehe Seite **141, 143, 147** >>

Strategie! 

★ Use a dictionary to find the correct German for a word and check both ways.

★ Work out meaning.

Lauter Laute: Aua! Igitt! Ach nein! Mensch!

mir *to me* • **dir** *to you* • **ihm** *to him* • **ihr** *to her* • **uns** *to us* • **euch** *to you* • **ihnen** *to them* • **Ihnen** *to you*
um … zu … *in order to …* • **seit** *since, for*

8 Austauscherlebnis

8A Wie war die Reise?

- describe a journey in the past
- compare one thing with another
- learn more about the perfect tense

Frau Schlüter: Hallo, Neil! Wie war die Reise?
Neil: Die Reise war furchtbar! Das Flugzeug ist 30 Minuten zu spät abgeflogen und wir sind erst um 14 Uhr in München angekommen.
Frau Schlüter: So ein Pech!
Neil: Der Flug war schlimm, aber die Zugfahrt war noch viel schlimmer! Ich bin fast zwölf Stunden unterwegs gewesen …
Frau Schlüter: Du Armer! Möchtest du deine Eltern anrufen?
Neil: Nein, danke. Ich habe mein Handy mitgebracht und habe meine Eltern schon angerufen.
Frau Schlüter: Möchtest du duschen?
Neil: Ja, bitte … ääh, ich habe mein Handtuch zu Hause vergessen. Haben Sie ein Handtuch …?
Frau Schlüter: Kein Problem – ich habe dein Zimmer fertig gemacht und ein Handtuch für dich vorbereitet.
Neil: Vielen Dank, Frau Schlüter.

1 **Hör zu und lies mit!**

2 **Lies den Dialog noch einmal und füll die Lücken mit den passenden Verbformen aus!**

Beispiel: **1 abgeflogen**

1. Das Flugzeug ist 30 Minuten zu spät ________ .
2. Wir sind erst um 14 Uhr in München ________ .
3. Ich habe mein Handy ________ .
4. Ich habe meine Eltern schon ________ .
5. Ich habe mein Handtuch zu Hause ________ .
6. Ich habe dein Zimmer fertig ________ .

gemacht mitgebracht
abgeflogen angerufen vergessen
angekommen

3 **Schreib die Sätze ins Perfekt um!**

Beispiel: **1 Ich habe meine Schultasche fertig gemacht.**

1. Ich mache meine Schultasche fertig.
2. Der Zug fährt um halb neun ab.
3. Mein Flugzeug kommt mittags in Düsseldorf an.
4. Er bringt seinen Koffer mit.
5. Sie ruft ihre Mutter an.
6. Ich verbringe zwei Tage in London.

Grammatik: Verben im Perfekt

To make the perfect tense in German, use an **auxiliary** verb (*haben* or *sein*) and a past participle.

- The past participle usually begins with **ge-** and goes at the end of the sentence.
- However, some verb participles don't begin with *ge-*.
- Examples of this are inseparable verbs beginning with a prefix such as **ver-**, and some verbs from other languages ending in **-ieren**.
  Ich habe mein Handtuch zu Hause vergessen.
- Most **separable** verbs have **-ge-** after their separable prefix, e.g. *abgefahren*, *angekommen*, etc.
  Das Flugzeug ist zu spät abgeflogen.
  Wir sind erst um 14 Uhr angekommen.

siehe Seite **144** >>

Möchtest du das Haus sehen, Paul?

Ja, sicher, Uwe. Es ist fast neu! Unser Haus ist viel älter.

Hier ist das Wohnzimmer.

Supertoll! Es ist riesig! Unser Wohnzimmer ist viel kleiner!

Und hier ist der Garten.

Prima! Es ist wunderschön! Unser Garten ist viel hässlicher.

Das Schlafzimmer ist im vierten Stock.

Toll. Im vierten Stock!!! Dieses Haus ist viel größer – unser Haus hat nur einen Stock!

Und das ist der Keller. Hier ist unser Bier.

Fantastisch! Deine Familie ist viel reicher – unser Keller ist leer.

Und hier ist unser Hund.

HILFE! UNSER HUND IST VIEL KLEINER!

4 **Vervollständige den Dialog! Übe ihn dann mit einem Partner/einer Partnerin!**

Beispiel: **A Wie war die Reise?**
B Furchtbar! Das Flugzeug ist …

A Wie war die Reise?
B ______________________
A Wann bist du in Hamburg angekommen?
B ______________________
A Möchtest du deine Eltern anrufen?
B ______________________
A Möchtest du ein Handtuch?
B ______________________

Left mobile at home.
Plane left 45 minutes late.
Brought towel with you.
Arrived in Hamburg at 4 p.m.

5 **Lies die Bildgeschichte und die Sätze unten! Sind sie richtig oder falsch?**

Beispiel: **1 falsch**

1. Uwes Haus ist älter als Pauls Haus.
2. Pauls Haus ist neuer als Uwes Haus.
3. Uwes Wohnzimmer ist größer als Pauls Wohnzimmer.
4. Uwes Garten ist schöner als Pauls Garten.
5. Pauls Hund ist viel größer als Uwes Hund.

6 **Schreib Vergleiche!**

Beispiel: **a Gertrud ist hässlicher als Claudia.**
***Oder:* Claudia ist schöner als Gertrud.**

Grammatik: comparatives

To say in German that something is bigger, smaller, better, more expensive, etc., you add **-er** to the adjective (smaller – *klein**er***; more beautiful – *schön**er***).

To say 'than' you use *als* (e.g. *kleiner* ***als*** – smaller than). Some adjectives change a little to make them easier to say (*teuer – teu**rer***) and/or add an umlaut (*lang – l**ä**nger*). Here are some other irregular ones.

*alt – **ä**lter (als)*
*groß – gr**ö**ßer (als)*
*gut – **besser** (als)*

siehe Seite **142** ➤➤

7 *extra!* **Schreib den Dialog zwischen Uwe und Paul weiter!**

Beispiel: **Uwe:** Das ist mein Mathelehrer, Herr Drossler.
Paul: Ach! Er ist hässlich! Aber mein Mathelehrer ist hässlicher …

8 **Übe deinen Dialog mit einem Partner/einer Partnerin!**

Beispiel: **A** Das ist …
B …

8B Reich mir bitte die Soße

- find out about typical German meals
- know what to say at mealtimes
- learn to use imperatives

1 a Sieh dir die Bilder und die Wörter an! Was passt zusammen?

Beispiel: **1 m**

1 Apfelmus
2 Bohnen
3 Bohneneintopf
4 Erbsen
5 Hähnchen
6 Hühnersuppe
7 Kartoffeln
8 Kuchen
9 Lammfleisch
10 Möhren
11 Obst
12 Quark
13 Rindfleisch
14 Schweinekoteletts
15 Tomatensuppe
16 Zwiebelsuppe

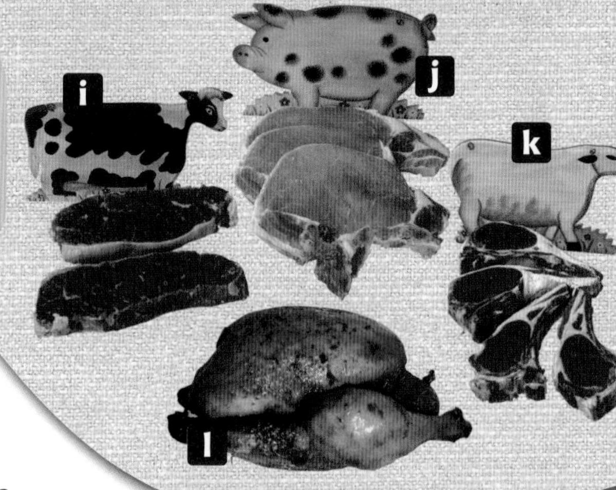

1 b Wie sagt man das? Rate mal und hör dann zu! Hattest du Recht?

2 Was gibt's zum Mittagessen? Hör zu und mach Notizen!

Beispiel: **Zwiebelsuppe ...**

Ich habe Hunger.
Was gibt's zum Mittagessen?
Als Nachtisch haben wir ... .
Danach gibt es ... .
Lecker!

3 Macht jetzt eure eigenen Dialoge! Benutzt die Bilder aus Übung 1a oben!

Beispiel: **A Was gibt es zum Mittagessen?**
B Heute haben wir ... .

4 a Lies die Postkarte! Sind die Sätze falsch oder richtig?

Beispiel: **1 falsch**

1 Als Vorspeise hat Peter Quark gegessen.
2 Tomatensuppe isst Peter nicht gern.
3 Als Hauptgericht hat er Schweinefleisch gegessen.
4 Das hat er gut gefunden.
5 Als Nachtisch gab es Schwarzwälder Kirschtorte.
6 Morgen gibt es Rindfleisch zum Abendessen.

Liebe Mutti,

gestern Abend habe ich bei meiner Gastfamilie gegessen. Es war meistens toll, aber als Vorspeise haben wir Tomatensuppe gegessen und das kann ich nicht leiden! Als Hauptgericht haben wir Schweinefleisch gehabt und danach Quark mit Apfelmus. Das Schweinefleisch hat mir sehr gut geschmeckt und der Quark war lecker. Morgen gibt es Rindfleisch – mein Lieblingsessen!

Dein Peter

4 b Schreib jetzt deine eigene Postkarte! Was hast du bei der deutschen Familie gegessen? Was wirst du morgen essen?

Beispiel: **Lieber Vati, gestern Abend habe ich bei meinem Austauschpartner gegessen ...**

5 Hör zu und lies mit!

Frau Fischer:	Reich mir bitte **das Salz**, Tina.
Tina:	Bitte schön. Und geben Sie mir **die Soße**, bitte.
Frau Fischer:	Hier ... **die Soße**.
Tina:	Hast du genug **Bohnen**, Fredi?
Fredi:	Ja, danke ... das reicht. Aber gib mir bitte **die Möhren**.
Tina:	Bitte schön. Karl ... noch ein bisschen **Rindfleisch**?
Karl:	Ja, bitte ... es ist lecker!

Karl:	Möchtest du noch etwas **Grießpudding**, Tina?
Tina:	Nee, nee, ist O.K. Ich habe genug gegessen. Aber gib mir auch **die Kirschen**, bitte.
Karl:	Bitte schön. Möchten Sie etwas trinken, Frau Fischer?
Frau Fischer:	Ja, gib mir **das Wasser**, bitte. Ich habe zu viel gegessen und ich habe Durst!
Fredi:	Bitte schön ... und reichen Sie mir bitte **den Apfelsaft**.
Frau Fischer:	Hier ... bitte schön.

6 Lies die Dialoge noch einmal! Was heißt das auf Deutsch?

Beispiel: **1 Reich mir ...**

1. Pass me the ...
2. It's delicious.
3. Would you like some more ...?
4. Would you like something to drink?
5. I've eaten enough.
6. I'm thirsty.

7 Füll die Lücken aus!

Beispiel: **1 *Reich* mir bitte die Butter.**

1. ______ mir bitte die Butter. (reichen)
2. ______ Sie geradeaus. (gehen)
3. ______ Sie die erste Straße links. (nehmen)
4. ______ Sie mir das Wasser, bitte. (geben)
5. ______ mir bitte die Bohnen. (geben)
6. ______ die zweite Straße rechts. (nehmen)

8 Ändere jetzt die fett gedruckten Wörter in Übung 5, um deinen eigenen Dialog zu machen!

Beispiel: **Martin: Reich mir bitte *das Brot*.**

9 *extra!* Kannst du andere Befehle erfinden?

Beispiel: **Nehmen Sie den Bus! Mach die Tür zu!**

Grammatik: imperatives

- The **imperative** is used for giving **orders** or **commands** (e.g. go away, come here), and is also used for instructions (e.g. in recipes).
- There are two main imperatives in German: the polite (*Sie*) form and the familiar (*du*) form.
- The imperative is similar to the normal verb, but the *du* form loses its *-st* ending, and sometimes the **vowel** in the verb changes or loses its umlaut.
- To say 'don't ...', just add *nicht* or *kein* after the imperative.

***du* form**	**familiar imperative**	***Sie* form**	**polite imperative**
du reichst	*reich*	*Sie reichen*	*reichen Sie*
du gibst	*gib*	*Sie geben*	*geben Sie*
du fährst	*fahr*	*Sie fahren*	*fahren Sie*

siehe Seite **146** >>

10 Lauter Laute: *sch* oder *ch*?

- Hör zu und sprich nach!

Reich mir das Rindfleisch, das Lammfleisch und das Hähnchen, bitte.
Und danach reich mir zwei Kuchen und eine Schale Grießpudding mit Kirschen.

8C Was meinst du?

- talk about buying presents
- learn how to report what people said
- learn how to use *dass*

Umfrage – gutes Geschenk oder schlechtes Geschenk?

Peter
Magda
Miriam
Sven
Ingrid
Wolfram
Trudi
Trixi
Isabelle

1 a Hör zu! Welches Geschenk ist das?

Beispiel: **Peter, c**

1 b Hör noch einmal zu und schreib für jede Person ***gutes Geschenk***, ***schlechtes Geschenk*** oder ***kommt drauf an***!

Beispiel: **Peter – Schokolade, gutes Geschenk**

Grammatik: *meinen, sagen, denken, finden + dass*

To report what people **think** or **say**, you can use the verbs *meinen*, *denken*, *sagen* or *finden*, followed by a comma and then ***dass***. The **verb** in the second part of the clause will have to go to **the end**.

Er sagt, ***dass*** *Schokolade ein tolles Geschenk* ***ist.***

Sie meint, ***dass*** *Plüschtiere langweilig* ***sind.***

siehe Seite **147** >>

2  **Wer meint was? Vervollständige die Sätze!**

Beispiel: **1** ***Trudi*** **denkt, dass ein Bierkrug ein doofes Geschenk ist.**

1. … denkt, dass ein Bierkrug ein doofes Geschenk ist.
2. … meint, dass Bücher ein tolles Geschenk sind.
3. … sagt, dass Bonbons ein schlechtes Geschenk sind.
4. Peter …
5. Miriam …
6. Ingrid …
7. Wolfram …
8. Trixi …
9. Isabelle …

Grammatik: *solange*

Remember, to say 'as long as' you can use ***solang(e)***. The verb also goes to the end of the clause with this word.

Er meint, dass CDs ein tolles Geschenk sind, ***solange*** *sie cool* ***sind****!*

… meint, dass … … sagt, dass … … denkt, dass …	*… thinks that …* *… says that …* *… thinks that …*
(Es) kommt drauf an.	*It depends.*
ein gutes/tolles Geschenk	*a good/great present*
ein schlechtes/furchtbares Geschenk	*a bad/awful present*
solange es gut **ist**	*as long as it's good*

3 **Wie findet dein(e) Partner(in) die unterschiedlichen Geschenke? Macht Interviews und macht Notizen!**

Beispiel: **A** **Wie findest du (Schokolade) als Geschenk?**
B **(Schokolade) finde ich ein gutes/schlimmes/tolles/furchtbares/doofes Geschenk.**

4 **Was hat dein(e) Partner(in) gesagt? Erzähl das den anderen in der Klasse!**

Beispiel: **Justin sagt, dass CDs ein furchtbares Geschenk sind, aber er meint, dass …**

5 Lies Katjas E-Mail! Sind die Sätze richtig oder falsch?

An: Anna Kärcher
Von: Katja Liebermann
Betr.: Geschenkideen

Liebe Anna,

es macht Spaß hier in Luzern – aber bald muss ich wieder nach Hause fahren. Und ich habe da ein Problem. Ich habe fast keine Geschenkideen für meine Familie! Ich wollte ein kleines Plüschtier für meine Schwester kaufen, aber sie ist schon zwölf und ich denke, dass sie keine Plüschtiere mag. Ich habe nichts für Vati gekauft, aber ich werde vielleicht ein Buch über die Gegend hier kaufen (hier ist es sehr schön und er liest gern). Was meinst du? Ich habe noch keine Ideen! Für Oma habe ich auch noch nichts gekauft, aber ich könnte eine Schachtel Pralinen für sie kaufen. Pralinen mag sie gern, aber hier sind sie sehr teuer! Meinst du, dass sie ein gutes Geschenk sind? Für Opa ist es leicht – wie üblich werde ich eine Flasche Schnaps kaufen! Aber hilf mir bitte mit den anderen! Und was möchtest du? Schreib bald zurück!

Deine Katja

1 Katja hat nichts für ihre Schwester gekauft.
2 Sie hat ein Buch für ihren Vater gekauft.
3 Sie wird vielleicht eine Schachtel Pralinen für ihre Oma kaufen.
4 Katjas Oma mag keine Pralinen.
5 Für ihren Opa wird Katja eine Flasche Schnaps kaufen.
6 Sie hat ein tolles Geschenk für Anna gekauft.

Grammatik: the future tense 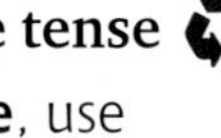

To form the **future tense**, use ***werden*** and an **infinitive**, which goes to the **end** of the clause.

*Ich **werde** ein Geschenk für meine Oma **kaufen**.*

siehe Seite **145** >>

6 Was kauft Magda für ihre Familie? Hör zu und füll die Tabelle aus!

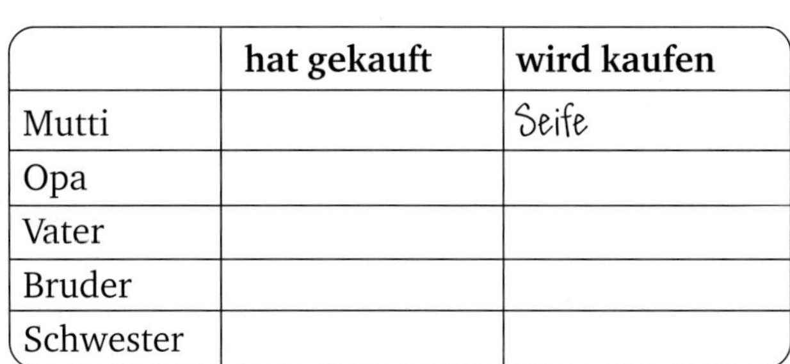

	hat gekauft	wird kaufen
Mutti		Seife
Opa		
Vater		
Bruder		
Schwester		

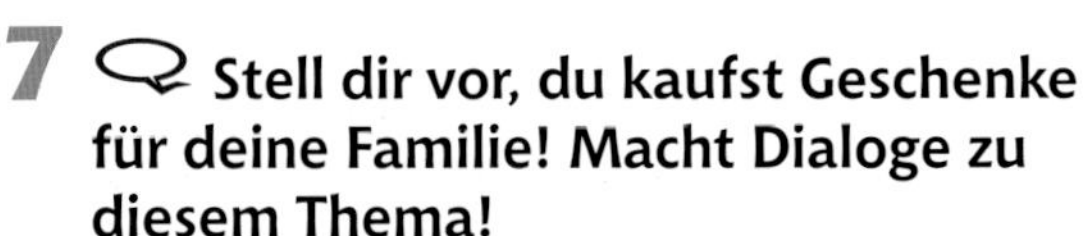

7 Stell dir vor, du kaufst Geschenke für deine Familie! Macht Dialoge zu diesem Thema!

Beispiel: **A** Was hast du als Geschenk für (deine Mutter) gekauft?
B Für (meine Mutter) habe ich … gekauft.
A Was wirst du für (deine Schwester) kaufen?
B Vielleicht werde ich … kaufen.

8 extra! Schreib eine Antwort auf Katjas E-Mail!

Beispiel: Liebe Katja,
danke für deine E-Mail … . Ich meine, dass … .
Du könntest … für (mich/deine Mutter) kaufen … .

8D Was bedeutet das?

- learn how to use a bilingual dictionary
- work out how to pick the word you need from a selection or dictionary entry

1 ***Now see if you can work out the correct German words for the following.***

a

chain

b

car sticker

c

ring

d

picture

e

badge

2 ***Now make sentences using some of the German words you have just looked up in Exercise 1.***

Beispiel: **a Diese Halskette ist sehr schön.**

Strategie! ***Learn to use detail in a bilingual dictionary and check back in the German-English section***

When you look up a word in the English-German part of a dictionary, you will often find that the word can be translated in more than one way.

For example, imagine that you would like to get a beer mug as a souvenir for your Dad, and you look up the word 'mug' in the dictionary. Here's the entry:

> **mug**[1], *s.* der Krug, Becher
> **mug**[2], 1. *s.* (*sl*) der Schnabel, das Maul; (*sl*) der Tölpel, Trottel. 2. *v.i.* (*sl*) büffeln. 3. *v.t.* überfallen

To help you work out which of these words you need, ask yourself the following questions:

- What do the little symbols and numbers by the entry mean?
- Is the word 'mug' with the meaning you want a noun or a verb?
- How can you work out which of the meanings listed is the right one?

Here's what the numbers and symbols tell you:

- mug[1] – the 1 here tells you there are two main meanings and this is the first. Words are usually listed with the most frequent meaning first.
- *s.* – this tells you that the first set of words listed are **substantives**, or **nouns**. These are usually listed with *der*, *die* or *das*, so that you can tell their **gender**.
- To find out the **plural** of a German noun, look it up in the German-English section of the dictionary (the plural is usually listed just after the singular form).
- (*sl*) – this tells you that this meaning is a slang word.
- *v.i.* or *v.t.* tell you that the word is a verb.

'Mug' can be a noun ('the beer is in the mug'), or a verb ('she was mugged'). The sense we are looking for here is the noun ('I'd like **a** beer mug for my Dad'), so we will want either meaning 1 or one of the nouns from the first section of meaning 2 – but which?

To find this out, look up each of the words in the German-English section of the dictionary. By doing this, you will often see from the examples given which word you want. In this case it is *Krug* – *Becher* is used more often to mean a container for other substances. *Schnabel* and *Maul* are slang words, meaning 'mug' as in 'his ugly mug', *Tölpel* and *Trottel* mean 'mug' in the sense of 'gullible person'.

Reisen	***Journeys***
abfahren	*to leave, depart*
abfliegen	*to take off (a plane)*
ankommen	*to arrive*
anrufen	*to telephone*
fertig machen	*to get (something) ready*
mitbringen	*to bring (along)*
duschen	*to have a shower*
verbringen	*to spend, pass (time)*
(zu Hause) vergessen	*to leave (behind), forget (at home)*
ein Handtuch vorbereiten	*to get a towel ready*

Vergleiche	***Comparisons***
alt/älter	*old/older*
groß/größer	*big/bigger*
hässlich/hässlicher	*ugly/uglier*
klein/kleiner	*small/smaller*
neu/neuer	*new/newer*
reich/reicher	*rich/richer*
schlimm/schlimmer	*bad/worse*
schön/schöner	*beautiful/more beautiful*
teuer/teurer	*expensive/more expensive*
gut/besser	*good/better*

zu Hause essen	***Eating at home***
noch ein bisschen (?)	*a bit more (?)*
reich(en Sie) mir (bitte) …	*(please) pass me …*
gib (geben Sie) mir (bitte) …	*(please) give me …*
Das reicht.	*That's enough.*

Geschenke	***Gifts***
der Bierkrug	*beer mug*
die Flasche	*bottle*
die Tafel	*bar, slab*
die Schokolade	*chocolate*
die Baseballmütze	*baseball cap*
die Tüte	*bag*
das T-Shirt	*T-shirt*
das Kölnischwasser	*eau de Cologne*
das Plüschtier	*cuddly toy*
das Buch	*book*
die CDs	*CDs*
die Bonbons	*sweets*

Grammatik:

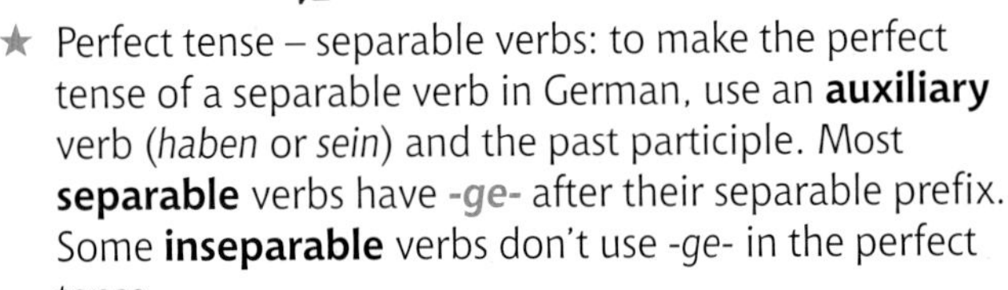

★ Perfect tense – separable verbs: to make the perfect tense of a separable verb in German, use an **auxiliary** verb (*haben* or *sein*) and the past participle. Most **separable** verbs have **-ge-** after their separable prefix. Some **inseparable** verbs don't use *-ge-* in the perfect tense.

Das Zug ist zu spät abgefahren.
Wir sind erst um 14 Uhr angekommen.
Ich habe meine Tasche ***vergessen****.*

★ Comparatives: to say in German that something is bigger, smaller, etc., add **-er** to most adjectives. Some are irregular and must be learnt. Use **als** for 'than'. For example:

schön – schöner (als) *teuer – teurer (als)*
gut – besser (als) *alt – älter (als)*

★ Imperatives: the **imperative** is used for giving **orders** or **commands** (e.g. go away, come here). There are two main imperatives in German: the polite (*Sie*) and the familiar (*du*) forms.

familiar	**polite**
reich	*reichen Sie*
fahr	*fahren Sie*

★ Reporting opinions: to report what people said or think, use the verbs *meinen*, *denken* or *sagen*, followed by a comma and then **dass**. The **verb** in the other part of the clause will have to go to **the end**.

Er sagt, ***dass*** *CDs ein furchtbares Geschenk* ***sind****.*

siehe Seiten **142, 144, 146, 147** >>

Strategie!

★ Learn to use detail in a bilingual dictionary and check back in the German-English section.

dass *that* • *separable prefixes:*
ab • **an** • **mit** • **um**

 **Lauter Laute:** *sch* oder *ch*?

Wiederholung

Kapitel 7 (Probleme? Siehe Seite 60–65!)

1 Sieh dir die Bilder an und schreib Sätze!

Beispiel: **1 Die rechte Hand tut weh.**

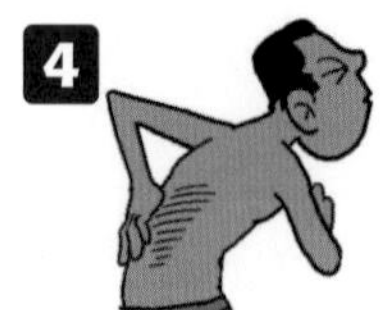

2 Schreib die Gesundheitsregeln richtig auf!

Beispiel: **1 Man soll auf den Markt gehen, um frisches Obst und Gemüse zu kaufen.**

1 Man soll auf den Markt gehen, um Schokolade und Bonbons zu kaufen.
2 Es ist wichtig, dass man von allem sehr viel isst.
3 Man soll nicht viel Sport machen, um dick zu werden.
4 Wir müssen nie Fisch oder Eier essen, um die richtigen Vitamine zu bekommen.
5 Wenn man zu viel isst, wird man fit bleiben!
6 Man soll gar kein Obst oder Gemüse essen.

Kapitel 8 (Probleme? Siehe Seite 70–73!)

3 Bring den Dialog in die richtige Reihenfolge!

Beispiel: **4, …**

1 Renate: Hier – die Kartoffeln. Möchten Sie etwas trinken?
2 Karl: Ja, danke – das reicht. Aber reich mir bitte die Kartoffeln.
3 Renate: So … ein Stück Apfelkuchen. Und ich werde noch etwas Apfelsaft trinken.
4 Karl: Reich mir bitte das Rindfleisch, Renate.
5 Frau Esders: Ich habe genug getrunken, aber ich werde ein Stück Apfelkuchen nehmen.
6 Renate: Das Rindfleisch … bitte schön. Hast du genug Soße?

4 a Lies die Postkarte und schau dir die Bilder an! Was passt zusammen?

Beispiel: **1 e**

Liebe Mutti,

es macht viel Spaß hier in Sylt, und ich habe so viele tolle Geschenke für die Familie gekauft! Ich habe eine Flasche Parfüm für Oma und ein Buch über Sylt für Opa gefunden, und für Tante Margrit habe ich eine tolle Sonnenbrille gekauft. Für Vati habe ich eine Flasche Schnaps gekauft, und für Lotte und Benno habe ich Plüschtiere gekauft. Und was werde ich für dich nach Hause mitbringen? Das ist eine Überraschung …

Deine Ursel

4 b Schreib einem Freund/einer Freundin in Deutschland! Was hast du für deine Familienmitglieder gekauft?

Beispiel: **Lieber Karl,
es macht viel Spaß hier in Margate …**

Ganz Leipzig träumt von den Olympischen Spielen

Leipzig hat sich für Deutschland um die Olympischen und Paralympischen Spiele 2012 beworben. Hier geben Jugendliche, die in Leipzig das Sportgymnasium besuchen, ihre Meinungen über die Spiele.

Christa, 16 Jahre, ist Turnerin. „Ich war auf dem Rathausplatz, als die nationale Entscheidung für Leipzig fiel", erzählt Christa. Hamburg, Frankfurt, Düsseldorf und Stuttgart waren geschlagen, Leipzig der Kandidat für Olympia. „Als Leistungssportlerin identifiziert man sich mit seiner Stadt", sagt Christa, die in Leipzig geboren ist. Sie sagt: „Ich wünsche Leipzig Erfolg, weil die Stadt es brauchen kann."

Christa, Turnerin: Sie wünscht Leipzig Erfolg.

Stefan, Judoka: Er will seinem großen sportlichen Vorbild nacheifern.

Stefan, 14 Jahre, ist Judoka. Im Moment geht Stefan in die 8. Klasse. Er fährt jeden Morgen mit der Straßenbahn 45 Minuten bis zum Sportgymnasium. Viele seiner Mitschüler sind ebenfalls Judokas. „Wir trainieren fünfmal in der Woche", verrät er. Sein sportliches Vorbild ist Udo Quellmalz. Quellmalz war 2000 Olympiasieger in Atlanta, mehrmaliger deutscher Meister und Weltmeister im Judo. Er ist einer von vielen Athleten, die aus der sächsischen Stadt kommen.

Christian, 17 Jahre, ist Schwimmer. Am Wochenende hat Christian häufig Wettkämpfe. Am Tag der Olympiaentscheidung war er gerade im Wasser, als der Sprecher die Wahl bekannt gab. „Ich konnte das zuerst gar nicht glauben. Ich habe mich riesig gefreut", sagt Christian. Sein persönliches Ziel: die Teilnahme bei Olympischen Spielen – spätestens 2012 in Leipzig.

Christian, Schwimmer: Er will an den Olympischen Spielen teilnehmen – spätestens in Leipzig.

Torsten, Radrennfahrer: Er träumt von den Olympischen Spielen in Leipzig.

Torsten, 16 Jahre, ist seit drei Jahren Radrennfahrer. Vorher hat er bereits verschiedene andere Sportarten ausprobiert. „Dann bin ich mal aus Spaß bei einem Radrennen mitgefahren", sagt Torsten. Er erreichte einen guten Platz und beschloss, mit dem Radsport weiter zu machen. Jetzt fährt er Straßenrennen und Mannschaftsverfolgung auf der Bahn. 2003 war sein erstes Wettkampfjahr. Die Bilanz: „Die Saison ist ganz gut gelaufen. Ich mache aber noch technisch-taktische Fehler."

Aus: *JUMA* 2/2004, Christian Vogeler, www.juma.de

1 Lies die Texte und beantworte die Fragen auf Englisch!

Beispiel: **1 Stefan says that his sporting icon is Udo Quellmalz.**

Who …

1. … says that his sporting icon is Udo Quellmalz?
2. … says that his personal goal is participating in the 2012 Olympics?
3. … says that as a top sports person you identify with your home town?
4. … says that the season has gone well, but that he still makes technical and tactical mistakes?
5. … wishes Leipzig success 'because the town can use it'?

9 Ich und andere

9A Wie findest du mich?

- describe people's personalities
- discuss people's good and bad qualities
- use correct adjectival agreement

sympathisch	*patient*
ehrlich	*mean*
geduldig	*selfish*
freigiebig	*lazy*
faul	*likeable, nice*
schüchtern	*moody*
selbstbewusst	*self-confident*
nervig	*generous*
launisch	*honest*
witzig	*helpful*
hilfsbereit	*irritating*
geizig	*hard-working*
fleißig	*fun, jolly*
selbstsüchtig	*shy*

Wolfgang

Ich bin meistens ehrlich und hilfsbereit, aber manchmal launisch und schüchtern.

1 a **Schau dir die Kästchen an! Welche Wörter passen zusammen? Benutze ein Wörterbuch, wenn du möchtest!**

Beispiel: **sympathisch – *likeable, nice***

1 b **Hör zu (1–4) und lies die Texte! Wer ist das?**

Who is … ?

1. … a bit selfish?
2. … normally hard-working?
3. … generous and patient?
4. … usually honest?
5. … occasionally irritating?
6. … nice and good fun?
7. … normally self-confident?
8. … a bit mean?
9. … a bit lazy?
10. … sometimes moody?

Sybille

Ich bin normalerweise selbstbewusst und fleißig, aber ab und zu bin ich arrogant und nervig.

Anna

Ich bin sympathisch und witzig, aber ein bisschen selbstsüchtig und geizig.

Markus

Ich bin freigiebig und geduldig, aber einige Leute finden mich etwas faul.

1 c **Lies die Texte aus Übung 1b noch einmal und hör zu (1–4)! Freunde reden über Wolfgang, Sybille, Markus und Anna. Welche Einzelheiten stimmen nicht? Mach eine Liste!**

Beispiel: **Wolfgang – faul/schüchtern**

2 **Wie seid ihr? Macht gegenseitig Notizen über euch! Vergleicht dann die Infos!**

Ich: Meistens witzig und fleißig. Ein bisschen arrogant.
Emma: Normalerweise sympathisch. Manchmal launisch und …

Beispiel: **A** **Ich denke, dass ich meistens fleißig bin. Was meinst du?**
B **Ja, ich finde dich fleißig. Und ich – wie findest du mich?**
A **Ich denke, dass du sympathisch bist.**
B **Danke! Aber ich denke, dass ich etwas launisch bin.**
A **…**

3 Lies die Texte! Wer sagt, dass ...

Beispiel: **1 Gudrun**

1 ... ihr Großvater ein witziger Mann ist?
2 ... seine Mutter eine nervige Frau ist, die oft ungeduldig ist?
3 ... ihr Vater ein geduldiger Mann ist?
4 ... ihre Mutter eine Frau ist, die fast alles macht?
5 ... ihre Eltern beide sympathische Leute sind?
6 ... sein Vater ein sympathischer Mann ist?

Ich finde meinen Vater toll! Er ist ein geduldiger, sympathischer Mann. Aber ich komme nicht so gut mit meiner Schwester aus – ich finde sie ein etwas selbstsüchtiges Mädchen, die immer an sich selbst denkt. Meine Mutter ist eine ehrliche Frau, die fast alles für uns macht.

Ulrike, 15

Die Mitglieder meiner Familie sind meistens sympathisch, aber meine Mutter ist eine nervige Frau, die oft sehr ungeduldig ist. Mein Vater ist ein sympathischer Mann und meine Geschwister sind toll – ich habe einen witzigen Bruder und eine freigiebige Schwester.

Andreas, 16

Ich habe eine tolle Familie, aber am liebsten mag ich meine Großeltern. Mein Großvater ist ein witziger Mann und meine Großmutter ist eine sehr nette Frau. Meine Mutter und mein Vater sind beide sympathische Leute, und nur meine Schwester ist etwas launisch.

Gudrun, 17

4 Füll die Lücken aus!

1 Mein Vater ist ein sympathisch___ Mann.
2 Ich habe einen nervig___ Bruder.
3 Ich habe einen arrogant___ Vater.
4 Meine Mutter ist eine freigiebig___ Frau.
5 Seine Eltern sind ehrlich___ Leute.
6 Sie hat einen geizig___ Großvater.

Grammatik: adjective endings after the indefinite article

When an adjective comes **after** its noun, it doesn't need an ending, e.g. *Meine Schwester ist faul.*

When it comes before its noun, it has to have the correct ending according to the noun's gender.

The ending will also change according to whether the noun is **nominative** or **accusative**.

After the **indefinite article** the endings are:

	masc	fem	neut	pl
nom	ein guter	eine gute	ein gutes	gute
acc	einen guten	eine gute	ein gutes	gute

siehe Seite **141** >>

5 Beschreib zwei Personen (z.B. deine Freunde, deine Familie, berühmte Leute, usw.)! Die Texte in Übung 3 können dir helfen.

Beispiel: **Ozzie Osbourne ist ein interessanter Mann, aber ...**

9B Pflichten und Rechte

- say what you are allowed to do
- talk about school rules
- use modal verbs in different tenses

Ich muss …	um neun Uhr ins Bett gehen. bei der Hausarbeit helfen. abwaschen und Staub saugen. mein Zimmer aufräumen.
Ich darf (nicht/keine) …	sehr spät nach Hause kommen. fernsehen. spätabends in die Disko gehen. laute Musik hören.
Mein (Stief-)Vater ist … Meine (Stief-)Mutter ist … Meine Eltern sind …	(nicht) sehr/so streng.

1 a Hör zu (1–8) und füll die Lücken aus!

Beispiel: **1 Karl *darf keine* laute Musik horen.**

1 Karl ______ ______ laute Musik hören.
2 Rudi ______ ______ bei der Hausarbeit helfen.
3 Anke ______ spätabends in die Disko gehen.
4 Babs ______ jede Woche ihr Zimmer aufräumen.
5 Elisabeth ______ nur eine Stunde pro Abend fernsehen.
6 Claudia ______ sehr spät nach Hause kommen!

Grammatik: *müssen* and *dürfen*

To say 'must' or 'have to', you use *müssen*.

To say 'allowed to', you use *dürfen*.

To say 'mustn't' or 'not allowed to', you **always** use *dürfen* and a **negative**:

*Ich **darf nicht** spät ausbleiben.* I mustn't/am not allowed to stay out late.

*Ich **darf kein** Bier trinken.* I mustn't/am not allowed to drink beer.

With a negative *müssen* means 'don't have to' (**not** 'mustn't'):

*Du **musst nicht** abwaschen.*
You don't have to wash up
(**not** 'you mustn't wash up'!)

*Du **musst nicht** früh dort sein.*
You don't have to arrive early
(**not** 'you mustn't arrive early'!)

siehe Seite **143** ➤➤

1 b Sind eure Eltern streng? Macht Dialoge!

Beispiel: **A Sind deine Eltern streng? Was musst du machen? Was darfst du nicht machen?**
B Nein, sie sind nicht streng. Ich darf …

2 a Und an der Schule? Wie ist es dort? Hör zu (1–6) und ordne die Bilder!

Beispiel: **1 e, …**

a

Man muss sich im Klassenzimmer gut benehmen.

b

Man darf nicht im Klassenzimmer essen.

c

Man darf während den Pausen nicht aus der Schule gehen.

d

Man muss die Hausaufgaben pünktlich machen.

e

Man muss pünktlich um acht Uhr in der Schule ankommen.

f

Man darf keine Handys ins Klassenzimmer bringen.

2 b **Hör noch einmal zu und schreib eine Meinung für jeden Dialog (1–6)!**

Beispiel: **1 anstrengend**

gerecht	blöd	dumm
anstrengend	fair	vernünftig

3 ***If you use an opposite verb (e.g. stay out late/come in early), sentences with* darf nicht *in them often mean the same as sentences containing* müssen*. Look at the sentences below and match up the ones that mean the same.***

Beispiel: **1 = 5**

1 Man darf nicht aus der Schule gehen.
2 Man darf sich nicht schlecht benehmen.
3 Man muss sein Handy draußen lassen.
4 Man muss sich gut benehmen.
5 Man muss in der Schule bleiben.
6 Man darf Handys nicht ins Klassenzimmer bringen.

4 **Seid ihr mit den Sätzen in Übung 3 einverstanden? Macht Dialoge!**

Beispiel: **A Man muss sein Handy draußen lassen – wie findest du das?**
B Das finde ich blöd.

Grammatik: the imperfect tense of modal verbs

To make the **imperfect** singular (simple past) tense of the modal verbs *müssen* and *dürfen*, just take away the umlaut on the first vowel and add **-te**.

musste (nicht) – 'had to'/'didn't have to'	***durfte (nicht)*** – '(wasn't) allowed to'
ich musste (nicht)	*ich durfte (nicht)*
du musstest (nicht)	*du durftest (nicht)*
er/sie/es/man musste (nicht)	*er/sie/es/man durfte (nicht)*

siehe Seite **145** >>

5 **Peter war in den 50er Jahren auf der Schule. Lies den Text! Sind die Sätze richtig oder falsch?**

Beispiel: **1 falsch**

1 Man durfte nur mit seinen Freunden oder Freundinnen sprechen.
2 Man durfte nur nach Ankunft des Lehrers ins Klassenzimmer gehen.
3 Man musste keine Mütze tragen.
4 Man musste sehr viele Hausaufgaben machen.
5 Peter hat das Leben auf der Schule Spaß gemacht.

Als ich auf der Schule war, war alles sehr streng! Man durfte überhaupt nicht in den Stunden sprechen. Man musste draußen vor dem Klassenzimmer auf den Lehrer warten. Und danach durfte man sich erst hinsetzen, nachdem der Lehrer sich hingesetzt hatte. Außerdem musste man den Lehrer immer mit „mein Herr“ anreden. Was sonst? Ah, ja – man musste eine Mütze tragen, und wenn man ohne Mütze zur Schule kam, musste man nach Hause gehen, um die Mütze zu holen! Zum Schluss musste man täglich mindestens drei Stunden Hausaufgaben machen. Mir hat das Leben auf der Schule gar keinen Spaß gemacht!

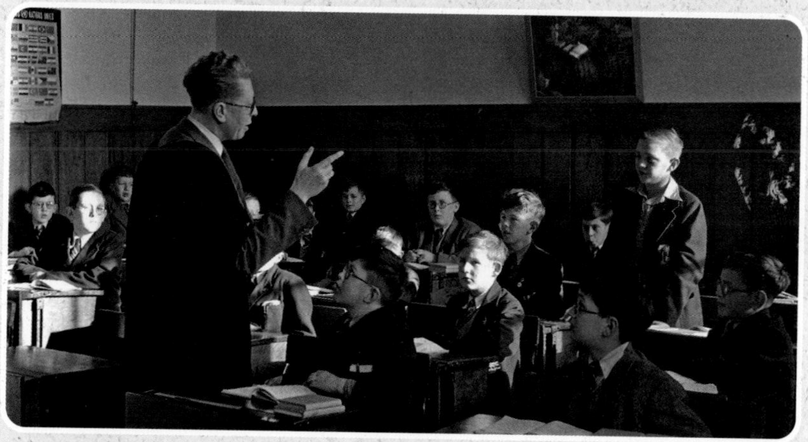

6 **Stell dir vor, du warst auf einer Horrorschule! Wie war es dort? Schreib ungefähr 60 Wörter!**

Beispiel: **In Horror Hall musste man Spinnen und Staub essen. Man musste um 4 Uhr morgens aufstehen und eine kalte Dusche nehmen. Der Direktor, Herr Drakula ...**

7 **Dein(e) Partner(in) überprüft deinen Text.**

9C Liebe Tante Claudia

- understand problem page letters
- use possessive adjectives correctly
- use grammar and context to understand text

1 a Hör zu (1–4) und lies mit!

Strategie! ***Using knowledge of word order to work out the meaning of sentences***

These letters contain some **complex language.** Look at these sentences:

Ich habe schlechte Noten bekommen.
Ich bin davon überzeugt, dass meine Eltern auch daran sterben werden.
Jetzt halte ich es mit ihr nicht mehr aus.

They all have verbs or separable prefixes at the end, and in some cases the word order is very different from the English, because of, for example, relative clauses and modals.

Also, in some of the sentences the time phrases have been placed at the beginning to change the emphasis.

Jetzt halte ich es mit ihr nicht mehr aus emphasises *jetzt* more than *ich halte es jetzt mit ihr nicht mehr aus*.

Finally, there are several new words in the texts. Try to work out their meanings from the context. For example, you probably don't know *wiege*, but in the sentence *ich wiege schon fast 60 Kilo* it is easy to work out.

Liebe Tante Claudia,

Liebe Tante Claudia,

hilf mir bitte! Ich esse zu viel Schokolade, Pommes frites, Hamburger usw. Ich weiß nicht, wie ich aufhören kann! Bald werde ich sehr dick sein, und ich habe Angst (ich wiege schon fast 60 Kilo!!!). Ich fange an, deprimiert zu werden, und ich habe mit niemandem darüber gesprochen.

Deprimiert, Düsseldorf

Liebe Tante Claudia,

hilf mir bitte! Meine Eltern rauchen beide, und ich habe Angst vor Lungenkrebs. Einige Familienmitglieder sind an Krebs gestorben und ich bin davon überzeugt, dass meine Eltern auch daran sterben werden. Kannst du mir helfen? Ich mache mir große Sorgen!

Tief besorgt, Innsbruck, Österreich

Liebe Tante Claudia,

Hilfe! Meine Freundin und ich haben seit gut drei Jahren eine Beziehung und wir sind total verliebt! Aber am letzten Tag des Schulsemesters hat sie mit meinem besten Freund geflirtet. Jetzt halte ich es mit ihr nicht mehr aus, aber ohne sie wird mein Leben sehr einsam sein! Was kann ich tun?

Trauriger Leser, Osterode im Harz

Liebe Tante Claudia,

hilf mir bitte – ich habe Angst vor Prüfungen. Nächste Woche muss ich eine Prüfung bestehen und ich habe große Angst. Es ist schwer zu beschreiben, aber bei Prüfungen wird mir irgendwie schwindlig und das letzte Mal war ich wirklich krank und ich habe schlechte Noten bekommen. Ist es ernsthaft? Und was kann ich tun?

Musikfan, Basel, Schweiz

1 b Richtig, falsch oder nicht im Text?

Beispiel: 1 falsch

1. „Deprimiert" hat Angst um ihren Freund.
2. Sie hat eine Katze, die Mitzi heißt.
3. „Tief besorgt" hat Angst, dass ihre Eltern an Lungenkrebs sterben werden.
4. Ihre Eltern trinken manchmal Rotwein.
5. „Trauriger Leser" kann seine Freundin nicht leiden.
6. Er hat sie mit seinem besten Freund flirten sehen.
7. „Musikfan" hat keine Angst vor Prüfungen.
8. Wenn er Prüfungen hat, fühlt er sich immer krank.

2 A spielt die Rolle von einer Person aus Übung 1a. B muss raten, wer das ist.

Beispiel: **A** **Meine Freundin hat mit meinem besten Freund geflirtet.**
B **Du bist „Trauriger Leser".**
A **Richtig.**

3 **Füll die Lücken mit dem richtigen Wort aus den Klammern aus!**

Beispiel: **1 Seine**

1 ______ Eltern rauchen beide. (Seine/Sein/Seinen)

2 ______ Eltern essen zu viel. (Unsere/Unser/Unseren)

3 ______ Mutter ist krank. (Meine/Meinen/Mein)

4 Er mag ______ Vater. (sein/seine/seinen)

5 Wie findet ihr ______ Mutter? (euer/eure/euren)

6 ______ Freund hat mit jemandem geflirtet. (Ihr/Ihren/Ihr)

Grammatik: possessive adjectives

The endings on possessive adjectives change according to whether the noun they refer to is masculine, feminine or neuter. Remember also that masculine words have a different ending in the accusative case

masc	fem	neut	pl
mein (mein**en**)	meine	mein	meine
dein (dein**en**)	deine	dein	deine
sein/ihr (sein**en**/ihr**en**)	seine/ihre	sein/ihr	seine/ihre
unser (unser**en**)	unsere	unser	unsere
euer (eur**en**)	eure	euer	eure
ihr (ihr**en**)	ihre	ihr	ihre
Ihr (Ihr**en**)	Ihre	Ihr	Ihre

siehe Seite **140** ≫

4 **Hör dir Tante Claudias Antworten an (1–4) und sieh dir die Briefe auf Seite 82 an! Welche Antwort passt zu welchem Brief?**

Beispiel: **Antwort 1 – Musikfan**

5 **Schreib deinen eigenen Brief an Tante Claudia! Beschreib ähnliche Probleme und schreib im Perfekt, im Präsens und im Futur! Die Sätze unten können dir helfen.**

Beispiel: **Liebe Tante Claudia,**
hilf mir bitte – ich habe Angst vor Spinnen …

Liebe Tante Claudia,
hilf mir bitte! Ich bin ein Fan von klassischer Musik und meine Freunde finden das komisch …

Hilf mir bitte!	*Help me, please.*
Ich esse zu viel …/habe zu viel … gegessen.	*I (have) eat(en) too much.*
Ich weiß nicht, wie …	*I don't know how …*
Bald werde ich …	*Soon I will …*
Ich habe Angst vor (+ Dativ) …	*I am afraid of …*
Ich fühle mich (deprimiert usw.)	*I feel (depressed, etc.)*
Ich fange an, deprimiert zu werden/ mich krank zu fühlen (usw.)	*I am starting to be depressed/feel sick.*
Ich habe mit niemandem darüber gesprochen.	*I haven't talked to anyone about it.*
Ich bin davon überzeugt, dass …	*I am convinced that …*
Ich mache mir Sorgen.	*I am worried.*
… wird sterben/krank werden.	*… will die/become sick.*
Er/Sie hat mit … geflirtet/geredet.	*He/She flirted with/talked to … .*
verliebt sein	*to be in love*
Ich kann … nicht leiden/aushalten.	*I can't bear/stand … .*
Ohne … wird mein Leben … sein.	*Without … my life will be … .*
Das letzte Mal/Letztes Jahr (usw.) war ich krank.	*The last time/Last year I was ill.*

9D Der perfekte Mensch!

- discuss the qualities of a good friend
- build word 'families' of adjectives and nouns

An: Rolf Maier
Von: Kai Lorenz
Betr.: idealen Freund

Lieber Rolf,

du hast mich gefragt, was die besten Eigenschaften eines idealen Freundes sind. Hier sind sie: Ehrlichkeit, Geduld, Hilfsbereitschaft, cool sein und keine Arroganz! Die meisten meiner Freunde haben mindestens zwei dieser Eigenschaften und meine Frau wird sie alle haben – wenn ich sie finde!

Dein Kai

1 Lies Kais E-Mail! Sind die Sätze richtig oder falsch?

Beispiel: **1 richtig**

1. Rolf hat Kai über die Eigenschaften eines idealen Freundes gefragt.
2. Kais idealer Freund ist geizig.
3. Er ist auch freigiebig.
4. Kais Freunde haben alle mindestens vier dieser Eigenschaften.
5. Kais Frau wird diese Eigenschaften haben.
6. Kai hat seine Frau schon gefunden.

2 Hör zu und füll die Lücken aus!

Beispiel: **1 *Witzigkeit* und *cool sein***

1. Für Yasmin sind ________ und ________ ________ am wichtigsten.
2. Peter findet ________ wichtig.
3. Er findet ________ auch wichtig.
4. Maria findet ________ und ________ wichtig.
5. Die beste Eigenschaft von Stefans Großvater war seine ________ .
6. Für Katja ist ________ ________ am wichtigsten.

3 Macht eine Liste von 10 Eigenschaften und macht Interviews über die fünf wichtigsten! Schreibt sie in der richtigen Reihenfolge auf!

Beispiel: **A Was sind die Eigenschaften eines guten Freundes?**
B Geduld und Freigiebigkeit. Und du – was sind für dich die Eigenschaften eines guten Freundes?
A Für mich sind sie ...

4 Wie ist ein guter Freund/eine gute Freundin? Wie war dein bester Freund/deine beste Freundin auf der Grundschule? Schreib mindestens 60 Wörter!

Beispiel: **Für mich sind Ehrlichkeit, ... die Eigenschaften eines guten Freundes. Mein bester Freund/Meine beste Freundin ist ... . Auf der Grundschule war mein bester Freund ... .**

Strategie! *Building word families of adjectives and nouns*

- Match the nouns of personality in Kai's E-mail to the adjectives you have learnt, e.g. *Ehrlichkeit – ehrlich*. Can you work out what each noun means?
- Choose other adjectives and try to predict how the noun will be formed (note down your guesses).
- Check in a dictionary to see whether your predictions were right.
- Group the nouns by their endings, then look at the endings on the related adjectives. Can you see any patterns?
- What are the equivalent endings in English to the German adjective and noun endings?

Leute beschreiben	***Describing people***
sympathisch	*likeable, nice*
ehrlich	*honest*
geduldig	*patient*
freigiebig	*generous*
faul	*lazy*
schüchtern	*shy*
selbstbewusst	*self-confident*
arrogant	*arrogant*
nervig	*irritating*
launisch	*moody*
cool	*cool*
witzig	*funny, witty*
hilfsbereit	*helpful*
geizig	*mean*
fleißig	*hard-working*
selbstsüchtig	*selfish*

Regeln	***Rules***
(nicht) streng	*(not) strict*
ins Bett gehen	*to go to bed*
bei der Hausarbeit helfen	*to help with the housework*
laute Musik hören	*to listen to loud music*
abwaschen	*to wash up*
Staub saugen	*to vacuum clean*
spätabends in die Disko gehen	*to go to the disco late in the evening*
sein Zimmer aufräumen	*to tidy one's room*
fernsehen	*to watch TV*
(spät) nach Hause kommen	*to stay out (late)*
(pünktlich) in der Schule ankommen	*to arrive (punctually) at school*
aus der Schule gehen	*to leave school*
(keine) Handys ins Klassenzimmer bringen	(not) *to bring mobile phones into the classroom*
(nicht) essen dürfen	*(not) to be allowed to eat*
die Hausaufgaben (pünktlich) machen	*to do one's homework (punctually)*
sich gut benehmen	*to behave oneself well*

Probleme	***Problems***
Hilf mir bitte!	*Help me, please.*
Ich weiß nicht, wie …	*I don't know how …*
Ich habe Angst vor (+ Dativ)	*I am afraid of …*
Ich fühle mich (deprimiert usw.)	*I feel (depressed, etc.)*
Ich fange an, deprimiert zu werden/mich krank zu fühlen.	*I am starting to be depressed/feel sick.*
Ich bin davon überzeugt, dass …	*I am convinced that …*
Ich mache mir Sorgen.	*I am worried.*

Grammatik: 

★ Adjective endings after the indefinite article:

	masc	fem	neut	pl
nom	ein gut**er**	eine gut**e**	ein gut**es**	gut**e**
acc	einen gut**en**	eine gut**e**	ein gut**es**	gut**e**

★ Modal verbs:
- To say 'must' or 'have to', you use *müssen*.
- To say 'allowed to', you use *dürfen*.
- To say 'mustn't' or 'not allowed to', you use *dürfen* and a **negative**.
- With a negative *müssen* means 'don't have to' (**not** 'mustn't').

★ The imperfect tense of *müssen* and *dürfen:*

müssen	***dürfen***
ich musste (nicht)	*ich durfte (nicht)*
du musstest (nicht)	*du durftest (nicht)*
er/sie/es/man musste (nicht)	*er/sie/es/man durfte (nicht)*

★ Possessives:

masc	fem	neut	pl
mein (mein**en**)	meine	mein	meine
dein (dein**en**)	deine	dein	deine
sein/ihr (sein**en**/ihr**en**)	seine/ihre	sein/ihr	seine/ihre
unser (unser**en**)	unsere	unser	unsere
euer (eur**en**)	eure	euer	eure
ihr (ihr**en**)	ihre	ihr	ihre
Ihr (Ihr**en**)	Ihre	Ihr	Ihre

siehe Seite **140, 141, 145** ➤➤

Strategie! ♻

★ Use knowledge of word order to work out the meaning of sentences.

★ Build word families of adjectives and nouns.

Possessive adjectives: **mein** *my* • **dein** *your (sing fam)* • **sein/ihr/sein** *his/her/its* • **unser** *our* • **euer** *your (pl fam)* • **ihr** *their* • **Ihr** *your (pl polite)*

10 Arbeit, Arbeit, Arbeit!

10A Meine Eltern geben mir nicht genug Geld!

- discuss pocket money
- talk about how much money you need
- learn more about dative pronouns

1 **Hör zu (1–6) und mach Notizen! Wer bekommt wie viel Geld insgesamt?**

Beispiel: **1 Ralf – 5,50 €**

2 **Hör noch einmal zu! Richtig oder falsch?**

Beispiel: **1 richtig**

1 Ralfs Eltern geben ihm 5,50 € pro Woche.
2 Ilses Eltern geben ihr 6 €.
3 Andreas und Bodos Eltern geben ihnen 10,90 €.
4 Brunos Geld reicht ihm nicht.
5 Erika bekommt 7,70 € die Woche.
6 Birgits Taschengeld reicht ihr.

3 **Spielt die Rollen von Herbert oder Maria und macht Interviews! Benutzt die Infos und die Fragen unten! Tauscht Rollen! Überprüft dann eure Antworten!**

Beispiel: **A Wie viel Geld bekommst du pro Woche?**
B …
A Wer gibt es dir?
B … gibt/geben mir …
A Reicht das dir?
B …

Infos:

A Herbert — Onkel € 6,25 — nicht genug

B Maria — Großeltern € 5,75 — reicht

Grammatik: indirect object pronouns (dative)

The indirect object pronoun is a shorthand way of saying 'to' or 'for me, you, him/her', etc. It is **never** missed out, even though we sometimes miss out some of the words in English.

*Gib **mir** das Buch.*
Give me the book (= give **to** me the book).

*Seine Eltern geben **ihm** 5 € die Woche.*
His parents give him (= give **to** him) 5 euros a week.

siehe Seite **143** >>

Strategie! ***Getting clues about meaning from words which change according to case, number or gender***

Having different cases for pronouns in German can help make the meaning of sentences a lot clearer than in English. Compare the following:

Give them to them. — *Gib sie ihnen.*
She gives it to it. — *Sie gibt es ihm.*

4 Welche Sätze bedeuten dasselbe?

1 Meistens bekomme ich genug Geld.
2 Meine Mutter gibt mir nicht viel Geld.
3 Mein Geld reicht mir nicht.
4 Ich habe nicht genug Geld.
5 Ich bekomme nicht viel Geld von meiner Mutter.
6 Im Großen und Ganzen reicht mir mein Geld.

5 Hör zu! Bring die Sätze in die richtige Reihenfolge!

Beispiel: **4, …**

1 Ich möchte mehr Geld haben, wenn ich erwachsen bin.
2 Ich habe einen einfachen Lebensstil.
3 Ich werde einen Porsche kaufen.
4 Ich werde nicht viel Geld brauchen.
5 Ich möchte anderen Leuten helfen, wenn ich erwachsen bin.
6 Ich werde ein gutes Einkommen brauchen.

6 Was möchtest du machen, wenn du erwachsen bist? Wirst du viel Geld brauchen, oder willst du anderen Leuten helfen? Benutze die Bilder unten! Schreib 60 Wörter zu diesem Thema!

Beispiel: **Wenn ich erwachsen bin, werde ich viel Geld brauchen, um … zu …/nicht viel Geld brauchen, weil …**

10B Mein Nebenjob

- talk about part-time jobs
- give opinions about jobs
- use different tenses in the same sentence

a **b** Nebenjob

1 Hör zu und lies die Texte! Wer macht was?

Beispiel: **1 c**

c **d** **e**

1 Ich arbeite am Wochenende in einem Supermarkt. Ich verdiene 15 € pro Woche. Das ist nicht viel, aber es reicht mir, weil ich meine Klamotten nicht selbst kaufe.

Ralf

2 Ich habe keinen Nebenjob, weil meine Eltern mir genug Taschengeld geben. Das finde ich toll, weil ich meinen Samstag lieber im Bett verbringe!

Julia

3 Im Moment habe ich keinen Nebenjob, weil ich für die Prüfungen lernen muss, aber normalerweise arbeite ich an einer Tankstelle. Es ist ätzend – langweiliger als die Prüfungen!

Markus

f

4 Ich arbeite auf einem Bauernhof und das gefällt mir, weil es interessant ist. Der Lohn ist nicht sehr gut, aber das ist für mich kein Problem, weil ich dort so gern arbeite.

Dennis

5 Ich mache drei- oder viermal in der Woche Babysitting. Das ist ein toller Nebenjob, weil ich fernsehen oder für meine Prüfungen lernen kann. Und die Kinder sind immer im Bett!

Ottilie

6 Ich trage jeden Morgen Zeitungen aus, von 6 bis 7 Uhr. Das ist für mich ein toller Nebenjob, weil ich viel Geld verdiene und ich es vor dem Schulanfang machen kann. Ich muss aber früh aufstehen!

Esther

2 Lies die Texte in Übung 1! Wer ist das?

Beispiel: **1 Dennis**

1. Wer arbeitet gern auf dem Bauernhof, weil es interessant ist?
2. Wer trägt gern Zeitungen aus, weil sie es vor dem Schulanfang machen kann?
3. Wer braucht nicht viel Geld, weil er seine Klamotten nicht kauft?
4. Wer arbeitet nicht gern an der Tankstelle, weil es langweiliger als die Prüfungen ist?
5. Wer hat keinen Nebenjob, weil ihre Eltern ihr genug Taschengeld geben?
6. Wer macht gern Babysitting, weil sie fernsehen kann?

Strategie! ***Looking for clues to help with meaning***

In the texts in Exercise 1 there are quite a few words that will be unfamiliar to you. Can you work out their meaning from the context they are in? For instance, you might not know the meaning of *Der Lohn ist nicht sehr gut* – but when someone is talking about the drawbacks of their job, what isn't likely to be very good?

Make a list of words you don't think you know, and then write what you think they might mean by the side of each. Then check in a dictionary – how often were you right?

3 a Seht euch die Bilder an und macht Notizen und Dialoge! Ihr könnt auch eure eigenen Gründe erfinden, warum ihr den Nebenjob gern oder nicht gern macht! Tauscht Rollen!

Beispiel: **A** Hast du einen Nebenjob?
B Ja, ich arbeite an einer Tankstelle.
A Arbeitest du gern dort?
B Nein.
A Warum?
B Weil ...

3 b Schreib Sätze in dein Heft! Schreib mindestens über zwei Leute!

Beispiel: Ralf arbeitet im Supermarkt. Er arbeitet nicht gern dort, weil ...

4 a Hör zu (1–6) und wähl jeweils ***Präsens***, ***Perfekt*** oder ***Futur***!

Beispiel: **1** Perfekt

4 b Was haben die Leute früher gemacht? Was machen sie jetzt ? Was werden sie in der Zukunft machen? Hör zu (1–3) und füll die Tabelle aus!

Name	früher	jetzt	in der Zukunft
Verena	d		
Stefan			
Gerhild			

Strategie! ***Using pictures to predict what you are going to hear in a listening activity***

Use any pictures accompanying a listening activity to predict what you are going to hear. For instance, looking at picture **a** below you might expect to hear the word *Haustier(e)*.

a 
b 
c 
d 
e 
f 
g 
h 
i 

4 c Lies die Sätze und vervollständige sie!

Beispiel: **1 Im Supermarkt hat Verena viele Leute kennen gelernt.**

1 Im Supermarkt hat Verena viele Leute ...
2 Sie möchte auf einem Bauernhof arbeiten, weil ...
3 Stefan hat in ... gearbeitet.
4 Jetzt arbeitet er in einer Bäckerei, aber ...
5 Gerhild hat gern als Babysitterin gearbeitet, weil ...
6 Sie möchte ...

der Lohn ist nicht gut | sie Tiere liebt | sie arbeiten und fernsehen konnte | kennen gelernt | selbst gemachte Geschenkartikel auf dem Markt verkaufen | Tankstellen und auf Bauernhöfen

5 ***Do you get enough pocket money, and if not, have you had a part-time job? If so, what was it like and why? Have you got one now, and what sort would you like to have in the future – and why?***

Look up the words you need to prepare a brief presentation on the topic and make notes about it. Then make the presentation and tape or video it if you like.

10C Die Zukunft

- talk about the sort of job you would like
- use infinitives with or without *zu*
- use word order to work out meanings

Kai
Wenn ich erwachsen bin, möchte ich in einem großen Büro arbeiten. Für mich ist Sicherheit wichtig und ich werde zum Beispiel eine Stelle in einem öffentlichen Amt suchen.
Daniela
Wenn ich erwachsen bin, habe ich die Absicht, im Freien zu arbeiten. Es ist mir egal, was ich mache, aber ich arbeite nicht gern in einem dunklen Raum mit verstaubten Akten und muffigen Leuten.
PORSCHE
Porsche Zentrum Aachen
Gereon
Wenn ich die Schule verlasse, habe ich vor, bei einer großen Autofirma zu arbeiten. Am liebsten möchte ich Rennfahrer werden, aber man muss realistische Ziele haben!

1 a Was sind deine Pläne für die Zukunft? Hör zu (1–6) und lies mit!

1 b Lies die englischen Sätze! Was heißt das auf Deutsch?

Beispiel: **1 Für mich ist Sicherheit wichtig.**

1. Security is important to me.
2. I am intending to work in the open air.
3. I am planning to work for a big car firm.
4. I would like to be an artist.
5. I think it is important to look for an interesting job.
6. I am planning to look for a job where I can help people.
7. You've got to have realistic goals.
8. You should try to make your dreams come true.

Grammatik: infinitive phrases

After modals and *werden* you **don't** use *zu* before the main verb.

After other verbs, and expressions like *die Absicht haben* and *vorhaben*, you **do** use **zu**.

Ich muss meine Hausaufgaben machen.

Ich habe vor, eine Stelle ***zu*** *suchen.*

Ich habe die Absicht, im Freien ***zu*** *arbeiten.*

siehe Seite **147** >>

1 c Vervollständige die Sätze! Egal wie …

Beispiel: **Wenn ich erwachsen bin, habe ich die Absicht, einen Job bei einer großen Autofirma zu suchen.**

1. Wenn ich erwachsen bin, habe ich die Absicht, einen Job …
2. Wenn ich erwachsen bin, werde ich bei einer …
3. Wenn ich die Schule verlasse, habe ich vor, …
4. Später möchte ich einmal …
5. Wenn ich die Schule verlasse, …
6. Wenn …

1 d Sieh dir die Texte über die Zukunft in Übung 1a noch einmal an! Mit welchen Sätzen bist du einverstanden? Mit welchen Sätzen bist du nicht einverstanden? Mach zwei Listen!

Beispiel:

Einverstanden	Nicht einverstanden
Man sollte versuchen, seine Träume zu verwirklichen.	Ich möchte in einem großen Büro arbeiten.

Später möchte ich einmal Künstler werden. Ich zeichne und male sehr gern, und meiner Meinung nach sollte man versuchen, seine Träume zu verwirklichen.

Kudret

Wenn ich erwachsen bin, habe ich vor, Modedesignerin zu werden. Ich weiß, dass viele Leute einen Arbeitsplatz in einer großen Fabrik bekommen, aber ich halte es für wichtig, einen interessanten Beruf zu suchen.

Ute

Johanna

Wenn ich erwachsen bin, möchte ich Lehrerin oder Ärztin werden. Meine Eltern sind beide Lehrer und ich habe vor, eine Stelle zu suchen, wo ich Leuten helfen kann.

2 **Spielt die Rollen von den jungen Leuten aus Übung 1 und macht Interviews in der Klasse! Schreibt auf, wer welche Rolle spielt!**

Beispiel: **A** **Was sind deine Pläne für die Zukunft?**
B **Ich habe vor, Modedesignerin zu werden.**
A **(Schreibt) B = Ute.**

Strategie! *Looking for clues to help with meaning*

It is always a good idea to listen to the **whole** of a German sentence before trying to decide the meaning because:

- many verbs are in **two parts**, the second part being at the end of the sentence or clause;
- modals and other verbs often send the verb they are with to the end of the sentence, or attract another verb to the beginning of the next clause.

*Wenn ich erwachsen **bin**, **habe** ich die Absicht, einen Job als Modedesigner zu **suchen**.*

*Wenn ich die Schule **verlasse**, **habe** ich **vor**, in einem großen Büro zu **arbeiten**.*

3 **Hör dir das Interview mit Ralf an! Welche der Sätze unten kommen im Interview vor?**

Beispiel: **1, ...**

1 Ich bin sicher, dass ich in keinem dunklen Büro arbeiten will.
2 Mir ist es egal, ob ich einen interessanten Job habe oder nicht.
3 Ich habe die Absicht, ins Ausland zu fahren, um einen Job zu suchen.
4 Ich habe die Absicht, Sänger zu werden.
5 Es interessiert mich nicht, reich zu werden.
6 Jetzt habe ich nur vor, Spaß bei der Arbeit zu haben!

Grammatik: adjective endings in the dative

In the dative (usually after prepositions like *bei*, *in*, *mit*, etc.) **adjectives** end in *-en*. The same ending is used for all genders in the plural.

masc	fem	neut	pl (m/f/n)
*in einem dunkl**en** Raum*	*bei einer groß**en** Autofirma*	*in einem öffentlich**en** Amt*	*mit muffig**en** Leuten*

siehe Seite **141** >>

4 **Und du? Was möchtest du später einmal machen und warum? Was ist wichtig? Was möchtest du unter keinen Umständen machen? Schreib ungefähr 100 Wörter zu diesem Thema!**

Beispiel: **Wenn ich die Schule verlasse, möchte ich einen interessanten Job haben ...**

10D Beim Studium oder im Beruf?

- talk about daily routine
- compare current with past routine

Grammatik: reflexive verbs

Reflexive verbs use a subject **and** an object pronoun. In the perfect tense the object pronoun goes before the past participle and any other information, e.g. time, place.

Ich *wasche* ***mich.***	I wash (myself).
Hast ***du dich*** *heute gewaschen?*	Have you washed (yourself) today?
Er/Sie *zieht* ***sich*** *an.*	He/She gets dressed (dresses him/herself).
Er/Sie *hat* ***sich*** *angezogen.*	He/She got dressed (dressed him/herself).

siehe Seite **144** >>

1 **Herbert redet über sein Leben in seinem neuen Job. Hör zu und schreib die Uhrzeiten auf!**

Ich stehe auf. 6.00

Ich wasche mich. ________

Ich ziehe mich an. ________

Ich verlasse das Haus. ________

Der Bus fährt ab. ________

Ich fange mit der Arbeit an. ________

Ich nehme den Bus nach Hause. ________

Ich komme zu Hause an. ________

2 **Und wie war es auf der Schule? Hör zu und mach Notizen!**

Beispiel: **ist aufgestanden – 7.00**

Ich habe mich angezogen. | Ich habe das Haus verlassen. | Der Schultag hat angefangen. | Ich bin aufgestanden. | Ich habe mich gewaschen. | Der Schultag war aus. | Ich bin zu Hause angekommen.

3 **Wie ist der Schultag bei euch? Und wie war es auf der Grundschule? Macht Dialoge zu diesem Thema!**

Beispiel: **A Wie ist deine Routine jetzt?**
B …
A Und wie war es auf der Grundschule?

4 **Schreib ungefähr 50 Wörter und vergleiche deinen jetzigen Schultag mit dem der Grundschule! Was war anders, als du auf der Grundschule warst?**

Beispiel: **Ich stehe um sieben Uhr auf, aber auf der Grundschule bin ich um acht Uhr aufgestanden. Damals war es viel besser …**

5 *extra!* **Wie wird dein Tagesablauf in der Zukunft aussehen? Schreib ungefähr 100 Wörter zu diesem Thema!**

Beispiel: **Ich werde um halb sechs aufstehen und meine Uniform anziehen. Dann werde ich zum Flughafen fahren. Dort werde ich mein Flugzeug …**

Taschengeld	***Pocket money***
(nicht) (viel) brauchen	*(not) to need (much)*
das Einkommen	*income*
das (Taschen)geld	*(pocket) money*
die Eltern	*parents*
pro Woche	*per week*
geben	*to give*
genug	*enough*
im Großen und Ganzen	*on the whole, in the main*
insgesamt	*all together*
mindestens	*at least*
normalerweise	*normally*
reich	*rich*
reichen (+ *dat*)	*to be enough*
wie viel	*how much*

Arbeit	***Work***
Babysitting machen	*to go babysitting*
der Bauernhof	*farm*
der Lohn	*pay, wages*
der Nebenjob	*part-time job*
der Supermarkt	*supermarket*
die Klamotten (*pl*)	*clothes (slang)*
die Tankstelle	*petrol station*
gefallen (+ *dat*)	*to please someone, to like*
kaufen	*to buy*
normalerweise	*usually*
ungefähr	*around, about*
verdienen	*to earn*
Zeitungen austragen	*to deliver newspapers, do a paper round*

Die Zukunft	***The future***
der Arbeitsplatz	*position, job*
der Arzt/die Ärztin	*doctor*
der Modedesigner/die Modedesignerin	*fashion designer*
der Plan	*plan*
der Traum	*dream*
der Lehrer/die Lehrerin	*teacher*
die Absicht haben	*to intend (to)*
vorhaben	*to plan (to)*
die Sicherheit	*safety, security*
die Zukunft	*the future*
das Ziel	*goal, aim*
(es ist mir) egal	*(I'm) indifferent, not bothered*
für wichtig halten	*to consider something important*
in einem Büro arbeiten	*to work in an office*
verlassen	*to leave*
verwirklichen	*to realise, put into practice*

Der Tagesablauf	***Daily routine***
aufstehen	*to get up*
sich waschen	*to wash*
sich anziehen	*to get dressed*
(das Haus) verlassen	*to leave (the house)*
abfahren	*to leave, depart*
anfangen	*to begin, start*
ankommen	*to arrive*

Grammatik:

★ Indirect object pronouns (dative): the indirect object pronoun is a shorthand way of saying 'to' or 'for me, you, him/her', etc.

*Gib **mir** das Buch.* Give me the book (= give **to** me the book).

★ Adjective endings in the dative: in the dative, adjectives **always** end in ***-en***, in the singular **and** in the plural.

*in einem dunkl**en** Raum*

*mit muffig**en** Leuten*

★ Reflexive verbs: reflexive verbs use a subject **and** an object pronoun.

***Ich** wasche **mich**.* I wash (myself).

***Er/Sie** hat **sich** angezogen.* He/She got dressed.

siehe Seite **141, 143, 144** >>

Strategie!

★ Look for clues to help with meaning.

★ Get clues about meaning from words which change according to case, number or gender.

★ Use pictures to predict what you are going to hear in a listening activity.

arbeiten *to work* • **bekommen** *to get* • **nehmen** *to take* • **kaufen** *to buy*
Indirect object pronouns: **mir** • **dir** • **ihm** • **ihr** • **uns** • **euch** • **ihnen** • **Ihnen**
Reflexive pronouns: **mich** • **dich** • **sich**

Wiederholung

Kapitel 9 (Probleme? Siehe Seite 80–83!)

1 Was muss man machen? Was darf man nicht machen? Schreib die Schulregeln richtig auf!

Beispiel: **1 Man *darf nicht* zu spät zur Schule kommen.**

1. Man muss zu spät zur Schule kommen.
2. Man darf sein Handy nicht draußen lassen.
3. Man muss sich schlecht benehmen.
4. Man darf nicht in der Schule bleiben.
5. Man muss in den Stunden sprechen.

2 Lies den Brief! Richtig oder falsch?

Beispiel: **1 falsch**

1. Claudia hat nicht genug Hausaufgaben.
2. Ihre Eltern finden sie unmöglich.
3. Ihre Eltern hatten mehr Hausaufgaben.
4. Wenn Claudia schlechte Noten bekommt, werden ihre Eltern zufrieden sein.

Liebe Tante Margrit,

hilf mir bitte – ich habe zu viele Hausaufgaben und ich habe großen Angst vor Stress. Meine Eltern finden mich unmöglich, weil sie selber in den 70er Jahren viel mehr Hausaufgaben hatten. Und wenn ich schlechte Noten in den Prüfungen bekomme, werden meine Eltern böse sein. Was kann ich tun? Hilf mir bitte!

Claudia (Essen, Deutschland)

Kapitel 10 (Probleme? Siehe Seite 86–89!)

3 Lies die Texte und schau dir die Bilder an! Was passt zusammen?

Beispiel: **1 c**

a

b

c

d

1 Meine Eltern geben mir 4,50 € pro Woche und meine Tante gibt mir 2,50 €. Für mich ist das nicht genug.

2 Meine Tante gibt mir 3,50 € und meine Eltern geben mir 2,50 € – also insgesamt 6 € die Woche. Im Großen und Ganzen reicht mir das.

3 Mein Vater gibt mir 5,50 € und mein Großvater gibt mir 3,25 €. Das reicht mir nicht, weil ich meine eigenen Klamotten kaufen muss.

4 Mein Vater gibt mir 2,50 € die Woche und meine Mutter gibt mir 3 €. Das reicht mir meistens, weil ich normalerweise nur Bonbons usw. kaufe.

4 Lies den Brief und vervollständige die Sätze!

Beispiel: **1 Babs bekommt kein Taschengeld.**

1. Babs bekommt kein _________.
2. Am Samstag arbeitet sie in einem _________.
3. Babysitten macht ihr _________.
4. Sie arbeitet nicht gern auf dem _________.
5. Babs verdient insgesamt _________.

Liebe Erika,

hast du einen Nebenjob? Ich bekomme kein Taschengeld, deshalb muss ich mein eigenes Geld verdienen und ich habe drei Nebenjobs. Am Samstag arbeite ich in einem Supermarkt und dort verdiene ich 5 €. Am Freitagabend mache ich normalerweise Babysitting. Beim Babysitten verdiene ich nur 3 €, aber es macht Spaß, weil ich fernsehen kann! Der dritte Nebenjob ist aber der schlimmste! Am Sonntag arbeite ich auf einem Bauernhof und das hasse ich, weil es stinkt! Dort verdiene ich 10 €!

Deine Babs

Umfrage: Was willst du?

Die Jugendlichen von heute streben nach Karriere und nach Familie, sagen Forscher. *JUMA* ist auf die Straße gegangen und hat selbst Jugendliche befragt.

Mario, 19 Jahre: Ich möchte wenig leisten, viel verdienen und Karriere machen. Am liebsten würde ich noch heute von zu Hause ausziehen. Eine Frau will ich später auch haben, und mindestens drei Kinder.

Philipp, 16 Jahre: Ich will unbedingt eine Familie gründen, weil ich selbst nie eine hatte. Heiraten muss ich meine Freundin nicht. Erfolg im Beruf ist mir wichtig. Mein Traum ist es, die ganze Welt zu sehen.

Esra, 12 Jahre: Karriere will ich nicht machen, aber schon einen guten Beruf haben. Etwas mit Computern finde ich gut. Wichtig ist mir die Freundschaft mit meiner Familie. Heiraten möchte ich später auch. Jetzt will ich Spaß haben.

Bahar, 13 Jahre: Zwei Kinder will ich später haben: einen Jungen und ein Mädchen. Meine Freunde und meine Familie sind mir wichtiger als der Beruf. Meine Mutter ist wie meine Freundin. Ich mag sie mehr als meinen Vater. Aber ein bisschen Karriere will ich machen. Tierärztin ist mein Traumberuf.

Sarah, 17 Jahre: Geld ist mir am wichtigsten im Leben, meine Freunde aber auch. Im Beruf will ich später gut sein. Ich möchte nämlich nicht als Hausfrau ohne eigenes Geld enden. Kinder will ich auch haben. Aber es ist wichtig, an sich selbst zu denken.

Svenja, 13 Jahre: Am wichtigsten in meinem Leben sind meine Freunde. Ohne sie wäre ich einsam. Zu meinen Eltern habe ich einen guten Kontakt. Ich will später eine eigene Familie haben. Natürlich auch Kinder, aber höchstens zwei. Mein Mann sollte mir im Haushalt helfen, denn ich möchte berufstätig sein. Am liebsten als Polizistin.

Sina, 14 Jahre: Ehrgeiz ist wichtig im Leben, aber Karriere muss ich später nicht machen. Ich will viel Zeit für Familie und Freunde haben. Und für mich selbst. Mich interessieren Menschenrechte und alles, was mit Kindern und Afrika zu tun hat. Außerdem bin ich gegen Atomkraft.

Aus: *JUMA* 3/2003, Annette Zellner, www.juma.de

1 Wer ist das?

Beispiel: **1 Sina**

1. Sie interessiert sich für Afrika und Kinder.
2. Geld ist ihr am wichtigsten und sie denkt an sich selbst.
3. Er will heiraten und mindestens drei Kinder haben.
4. Er möchte Spaß haben und mit Computern arbeiten.
5. Sie will nicht mehr als zwei Kinder haben.
6. Er hat keine eigene Familie und möchte viel reisen.
7. Sie will einen Jungen und ein Mädchen haben.

11 Los geht's!

11A Wohin denn?

- discuss what you could do
- learn how to use the conditional
- learn how to write for information

a *Aktives Strandleben in Skagen, Dänemark*

b *Wandern in den Schweizer Alpen*

1 a **Eine Jugendgruppe aus Hannover diskutiert einen Ausflug. Hör zu und sieh dir die Fotos an! Wie ist die richtige Reihenfolge?**

Beispiel: **b** Wandern in den Schweizer Alpen

c *Geschäfte und Geschichte in der schönen Hauptstadt Österreichs*

1 b **Hör noch einmal zu! Was sind die Vor- und Nachteile von jedem Ort? Füll die Tabelle aus!**

Beispiel:

Bild	Vorteil(e)	Nachteil(e)
b	8, 4	13

d *Freiwillige Umweltarbeit in Halle, Ostdeutschland*

Vorteile

1. Camping nicht teuer
2. gut für die Umwelt
3. interessant für alle
4. Jugendherberge billig
5. keine Unterkunftskosten
6. viel Spaß und nicht weit weg
7. interessante Stadt mit guten Geschäften
8. schönes Wetter und frische Luft

Nachteile

9. harte Arbeit
10. keinen Spaß bei schlechtem Wetter
11. nicht für eine ganze Woche
12. schon dreimal dort
13. zu langweilig und weit weg
14. zu weit weg und Hotel zu teuer

e *Spaß im Erlebnispark Heide-Park, Deutschland*

1 c **Macht Dialoge!**

Beispiel:
A Wohin würdest du gern fahren?
B Ich würde gern in die Schweiz fahren.
A Warum?
B Ich könnte in den Alpen wandern. Und du?

1 d *extra!* **Schreib Sätze mit *weil*!**

Beispiel: **Ich würde gern in die Schweiz fahren, weil ich in den Alpen wandern könnte.
Ich würde nicht in einen Freizeitpark gehen, weil ich schon sehr oft dort war.**

Ich würde gern/lieber nach X gehen.
Das würde Spaß machen.
Das wäre teuer (usw.).
Wir könnten das machen/nach X gehen/fahren.
Ich hätte (keine) Lust dazu.
Das wäre gut.

Lauter Laute: a/ä, o/ö, u/ü

An umlaut makes a big difference to the meaning, e.g. ich hatte = *I had (imperfect tense),* ich hätte = *I would have (conditional tense).*

- *Hör zu und sprich nach!*

Grammatik: conditional
(der Konditional)

The conditional is used to say 'would do'.

It is normally formed using **würde** + infinitive.

ich	**würde**	*(gern) machen*
du	**würdest**	*(nicht gern) gehen*
er/sie/es/man	**würde**	*schreiben*
wir	**würden**	*fahren*
ihr	**würdet**	*mitkommen*
sie/Sie	**würden**	*kosten*

Some common verbs shorten *würde* + infinitive to just one word.

ich ***hätte****/wir* ***hätten*** (I/we would have)
ich ***wäre****/wir* ***wären*** (I/we would be)
ich ***könnte****/wir* ***könnten*** (I/we could/would be able to)
ich ***möchte****/wir* ***möchten*** (I/we would like to)

siehe Seite **145** >>

2 a Hör noch einmal zu (1–6)! Schreib *a* oder *b*!

1 a ich hatte
b ich hätte
2 a wir konnten
b wir könnten
3 a er war
b er wäre
4 a es wurde
b es würde
5 a ich mochte
b ich möchte
6 a wir mussten
b wir müssten

2 b Hör zu und sprich nach! Füll dann die Lücken aus!

1 Wir ___________ gern Informationen.
2 Ich ___________ einen Brief schreiben.
3 Das ___________ toll.
4 Wir ___________ im Juli losfahren.
5 Was ___________ du machen?

3 a Die Gruppe schreibt Briefe an verschiedene Orte, um Informationen zu bekommen. Lies Carmens Brief!

Abs: **C. Hardinger**
Eulengasse 13
30456 Hannover

Hannover, **3. April**

Sehr geehrte Damen und Herren!

Unsere Jugendgruppe hat jedes Jahr einen Ausflug gemacht und dieses Jahr haben wir beschlossen, **einen Campingurlaub** zu machen. Ich hätte gern Informationen über **Ihren Campingplatz**, zum Beispiel **Lage, Preise und Freizeitmöglichkeiten.**

Wir sind **15** Jugendliche und **3** Erwachsene aus **Hannover** und wir möchten **eine Woche** in Ihrer Gegend verbringen. Wir würden **mit dem Bus** fahren und am **20. Juli** ankommen. Wir möchten gern **6 Nächte** bleiben.

Ich danke Ihnen im Voraus für die Auskunft.

Mit freundlichen Grüßen

Ihre Carmen Hardinger

3 b Schreib einen ähnlichen Brief/eine E-Mail an einen der folgenden Orte! Ändere die fett gedruckten Wörter! Schlag eventuell im Wörterbuch nach!

- ein Campingplatz in Deutschland
- eine Jugendherberge in der Schweiz
- ein Hotel in Österreich
- ein Umweltprojekt in Deutschland

11B Haben Sie Platz?

- learn how to book accommodation
- understand information about holiday accommodation
- learn more about separable verbs

1 **Hör zu und sieh dir die Bilder an! Welche zwei Bilder passen?**

2 **Seht euch die Kästchen an und macht Dialoge!**

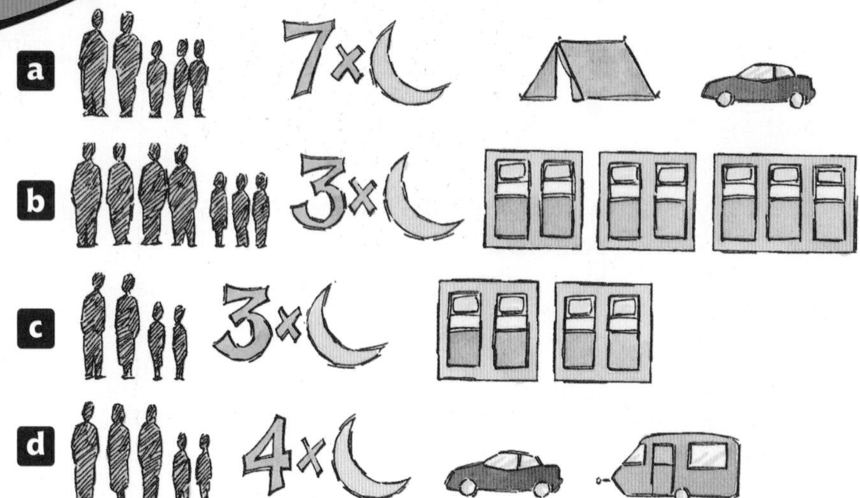

das Hotel/der Campingplatz

Kann ich Ihnen helfen?

Für wie viele Personen?

Für ein Zelt, einen Wohnwagen oder ein Wohnmobil?

Wann kommen Sie an?

Wie viele Nächte werden Sie bleiben?

Hätten Sie noch einen Wunsch?

Auf welchen Namen soll ich reservieren?

Ich habe alles reserviert.

der Gast

Ich möchte ein/zwei Zimmer/ einen Platz reservieren.

Haben Sie Platz?

Was kostet ...?

ein Einzelzimmer/ Doppelzimmer/ Dreibettzimmer

für ein Zelt/einen Wohnwagen/ ein Wohnmobil

für zwei Erwachsene/Kinder

Wir kommen am 25. Juli an.

eine Nacht/zwei Nächte

Haben Sie einen Parkplatz?

Gibt es ein Schwimmbad?

Grammatik: ***trennbare Verben*** 

Remember that separable verbs join up in the infinitive.

*Wir **kommen** um 17 Uhr **an**.*

*Wir werden um 17 Uhr **ankommen**.*

If you need **zu** with the infinitive, it goes after the separable prefix. (See pages 64, 90 for a reminder of when to use *zu*.)

*Wir hoffen, um 17 Uhr **anzukommen**.*

Remember that in the perfect tense the **-ge-** part of the past participle also separates the prefix from the rest of the verb.

*Ich bin um 17 Uhr **angekommen**.*

siehe Seite **147** >>

3 **Schreib einen Brief (oder eine E-Mail) an ein Hotel oder einen Campingplatz, um eine Reservierung zu machen! Stell auch mindestens eine Frage! Wähl die richtigen Verbformen, Anfang und Ende für deinen Brief. Dein(e) Partner(in) überprüft deine Antworten.**

Hier sind einige Vorschläge:

Campingplatz Sonnenwald

12.08–16.08

Hotel Bergweg

27.07–30.07

A

Herzlich willkommen in der Jugendherberge Aachen!

Die im Herbst 1998 vollständig modernisierte Jugendherberge Aachen bietet ihren Gästen eine moderne Innenausstattung und ein großzügiges Raumangebot. Das schöne Bistro mit Sonnenterrasse, die neuen Tagungsräume und nicht zuletzt die große Zahl behindertenfreundlicher Zimmer sorgen dafür, dass alle Gästegruppen sich hier richtig wohl fühlen können.

PREISLISTE

Übernachtung mit Frühstücksbüfett	€ 21,10
Familienermäßigung	-30%
Einzelzimmerzuschlag	€ 13,50
Doppelzimmerzuschlag	p.P. € 5,10
Mittagessen/Abendessen	je € 5,00
Lunchpaket	€ 4,95

Angaben ohne Gewähr

B

Das Hotel Granus ist ein völlig neu ausgebautes Privat-Hotel im Herzen Berlins. In zentraler Lage haben Sie die Möglichkeit, das aufregende Leben der Stadt zu erfahren sowie die Ruhe in unserem Hof zu genießen. Zahlreiche Sehenswürdigkeiten (Tiergarten, Brandenburger Tor, Zoo, Potsdamer Platz, Kurfürstendamm und vieles mehr) befinden sich ganz in der Nähe des Hotels.

Unsere Preise:

Einzelzimmer	ab € 59
Doppelzimmer	ab € 77
Dreibettzimmer	ab € 93
Vierbettzimmer	ab € 103
Zusatzbett	ab € 15
Parkplatz	ab € 6

Alle Preise inkl. reichhaltiges Frühstücksbüfett und MwSt.
Preisänderungen vorbehalten.
Sonderpreise für Dauergäste und Reisegruppen auf Anfrage.

4 Lies die Sätze! Richtig oder falsch?

1. Die Jugendherberge ist altmodisch.
2. Familien können dreißig Prozent billiger übernachten.
3. Wenn man ein Einzelzimmer hat, muss man mehr bezahlen.
4. Das Hotel ist nicht in der Stadtmitte.
5. Berlins Sehenswürdigkeiten sind nicht weit vom Hotel.
6. Man kann am Hotel kostenlos parken.

5 Lies die Texte noch einmal und beantworte die Fragen auf Deutsch!

Beispiel: **1 Ein Zimmer für zwei Personen kostet (mindestens) 77 €.**

1. Was kostet ein Zimmer für zwei Personen im Hotel?
2. Warum wäre das Hotel für Touristen gut?
3. Welche Mahlzeiten sind im Preis inklusive?
4. Was hat man 1998 in der Jugendherberge gemacht?
5. Was muss man dort pro Nacht bezahlen, wenn man ein Einzelzimmer möchte?
6. Warum wäre diese Jugendherberge für Behinderte ideal?

Strategie! *Reading unfamiliar texts*

When reading an unfamiliar text:

- use a dictionary, but don't look up every unknown word;
- look at the questions to find out what you need to know and therefore which words you need to look up;
- remember to break down compound nouns to work out meanings.

6 Stellt mindestens fünf Fragen und beantwortet sie! Die Fragen und Antworten aus Übung 5 können euch helfen.

Beispiel: **A Was kostet ein Einzelzimmer im Hotel?**
B Das kostet ab 59 €.

11C Probleme, Probleme!

- ask about campsite facilities
- report problems
- learn more about forming questions

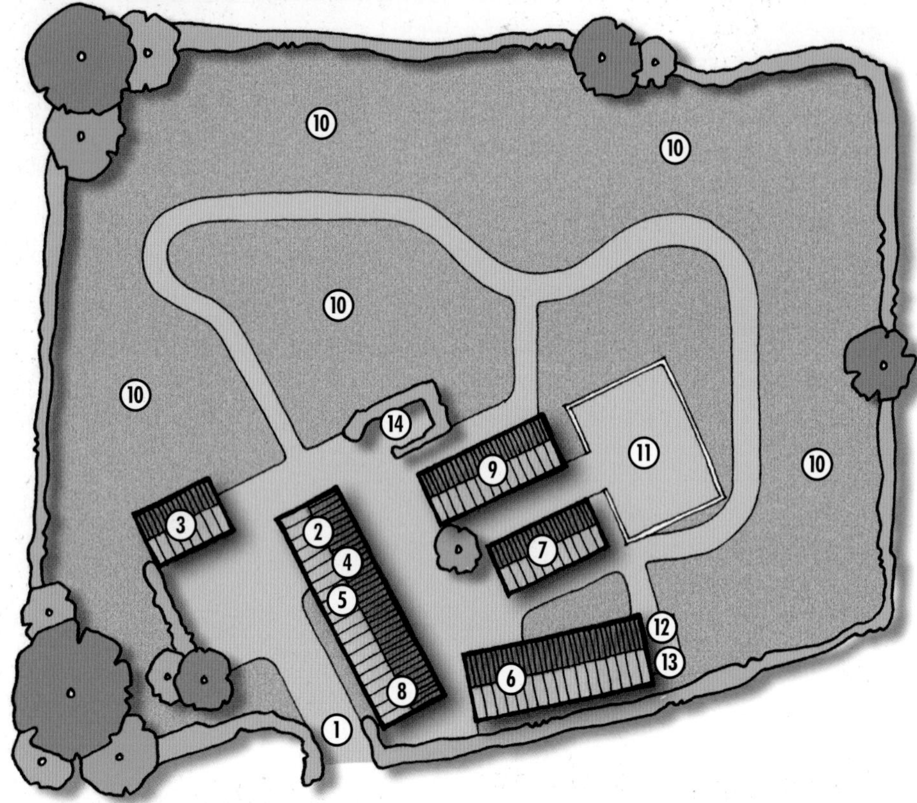

Schlüssel:

 **1** Einfahrt

 **2** Telefonzellen

 **3** Rezeption

 **4** Gasverkauf

 **5** Kiosk (Lebensmittel, Zeitungen)

 **6** Sanitäranlagen (Waschbecken, Duschen, Toiletten)

 **7** Waschhaus (Waschmaschinen, Wäschetrockner, Geschirrspülbecken)

 **8** Tischtennis

 **9** Restaurant

 **10** Stellplätze (Zelte, Wohnmobile, Wohnwagen)

 **11** Kinderspielplatz

 **12** Stromanschluss

 **13** Wasserstelle

 **14** Müllcontainer

1 a Hör zu und sieh dir den Plan und den Schlüssel an! Was erwähnt man? Schreib die Nummern auf!

Beispiel: **10, ...**

1 b Hör noch einmal zu! Welche Fragen hörst du? Mach Notizen!

Beispiel: **Wie lange werden Sie bleiben?**

1 c Wie sind die Antworten auf die Fragen? Mach Notizen!

1 d Stellt Fragen und beantwortet sie!

Beispiel: **A Wie lange werden Sie bleiben?**
B Wir werden fünf Nächte bleiben.

2 *extra!* **Schreib eine Frage (oder mehrere Fragen) für jedes Fragewort im Grammatik-Kästchen! Schreib mindestens eine Frage im Perfekt, eine im Futur und eine im Konditional. Dein(e) Partner(in) überprüft deine Fragen.**

Grammatik: questions

- To form a question, the subject and verb change places.
- Sometimes you also put a question word at the beginning.
- Most question words begin with *w*.
- Intonation also helps to identify questions.
- Remember that you can often use part of the language of a question in your answers.

Make sure you know the meaning of these question words.

was *warum*
wer *wann/um wie viel Uhr*
wo *wie viel(e)*
wie *wie lange*

siehe Seite **147** >>

3 Die Gäste im Katzenhotel rechts haben Probleme. Hör zu (1–8)! Was passt zusammen?

Beispiel: **1 d**

Kann ich Ihnen helfen?
Was (genau) ist das Problem?
Kann ich einen Tisch reservieren?
... funktioniert nicht
... ist schmutzig/kaputt
... ist zu kalt/heiß/laut.

Ich habe	den Schlüssel meine Brille	verloren. kaputt gemacht.
Es gibt	keinen Haartrockner. keine Handtücher.	

a Der Haartrockner funktioniert nicht.

b Die Gäste im nächsten Zimmer sind zu laut.

c Es tut mir Leid, ich habe die Lampe kaputt gemacht.

d Das Badezimmer ist schmutzig und es gibt keine sauberen Handtücher.

REZEPTION

e Ich habe meine Brille verloren. Hat man sie vielleicht gefunden?

f Ich werde heute Abend drei Gäste zum Essen einladen. Kann ich bitte einen Tisch reservieren?

g Der Fernseher ist kaputt!

h Das Zimmer ist zu kalt.

4 a Was ist das Problem? Macht Sätze! Dein(e) Partner(in) überprüft.

Beispiel: **a Die Dusche ist kaputt./Die Dusche funktioniert nicht.**

Strategie! Using connectives

Remember, there are many different connectives you could use to link sentences:
und, aber, oder
wenn, weil, dass
der, die, das, etc. (relative pronouns)

4 b Macht einen witzigen Dialog in einem furchtbaren Hotel!

Beispiel: **A Rezeption. Kann ich Ihnen helfen?**
B Ja, ... funktioniert nicht.
A Was genau ist das Problem?

5 Es gibt Probleme im Urlaub (im Hotel/auf dem Campingplatz). Schreib eine Postkarte an einen Freund/eine Freundin!

Beispiel: **Liebe Katrin!**

Das Wetter hier ist gut, aber ich habe ... verloren, aber morgen, wenn ..., werde ich ... Das Hotel, in dem wir wohnen, ...

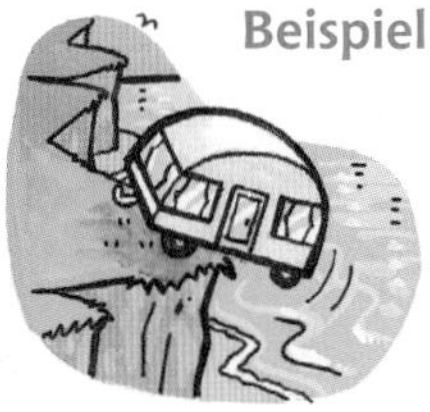

11D Das geht nicht!

- write a letter of complaint
- learn how to improve your writing

1 Lies den Brief und beantworte die Fragen auf Englisch!

1 List the problems Jakob had at the Hotel Seeblick.

2 What does he say and ask for at the end of the letter?

Arnold Niemeyer (Direktor)
Hotel Seeblick
Seestraße 76
54321 Klarstadt

Hannover, 12. Juni

Sehr geehrter Herr Niemeyer,

ich habe drei Tage, vom 10. bis zum 12. Mai, in ihrem Hotel verbracht und ich habe viele Probleme gehabt. Als ich am ersten Tag angekommen bin, hat der Fernseher gar nicht funktioniert und ich habe meine Lieblingssendung nicht gesehen. Niemand hat den Fernseher repariert. Das finde ich furchtbar!

Am zweiten Tag hat die Empfangsdame meinen Schlüssel verloren und ich bin ziemlich spät ins Bett gegangen, aber die Nachbarn waren zu laut und ich habe wenig geschlafen. Am nächsten Morgen habe ich kein Frühstück bekommen, weil es zu spät war. Meiner Meinung nach geht das nicht.

Bald werden Sie keine Gäste mehr haben. Wenn die Bedienung weiterhin so schlecht bleibt, werde ich Ihr Hotel nie wieder besuchen. Wann kann man die Lösung dieser Probleme erwarten? Ich hoffe auf eine baldige Antwort und eine Entschuldigung.

Ihr Jakob Kreuzer

Grammatik: *when*

Wann, *wenn* and *als* all mean 'when'. What's the difference between them?

Explain to your partner.

2 Füll die Lücken aus!

1 ________ es regnet, werden wir nicht auf der Terrasse essen.

2 Sie ist zur Polizei gegangen, ________ sie ihr Portmonee verloren hat.

3 ________ können wir das Schwimmbad benutzen?

siehe Seite **146, 147** >>

3 Schreib einen ähnlichen Brief an ein Hotel oder einen Campingplatz! Benutze Wörter aus dem Brief in Übung 1!

Hier sind einige Vorschläge:

Strategie! *Improving your writing*

- Think carefully about what you are going to write and remember to edit and redraft your work.
- Adapt language you already know.
- Think about whether you should use *du* or *Sie*.
- Use a range of tenses to add variety to your writing.
- Try to vary the word order, e.g. start some sentences with a time phrase or a *wenn* clause.
- Give opinions.
- Use connectives to link sentences and paragraphs.
- Use a dictionary to check that what you have written is accurate.

Wohin denn?	***Where to?***
Ich würde gern/lieber nach X gehen.	*I'd like/prefer to go to X.*
Das würde Spaß machen.	*That would be fun.*
Das wäre zu teuer.	*That would be too expensive.*
Wir könnten das machen/nach X fahren.	*We could do that/go to X.*
Ich hätte (keine) Lust dazu.	*I'd (not) like to do that.*
Das wäre gut.	*That would be good.*

Reservierungen	***Reservations***
Kann ich Ihnen helfen?	*Can I help you?*
Für wie viele Personen?	*For how many people?*
Wann kommen Sie an?	*When are you arriving?*
Wie viele Nächte werden Sie bleiben?	*How many nights will you stay?*
Hätten Sie noch einen Wunsch?	*Would you like anything else?*
Auf welchen Namen soll ich reservieren?	*What name shall I book under?*
Ich habe alles reserviert.	*I've reserved everything.*
Ich möchte ein/zwei Zimmer reservieren.	*I'd like to book one room/two rooms.*
Ich möchte einen Platz/Stellplatz reservieren.	*I'd like to reserve a pitch.*
Haben Sie Platz?	*Have you room?*
Was kostet …?	*How much is …?*
ein Einzelzimmer/Doppelzimmer/Dreibettzimmer	*a single/double/3-bed room*
für ein Zelt/einen Wohnwagen/ein Wohnmobil	*for a tent/a caravan/a motor-home*
für zwei Erwachsene/Kinder.	*for two adults/children.*
Wir kommen am 25. Juli an.	*We are arriving on 25th July.*
eine Nacht/zwei Nächte	*one night/two nights*
Haben Sie einen Parkplatz?	*Have you got a car park?*
Gibt es ein Schwimmbad?	*Is there a pool?*

Probleme	***Problems***
Was (genau) ist das Problem?	*What (exactly) is the problem?*
Kann ich einen Tisch reservieren?	*Can I book a table?*
… funktioniert nicht.	*… isn't working.*
… ist schmutzig/kaputt/zu kalt/heiß/laut.	*… is dirty/broken/too cold/hot/noisy.*
Ich habe den Schlüssel/meine Brille verloren/kaputt gemacht.	*I've lost/broken the key/my glasses.*
Es gibt keinen Haartrockner/keine Handtücher.	*There's no hair drier/There are no towels.*

Grammatik:

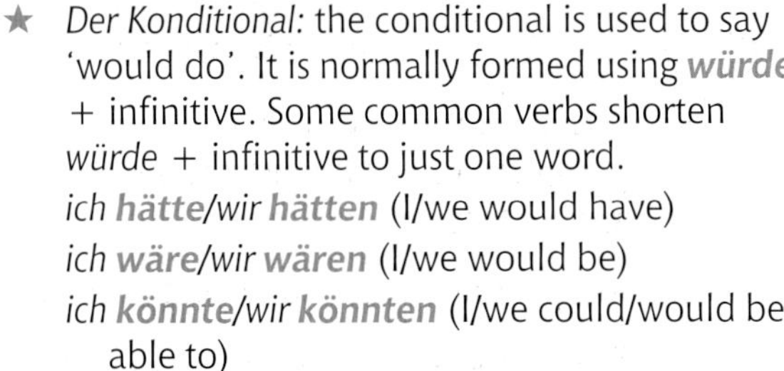

★ *Der Konditional:* the conditional is used to say 'would do'. It is normally formed using **würde** + infinitive. Some common verbs shorten *würde* + infinitive to just one word.

ich ***hätte****/wir* ***hätten*** (I/we would have)
ich ***wäre****/wir* ***wären*** (I/we would be)
ich ***könnte****/wir* ***könnten*** (I/we could/would be able to)
ich ***möchte****/wir* ***möchten*** (I/we would like to)

★ Separable verbs (*trennbare Verben*): remember that separable verbs join up in the infinitive.
Wir werden um 17 Uhr ***ankommen****.*

If you need **zu** with the infinitive, it goes after the separable prefix.
Wir hoffen, um 17 Uhr ***anzukommen****.*

★ Questions:

was	*warum*
wer	*wann/um wie viel Uhr*
wo	*wie viel(e)*
wie	*wie lange*

★ When: *wann, wenn* and *als* all mean 'when'. (*wann* = question; *wenn* = whenever/if; *als* = single time in the past)

siehe Seite **145–147** >>

Strategie!

★ Read unfamiliar texts.
★ Use connectives.
★ Improve your writing.

wenn, wann, als *when* • **was** *what* • **warum** *why* • **wer** *who* • **um wie viel Uhr** *at what time* • **wo** *where* • **wie viel(e)** *how much/many* • **wie** *how* • **wie lange** *how long*

Lauter Laute: a/ä, o/ö, u/ü

12 Überall Touristen

12A Ferienziel Deutschland

- talk about holiday destinations
- use correct word order
- use present and future tenses

1 a Hör zu (1–4)! Wer spricht?

Beispiel: **1 Sofia**

1 b Lies die Texte! Wer sagt das?

Beispiel: **a Ali**

a Mir gefällt es in Hamburg, weil ich dort viele Verwandte und Freunde habe. Bei jedem Wetter gibt es viel zu tun und wir langweilen uns nie. Ich freue mich schon auf die Ferien!

b Wir fahren jedes Jahr mit dem Auto zu einem süddeutschen Bauernhof. Das macht viel Spaß, weil wir dort reiten und Rad fahren können.

c Diesen Sommer fahren wir nicht nach Spanien. Wir werden nicht weit von Köln am Rhein campen und wir hoffen, dass das Wetter gut sein wird.

d Normalerweise fahren wir mit dem Zug auf die Insel Sylt, die in der Nordsee liegt, aber nächstes Jahr möchte ich mal ins Ausland fliegen.

Boris

Ali

Dorothea

Sofia

1 c Hör noch einmal zu! Richtig oder falsch?

Beispiel: **1 falsch**

1. Sofia macht Urlaub in Norddeutschland.
2. Sie mag Pferde.
3. Dorothea wird in einem Hotel am Rhein übernachten.
4. In den Sommerferien kauft sie in Köln ein.
5. Man kann mit dem Zug nach Sylt fahren.
6. Boris hat keine Lust, jeden Sommer auf Sylt zu verbringen.
7. Ali wird dieses Jahr nicht nach Hamburg fahren.
8. Bei schlechtem Wetter gibt es in Hamburg nichts zu tun.

Grammatik: present and future tenses

Remember, the **present** tense is used for things that

- are happening now (*er* ***spielt*** *Tennis im Park*);
- happen regularly (*sie* ***geht*** *jeden Tag zu Fuß zur Schule*).

You can also use the present tense (usually with a time phrase) to refer to the future.

Nächstes Jahr ***fahre*** *ich ins Ausland.*

The **future** tense is used for things that will happen or will be happening. It is formed by the present tense of the verb ***werden*** + infinitive.

Look out for clues that help to indicate the future (*nächsten Sommer, nächstes Jahr*).

siehe Seite **143, 145** >>

2 **Was machen diese Personen? Macht Sätze im Präsens und im Futur!**

Beispiel: **A** **Was macht Carsten in den Sommerferien?**
B **Er fährt mit dem Bus nach Berlin.**
Wann wird Steffi nach Sylt fahren?
A **Sie wird …**

Steffi | Carsten | Meryem | Göker

wo? wann? was? wie? wer?

in den Sommerferien/ Herbstferien/ …

im April/August/ Oktober/…

machen, fahren, bleiben, fliegen

Grammatik: ***Wortstellung* (word order)**

- Adverbs and adverbial phrases follow this order: time, manner, place (when, how, where).
- The verb is the second idea in a main clause.
- infinitives go to the end of a main clause.

Ich	*werde*	*morgen*	*mit dem Bus*	*in die Stadt*	*fahren.*
first idea	second idea verb in present	time	manner	place	infinitive

siehe Seite **146** >>

3 **a** **Was kann man auf der Insel Rügen machen? Erzähl deinem Partner/deiner Partnerin davon!**

Beispiel: **Man kann … Es gibt … Die Insel hat …**

Ich werde mit dem Bus fahren.
Sie fährt mit der Bahn.
Wir fliegen nach Hamburg/Sylt.
Wir fahren auf **einen** Bauernhof/Campingplatz.
Er wird auf **einem** Bauernhof/Campingplatz bleiben.
Sie mietet eine Ferienwohnung.
Ich übernachte in einem Hotel/in Hotels.
in Nordostdeutschland/im Südwesten

Man kann …	Rad fahren, segeln, windsurfen, wandern, schwimmen, reiten.
Du wirst …	einkaufen gehen, Ausflüge machen, das Schloss besichtigen.

Entdecken Sie Rügen – Deutschlands größte Insel!
Diese schöne Insel hat weiße Felsen, grüne Alleen, alte Fischerhäuser, sandige Strände und vieles mehr.

der Felsen (-) – *cliff*

3 **b** *extra!* **Stell dir vor, du fährst nach Rügen! Was wirst du machen? Warum?**

Beispiel: **Es gibt weiße Felsen, die sehr schön sind. Ich werde sie fotografieren, weil sie sehr interessant sind …**

12B Bei den Nachbarn

- describe a holiday in the past
- give opinions about something in the past
- use the perfect and imperfect tenses

1  **Lies die Broschüre über Luzern und beantworte die Fragen auf Englisch!**

1 How long does the Luzern walking tour last?
2 Is the *Rigi* a ship, a mountain or a restaurant?
3 What eras of transport and communication can you see in the *Verkehrshaus?*

2 a Benno ist letzten Sommer nach Luzern gefahren. Hör zu, sieh dir die Broschüre in Übung 1 an und wähl die richtigen Antworten!

Beispiel: **1 Er hat einen *Stadtrundgang* gemacht.**

1 Er hat einen Stadtrundgang / eine Bustour gemacht.
2 Das war sehr interessant / langweilig.
3 Sie sind auch in die Schule / ins Museum gegangen.
4 Die Kapellbrücke hat er toll / doof gefunden.
5 Später ist er mit dem Schiff / Schlitten und mit der U-Bahn / Bergbahn auf die Rigi gefahren.
6 Der Spaziergang / Die Fahrt hat 90 Minuten gedauert.
7 Von der Rigi aus konnte man viele Schweizer Seen / Deutschlands Nordseeküste sehen.
8 Benno und seine Mutter wollten den Flughafen / das Theater besuchen, …
9 … aber sie mussten mit den anderen ins Restaurant / ins Verkehrshaus gehen.
10 Es gab dort viel zu tun / essen und alle haben sich amüsiert.

2 b Macht einen Dialog zwischen Benno und einem Freund/einer Freundin! Was hat Benno gemacht, wo war er, wie war das?

Beispiel: **A Wo warst du in den Ferien?**
B Ich war in Luzern. Das war interessant.

Das war toll/interessant/langweilig.
Ich habe es gut gefunden.
Wir haben uns amüsiert.

Luzern

Unsere Touristen-Tipps!

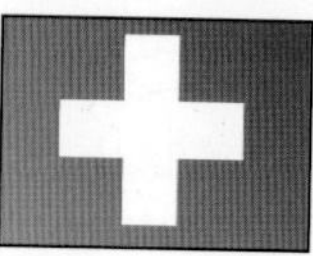

- Stadtbummel
  Sie erfahren Wichtiges, Witziges und Wahres über die Geschichte Luzerns.
  Treffpunkt: Tourist Information, 9.45 Uhr.
  Dauer: ca. 2 Stunden

Die Kapellbrücke, das Wahrzeichen Luzerns

- Ausflug auf die Rigi
  - atemberaubender Panoramablick
  - über 100 km Wander- und Spazierwege
  - mit Schiff und Bergbahn in 90 Minuten erreichbar

Die Rigi (1800m ü. M.)

- verkehrshaus.ch
  - Museum von Verkehr und Kommunikation – gestern, heute und morgen
  - Der neueste Flugsimulator erlaubt Drehungen um 360 Grad!
  - Planetarium mit digitaler Technik
  - IMAX-Filmtheater präsentiert überwältigende Dokumentarfilme.

Altes Flugzeug im Verkehrshaus

2 c Schreib eine Postkarte aus Luzern!

Beispiel: **Hallo Susi!**
Gestern haben wir einen Stadtbummel in Luzern gemacht. Das war …

2 d *extra!* **Was genau hat Benno gemacht? Schreib zehn Sätze, aber ein Satz muss falsch sein! Dein(e) Partner(in) muss den falschen Satz finden, wenn du die Sätze sagst.**

Beispiel: **A Er hat ein paar Tage in Luzern verbracht. Er ist am Abend im Hotel angekommen. Er hat keinen Stadtbummel gemacht.**
B Das ist falsch! …

Salzburg

Unsere Touristen-Tipps!

Mozarts Geburtshaus

Hier ist am 27. Januar 1756 Wolfgang Amadeus Mozart geboren.

Das Schloss Hellbrunn

Das Schloss Hellbrunn mit dem weitläufigen Park und den Wasserspielen ist einzigartig in Europa.

Zoo Salzburg

Im Salzburger Tiergarten leben über 400 Tiere.

Fotos: Zoo Salzburg

Auf dem Duerrnberg

Im Sommer Salzburgs längste Rodelbahn mit 2,2 km! Im Winter ein beliebtes Skigebiet.

Bergrestaurant mit Skimuseum ganzjährig geöffnet!

3 a **Seht euch die Broschüre an! Eine(r) von euch ist Tourist(in) in Salzburg. Erzähl, was du gemacht hast und wie das war!**

Beispiel: **Ich habe Mozarts Geburtshaus besucht. Für mich war das ziemlich langweilig, aber meine Eltern haben es interessant gefunden.**

Grammatik: past tenses

★ **Perfect tense**

The perfect is used for things that

- happened (I went to Italy – *ich bin nach Italien gefahren*);
- have happened (I have been to Italy – *ich bin nach Italien gefahren*);
- did happen (I did go to Italy – *ich bin nach Italien gefahren*).

It consists of two parts: the auxiliary (*haben* or *sein*) + past participle (*ge…t/ge…en*).

The past participle usually goes at the end of the clause.

★ **Imperfect tense**

The imperfect is also used to talk about the past, especially

- modal verbs (*ich musste, ich konnte, ich durfte, ich sollte, ich wollte*);
- to say 'was/were'; 'there was/were' (*es war, wir waren; es gab*);
- to say 'had' (*ich hatte, wir hatten*).

siehe Seite **144–145** >>

3 b **Schreib eine kurze E-Mail aus dem Urlaub in Salzburg!**

Beispiel: **Hallo Oliver!**
Wir verbringen ein paar Tage in Salzburg und ich habe mich gestern gut amüsiert, weil ich mit einer Rodelbahn gefahren bin! ... Wenn das Wetter gut ist, werden wir morgen ...

4 **Macht Dialoge! Stellt folgende Fragen!**

- Wohin bist du in den Ferien gefahren? (nach Blackpool/nach Portugal/an die Küste/…)
- Wie bist du gefahren? (mit dem Auto/…)
- Was hast du gemacht?/Was gab es zu tun?
- Wie war das?

5 **Lauter Laute: r, ch**

- *These are sounds that can make you sound much more German. Practise them with these sentences.*
  - Ach, Michael, hast du dich nicht gewaschen?
  - Doch! Das habe ich wirklich gemacht und jetzt brauche ich ein Handtuch.
  - Ich auch! Das große rosa-rote Handtuch rechts im Schrank ist für mich. Ich reiche dir das grüne.

12C Katastrophal!

- describe disastrous holiday experiences
- use past, present and future tenses
- use time phrases

a
Mein Vater hat sein Portmonee verloren, oder jemand hat es gestohlen.

b
St. Jean
Complet
camp
Der Campingplatz war schon voll besetzt.

c
KRANKENWAGEN
Ich habe einen Unfall gehabt und ich musste ins Krankenhaus.

d
Das Hotel war schmutzig und laut!

e

ADAC

Wir haben eine Panne auf der Autobahn gehabt.

f
Das Wetter war furchtbar! Es hat die ganze Zeit geregnet.

g

Il Rist...nte

Das Essen im Restaurant war so schlecht. Ich war die ganze Zeit krank.

1 a **Hör zu (1–7)! Was passt zusammen?**

Beispiel: **1 c**

1 b **Hör noch einmal zu! Wie viele Zeit-Wörter hörst du? Kopiere die Tabelle und mach Notizen!**

Beispiel:

	Vergangenheit	Präsens	Futur
1	letztes Jahr		

1 c *extra!* **Hör noch einmal zu! Wo waren die Leute? Was ist passiert?**

Beispiel: **1 Sie waren in einer Ferienwohnung im Schwarzwald. Das Mädchen ist reiten gegangen und hat einen Unfall gehabt. Sie musste zwei Wochen im Krankenhaus bleiben.**

normalerweise
letzten/nächsten Sommer/August
letztes/nächstes Jahr
im Juli/Sommer/Winter
zu Weihnachten/Ostern
das nächste Mal

2 a **Macht Dialoge! Wählt eine der Situationen unten.**

Beispiel: **A** **Was machst du normalerweise in den Ferien?**
B **Normalerweise fahren wir mit dem Wohnwagen nach Frankreich.**
A **Was hast du letztes Jahr gemacht?**
B **In den letzten Ferien haben wir zwei Wochen in einem Hotel in Italien verbracht.**
A **Wie war das?/Was ist passiert?**
B **Das war katastrophal! Das Badezimmer im Hotel war schmutzig und das Essen war furchtbar! Ich war die ganze Zeit krank.**
A **Was wirst du nächstes Jahr machen?**
B **Nächsten Sommer werden wir in Deutschland bleiben. Wir werden im Schwarzwald campen.**

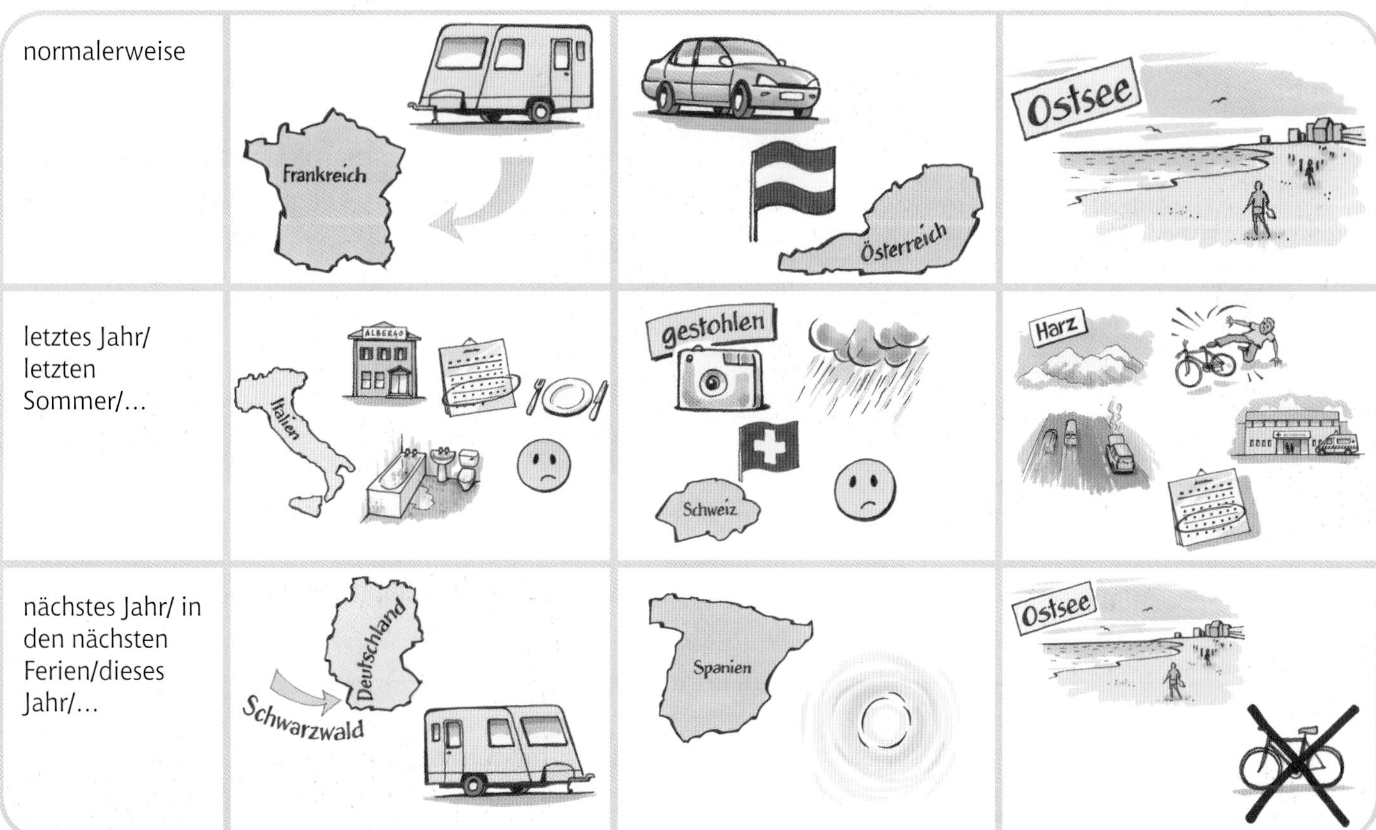

2 b **Wähl eine der Situationen aus Übung 2a und schreib einen kurzen Bericht!**

Beispiel: **Normalerweise fahren wir mit dem Wohnwagen nach Frankreich, aber letztes Jahr haben wir zwei Wochen in einem Hotel in Italien verbracht ...**

3 **Beschreib einen katastrophalen Urlaub! Schreib etwa 100 Wörter! Benutze Situationen von den Seiten 108–109 oder erfinde weitere Situationen!**

Tipps!

- Wer ist das? *(Du? Ein(e) Freund(in)? Eine bekannte Persönlichkeit?)*
- Was macht diese Person normalerweise?
- Wohin ist sie *(letztes Jahr/letzten Sommer)* gefahren? Mit wem? Wie lange?
- Wie war das? Was ist passiert? Warum?
- Was wird diese Person nächstes Jahr machen? Warum?

12D Das wäre ideal!

- talk about an ideal holiday
- use the conditional

1 Hör zu und lies das Gedicht mit!

2 Ihr habt einen Preis in einem Pop-Magazin gewonnen: ein Wochenende mit einem Star! Welchen Star würdet ihr wählen? Wohin würdet ihr mit ihm/ihr gehen? Diskutiert mit einem Partner/einer Partnerin!

Beispiel: **A** **Welchen Star würdest du wählen?**
B **Ich würde die Sängerin X/den Filmstar Y/den Sportstar Z wählen. Wir würden nach .../in die .../zum ... gehen.**

Grammatik: ***der Konditional*** 

Remember, the conditional is used for things that would happen or would be happening. It is formed by *würde(n)* + infinitive.

Some verbs are often shortened, e.g. *würde sein = wäre; würden haben = hätten.*

siehe Seite **145** >>

3 Schreib über deinen idealen Urlaub! Die Fragen im Kästchen helfen dir.

Was machst du gern im Urlaub?
Wohin bist du schon gefahren?
Wie wäre dein idealer Urlaub?
Wohin würdest du fahren? Mit wem?
Wohin würdest du **nicht** fahren? Warum?
Und mit wem würdest du **nicht** fahren? Warum?

Ich habe im Lotto gewonnen.
Ich bin jetzt sehr reich geworden.
Ich bleibe nicht mehr zu Hause.
Ich möchte auf Urlaub gehen.

Wohin denn? Das ist die Frage!
Ich schaue im Internet nach.
Österreich? Liechtenstein? Schweiz?
Dort spricht man wenigstens Deutsch!

Ich reise auch gerne ins Ausland.
Australien wäre sehr schön.
Im Barossatal gibt's viele Deutsche:
Da würde ich mich sicher freuen!

Ich könnte nach Afrika fliegen –
Den Kontinent kenne ich noch nicht.
Im Südwesten gibt es noch Teile,
Wo man gutes Deutsch spricht!

Aber was wäre wichtig für mich?
Was hat mir denn immer gefallen?
Mein idealer Urlaub: wo wäre das?
Das könnte irgendwo sein!

Das Wichtigste ist nicht das „Wo".
Das „Wie" und „Wie viel" sind egal.
Mit Freunden muss man zusammen sein!
Mit ihnen, das wäre ideal!

In den Ferien	***In the holidays***
Ich werde mit dem Bus fahren.	*I'll go by bus.*
Sie fährt mit der Bahn.	*She's going by rail.*
Wir fliegen nach Hamburg/Sylt.	*We're flying to Hamburg/Sylt.*
Wir fahren **auf einen** Bauernhof/Campingplatz.	*We're going **to a** farm/campsite.*
Er wird **auf einem** Bauernhof/Campingplatz bleiben.	*He's going to stay **on a** farm/campsite.*
Sie mietet eine Ferienwohnung.	*She's renting a holiday appartment.*
Ich übernachte in einem Hotel/in Hotels.	*I'm staying in a hotel/in hotels.*
in Nordostdeutschland	*in northeast Germany*
im Südwesten	*in the southwest*
man kann .../du wirst ...	*you can/will ...*
Rad fahren, segeln, windsurfen, wandern, schwimmen, einkaufen gehen, Ausflüge machen, das Schloss besichtigen.	*go cycling, go sailing, windsurf, hike, swim, go shopping, go on trips, visit the castle.*

Wie war das?	***What was it like?***
Das war toll/interessant/langweilig.	*It was great/interesting/boring.*
Ich habe es gut gefunden.	*I found it good.*
Wir haben uns amüsiert.	*We enjoyed ourselves.*

Wann?	***When?***
normalerweise	*normally*
letzten/nächsten Sommer/August	*last/next summer/August*
letztes/nächstes Jahr	*last/next year*
im Juli	*in July*
im Sommer/Winter	*in the summer/winter*
zu Weihnachten/Ostern	*at Christmas/Easter*
das nächste Mal	*next time*

Grammatik: 

★ Present and future tenses: the **present** tense is used for things that
- are happening now (*er **spielt** Tennis im Park*);
- happen regularly (*sie **geht** jeden Tag zu Fuß zur Schule*).

You can also use the **present** tense (usually with a time phrase) to refer to the **future**.

***Nächstes Jahr** fahre ich ins Ausland.*

The **future** tense is used for things that will happen or will be happening.

It is formed by the present tense of **werden** + infinitive.

Look for clues that help to indicate the future (*nächsten Sommer, nächstes Jahr*).

★ Word order (*Wortstellung*): adverbs and adverbial phrases follow this order – time, manner, place (when, how, where).

The verb is the second idea in a main clause.

Infinitives go to the end of a main clause.

Ich	*werde*	*morgen*	*mit dem Bus*	*in die Stadt*	*fahren.*
first idea	second idea verb in present	time	manner	place	infinitive

★ Past tenses

The **perfect tense** is used for things that
- happened (I went to Italy – *ich bin nach Italien gefahren*);
- have happened (I have been to Italy – *ich bin nach Italien gefahren*);
- did happen (I did go to Italy – *ich bin nach Italien gefahren*).

It consists of two parts: the auxiliary (*haben* or *sein*) + past participle (*ge...t/ge...en*).

The past participle usually goes at the end of the clause.

The **imperfect tense** is also used to talk about the past, especially
- modal verbs (*ich musste, ich konnte, ich durfte, ich sollte, ich wollte*);
- to say 'was/were'; 'there was/were' (*es war, wir waren; es gab*);
- to say 'had' (*ich hatte, wir hatten*).

★ Conditional: the conditional is used for things that would happen or would be happening.

It is formed by **würde(n)** + infinitive.

Some verbs are often shortened (e.g. *würde sein = wäre; würden haben = hätten*).

siehe Seite **143–146** ➤➤

Lauter Laute: r, ch

normalerweise *usually* • **letzten Sommer** *last summer* • **nächsten August** *next August* • **letztes/nächstes Jahr** *last/next year* • **im Juli** *in July* • **im Sommer/Winter** *in summer/winter* • **das nächste Mal** *the next time*

Wiederholung

Kapitel 11 (Probleme? Siehe Seite 98, 101–102!)

1 Bring den Dialog in die richtige Reihenfolge!

Beispiel: **3, 5, …**

1 – Für zwei Erwachsene und ein Kind.
2 – Am 25. Juli … und wie viele Nächte werden Sie bleiben?
3 – Ich möchte ein Zimmer reservieren.
4 – Mein Name ist Schmidt.
5 – Wann kommen Sie an?
6 – Auf welchen Namen soll ich reservieren?
7 – Wir hoffen, drei Nächte zu bleiben, aber wir haben keine festen Pläne gemacht.
8 – Das ist kein Problem. Und das Zimmer wäre für wie viele Personen?
9 – So, Herr Schmidt. Ich habe alles reserviert. Auf Wiederhören.
10 – Danke. Auf Wiederhören.
11 – Prima. Das nehme ich, danke.
12 – Wir werden am 25. Juli ankommen.
13 – Also, wir haben ein Dreibettzimmer mit Dusche zu 80 .

2 Sieh dir die Bilder und Texte an und schreib Sätze! Setz die Verben in die richtige Zeitform!

Beispiel: **a Gestern habe ich den Schlüssel verloren.**

a gestern 

b morgen  wenn

c  schlafen, weil  nächstes Zimmer

d nächsten Sommer gern aber müssen bleiben  ,

Kapitel 12 (Probleme? Siehe Seite 104–105, 108–109!)

3 Ordne die Sätze! Beginn mit dem fett gedruckten Wort!

Beispiel: **1 Sie ist letzte Woche mit der Bahn nach Berlin gefahren.**

1 nach Berlin ist Woche mit Bahn der **Sie** gefahren letzte.
2 dem fahren **Ich** Italien würde nach nicht gern Bus mit.
3 nächsten Hamburg **Ich** mit Montag fliege Mutter nach meiner.
4 **Im** zusammen Bauernhof wir einen August auf fahren.
5 werden **Im** wir einem auf zwei bleiben Schwarzwald Campingplatz Wochen.
6 Nordostdeutschland würde **Nächstes** Ferienwohnung ich gern in mieten eine Jahr.

4 Du bist ein Mars-Mensch! Beschreib deine letzten Ferien! Was würdest du in den nächsten Ferien (nicht) gern machen?

Beispiel: **Letztes Jahr bin ich nach Jupiter gefahren. Das war toll, weil … .**
Jeden Tag habe ich …

letztes Jahr

nächstes Jahr

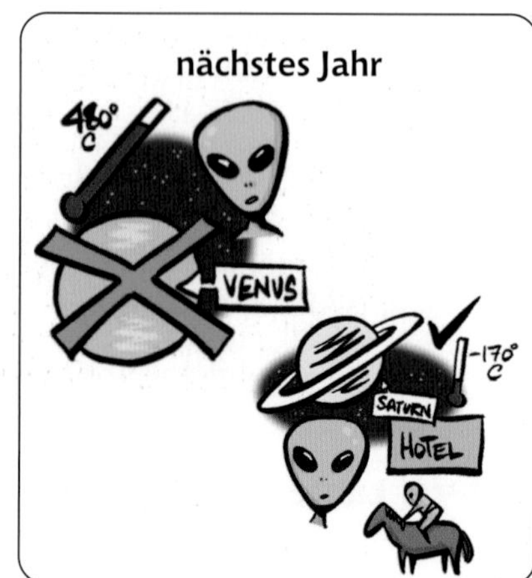

Weltraumtourismus

Schon seit vielen Jahren versuchen eine Menge Leute zum Mond, zum Mars und zu anderen Planeten zu reisen oder überhaupt in den Weltraum zu kommen. Aber dafür müssen sie mindestens ein knappes Jahr trainieren, um für den Weltraum fit zu sein, und zu anderen Himmelskörpern zu fliegen, wird wohl noch lange ein Traum bleiben. Der erste Weltraumtourist war der Amerikaner Dennis Tito, der am Samstag dem 28. April 2001 startete.

Der 60-jährige Millionär bezahlte 20 Millionen Dollar dafür, dass er von der Gagarin-Rampe in dem Raumschiff Sojus-TM in den Weltraum starten durfte.

Nun ist mit Mark Shuttleworth der zweite Tourist im All gewesen. Er konnte sogar an Experimenten teilnehmen. Der Start war am 26.04.2002. Die Landung erfolgte am 5.05.2002. Als Andenken kaufte er vor lauter Begeisterung gleich noch die Landekapsel dazu. Über einen Souvenirshop verfügt die *International Space Station* noch nicht.

Strategie! *Understanding longer sentences*

Some texts have quite long and complex sentences. You need to use context and grammar (especially knowledge of word order) to understand them and split them up into smaller chunks.

A good place to start is by spotting the verbs and then working out what goes with each one.

Remember, connectives are also used to break down long sentences.

1 Was heißt das auf Deutsch?

1 to be fit for space
2 in the Soyuz-TM spaceship
3 the second tourist in space
4 to take part in experiments

2 Beantworte die Fragen!

1 Was würdest du bezahlen, um Weltraumtourist zu werden?
2 Stell dir vor, du hast eine Weltraumfahrt gemacht! Erzähl, was du gesehen und gemacht hast!
3 Was würdest du als Andenken an den Weltraum kaufen?

3 *Research.*

1 Find out some facts about one of these German-speaking countries or regions.

a *das Barossatal, Australien*

b *Namibia, Südwestafrika*

c *Liechtenstein, Europa*

2 Prepare a presentation on your research findings, using visuals/ICT, if possible. Try to include the following details.

- Einwohner
- Hauptstadt
- Sehenswürdigkeiten
- Wetter
- Essen
- Feste und Bräuche

1 **Was passt zusammen? Schreib die Sätze auf!** (◄◄ S. 6–7)

Beispiel: **1 c Ich sehe gern fern.**

1 Ich sehe — **a** gern Rollschuh?
2 Was machst — **b** lieber ins Kino.
3 Am liebsten — **c** gern fern.
4 Fährst du — **d** spielt nicht gern am Computer.
5 Meine Schwester — **e** gehen wir einkaufen.
6 Wir gehen — **f** du gern?

2 a **Lies den Text und sieh dir die Bilder an! Wie ist die richtige Reihenfolge?** (◄◄ S. 8–9)

Beispiel: **c, …**

Ich habe den Morgen zu Hause verbracht. Ich habe am Computer gespielt und ein paar Popsongs heruntergeladen. Dann habe ich Musik gehört. Am Nachmittag habe ich im Park Sport getrieben – ich bin Rollschuh gefahren und habe Fußball gespielt. Danach habe ich bei Burger-Bar gegessen. Am Abend habe ich stundenlang ferngesehen.

stundenlang – *for hours*

2 b **Was heißt das auf Deutsch?** (◄◄ S. 8–9)

Beispiel: **1 Ich habe den Morgen im Park verbracht.**

1 I spent the morning in the park.
2 I downloaded a few computer games.
3 Then I ate at 'Burger-Bar'.
4 In the afternoon I watched television for hours and hours.

3 **Sieh dir die Bilder an und schreib Sätze!** (◄◄ S. 10–11)

Beispiel: **1 Am Freitag bin ich in den Supermarkt gegangen. Das war ganz langweilig.**

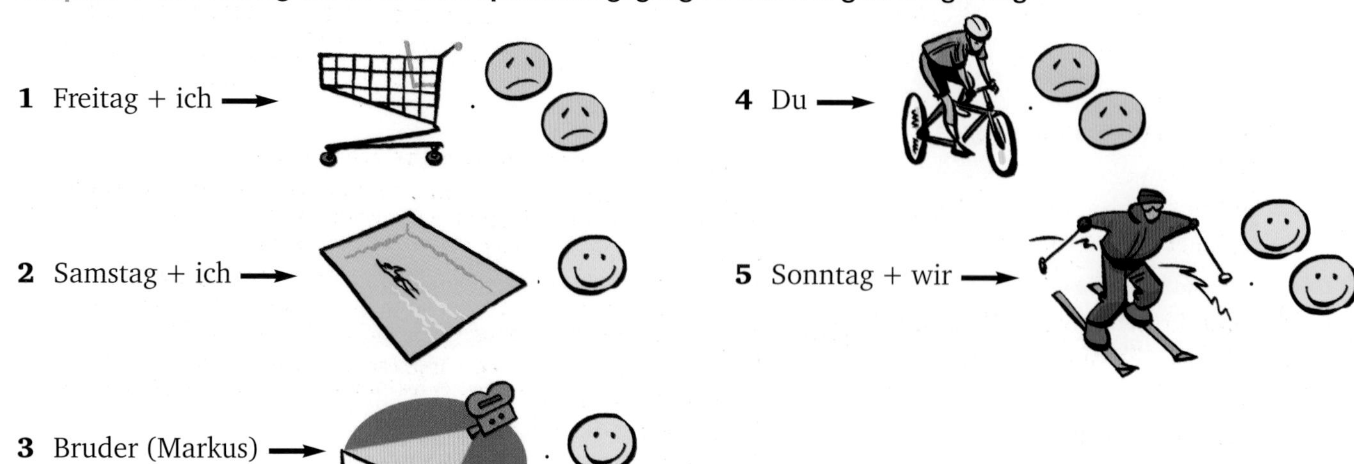

1 **Finde die sechs Hobbys heraus und ergänze die Sätze!** (◄◄ S. 6–7)

Beispiel: **1** ***Fußball:* Ich *spiele* gern *Fußball.***

1 __________: Ich __________ gern __________ .

2 __________: Du __________ am __________ .

3 __________: Wir __________ nicht __________ .

4 __________: Meine Freundin Frauke __________ am liebsten __________ .

5 __________: Ich __________ lieber __________ .

6 __________: Mein Bruder __________ gern ins __________ .

2 **Lies die E-Mail! Richtig (R), falsch (F) oder nicht im Text (NT)?** (◄◄ S. 8–9)

Beispiel: **1 F**

1 Am Samstag hat Alex stundenlang ferngesehen.
2 Er sieht am liebsten Sportsendungen.
3 Er hat keinen Hamburger gegessen.
4 Er hat den ganzen Tag am Computer verbracht.
5 Im Park hat er alleine Sport getrieben.
6 Am Sonntag hat er den ganzen Tag zu Hause verbracht.

An: Martin Sautter
Von: Alex Jenne
Betr.: Mein Wochenende

Letztes Wochenende habe ich nichts Interessantes gemacht. Zuerst habe ich am Samstag ein bisschen ferngesehen. Ich habe eine Sportsendung und einen Film gesehen. Dann habe ich Spagetti gegessen. Danach habe ich Probleme mit meinem Computer gehabt. Das hat mich so genervt!

Es hat aber Spaß gemacht, am Nachmittag Fußball mit meinen Freunden im Park zu spielen. Und am Sonntag? Ich war so müde, ich bin den ganzen Tag im Bett geblieben! Das war so langweilig!

Bis bald!

Alex

3 **Lies Bernds E-Mail und schreib eine Antwort darauf!** (◄◄ S. 10–11)

Beispiel: **Hi, Bernd!**

Normalerweise ...

An: meinen neuen Mailfreund/meine neue Mailfreundin
Von: Bernd Richter
Betr.: Was machst du am Wochenende?

He, du da!

Wie geht's? Was machst du am Wochenende?

Normalerweise gehe ich mit meinen Freunden aus. Meistens fahren wir in die Stadt und gehen ins Kino oder ins Café im Einkaufszentrum. Das ist nicht schlecht.

Letztes Wochenende aber sind wir schwimmen gegangen. Das war fantastisch! Es gibt ein sehr modernes Freibad in der Stadtmitte. Wir haben den ganzen Nachmittag da verbracht.

Und du? Was machst du normalerweise? Was hast du letztes Wochenende gemacht? Wie war es? Hat es viel Spaß gemacht?

Schreib bald wieder! Tschüs!

Bernd

1 **Sieh dir die Bilder an und füll die Lücken aus!** (◄◄ S. 14–15)

Beispiel: **1 Ich trage eine Jeans. *Sie* ist blau.**

1 Ich trage eine Jeans. __________ ist blau.

2 Bettina trägt einen __________. __________ ist __________.

3 Thomas trägt __________ __________. Sie ist __________.

4 Meine Schuhe sind cool! __________ sind rosa, __________ und __________.

2 **Richtig (R), falsch (F) oder nicht im Text (NT)?** (◄◄ S. 16–17)

Beispiel: **1 R**

Ich finde eine Schuluniform total blöd! Ich muss ein weißes oder ein graues Hemd, eine Krawatte, eine schwarze Hose und schwarze Schuhe tragen. Das sieht doof aus!

Alex

Ellie

Das finde ich nicht. Ich mag meine Schuluniform. Ich muss eine schwarze Hose oder einen schwarzen Rock tragen, das stimmt, aber ich darf auch ein Sweatshirt tragen und muss keine Krawatte tragen. Meine Schuluniform sieht cool aus.

1. Alex dislikes school uniform.
2. He would prefer to wear jeans.
3. Black trousers are compulsory for boys.
4. Ellie is unhappy about her school uniform.
5. She can choose between trousers and a skirt.
6. She does not like ties.

3 **Sie dir die Bilder unten an und schreib kurze Beschreibungen!** (◄◄ S. 18–20)

Beispiel: **Annika trägt ein gelbes Oberteil. Es ist nicht schlecht, aber ich finde es altmodisch ...**

1 Sieh dir die Bilder an, korrigiere die Sätze und schreib sie richtig auf! (◀◀ S. 14–15)

Beispiel: **1 Anne trägt einen *Rock*. *Er* ist *kurz* und *grün*. Sie trägt auch ein Hemd. *Es* ist gelb.**

Strategie!

Note: some of the mistakes in Exercise 1 are grammatical!

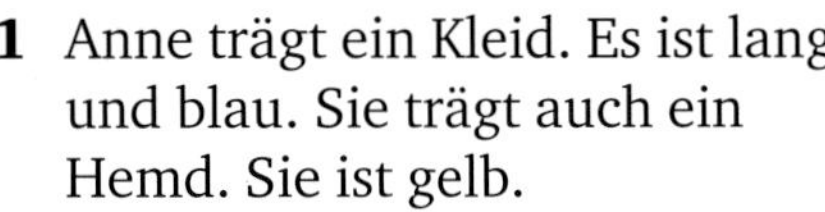

1 Anne trägt ein Kleid. Es ist lang und blau. Sie trägt auch ein Hemd. Sie ist gelb.

2 Philipp trägt eine Jeans. Es ist schwarz. Sie trägt auch ein Sweatshirt. Er ist rot.

3 Karla trägt ein Kleid. Es ist weiß. Sie trägt auch einen Mantel. Er ist kurz und schwarz.

2 Bist du für oder gegen die Schuluniform? Schreib einen Bericht! (◀◀ S. 16–17)

Beispiel:

Ich bin für die Schuluniform. Normalerweise müssen wir …

Ich bin gegen die Schuluniform. Ich muss …

3 a Lies den Brief! Was heißt das auf Deutsch?

1 I bought new clothes.
2 firstly
3 It's too short!
4 I like my blue skirt.
5 too expensive
6 because I've got no money left and no clothes

Ich habe neue Klamotten für das Popkonzert gekauft, aber alles ist schief gegangen. Zuerst habe ich ein schönes Oberteil gekauft, aber es ist zu kurz! Danach habe ich gestreifte Socken gekauft, aber sie sind zu lang! Und mein blauer Rock gefällt mir gut, aber er war zu teuer. Jetzt gehe ich nicht zum Konzert, weil ich kein Geld mehr habe und keine Klamotten!

schief gegangen – *went wrong*

3 b Schreib deinen eigenen Brief! (◀◀ S. 18–20)

Beispiel:

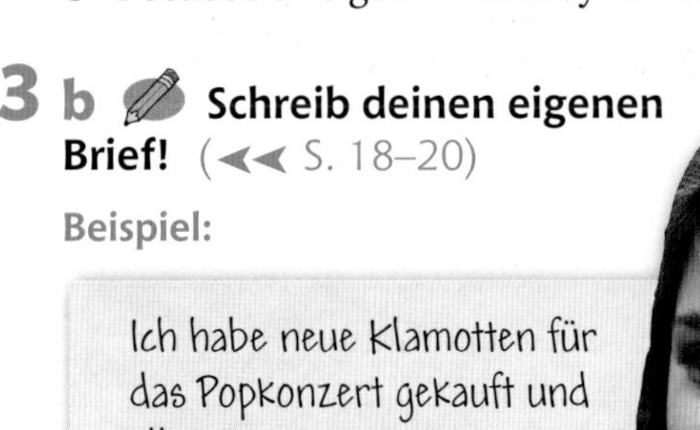

Ich habe neue Klamotten für das Popkonzert gekauft und alles ist gut gegangen. Zuerst habe ich …

1 **Schreib die Sätze richtig auf!** (◄◄ S. 24–25)

Beispiel: **1 Ich gehe in den Supermarkt und kaufe Shampoo.**

1. Shampoo Ich und kaufe in den Supermarkt gehe
2. kaufe Ich Sportgeschäft und ins Sportschuhe gehe
3. im Schreibblock kaufe einen Schreibwarenladen Ich
4. einkaufen Kaufhaus und Supermarkt im Ich im gehe
5. der Wurst Metzgerei kaufst Du in
6. in die Apfeltorte Sie geht und kauft eine Konditorei

2 a **D'Artagnan und die drei Musketiere. Schreib die Sätze richtig auf!** (◄◄ S. 26–27)

Beispiel: **1 Wir treffen uns um 13.00 Uhr hinter der Telefonzelle.**

2 b **Wie beantworten die Musketiere die Frage: Wo gehst du hin?** (◄◄ S. 26–27)

Beispiel: **1 Ich gehe um 13.00 Uhr hinter die Telefonzelle.**

3 a **Lies die E-Mail ans Restaurant! Schreib dann noch eine E-Mail ans Restaurant! Ersetze die unterstrichenen Wörter!** (◄◄ S. 28)

Beispiel: **Ich möchte einen Tisch für *Samstagnachmittag* …**

Ich möchte einen Tisch für Freitagabend für zwei Personen reservieren. Ich möchte gegen acht Uhr essen. Haben Sie Rauchertische auf der Terrasse? Schicken Sie mir bitte die Speisekarte, weil ich allergisch gegen Eier, Käse und Milch bin.

Ich bedanke mich im Voraus.

Ich bedanke mich im Voraus. – *Thank you in advance.*

3 b **Jetzt bist du im Restaurant mit zwei Freunden. Schreib die drei Bestellungen auf!** (◄◄ S. 28–30)

Beispiel: **Als Vorspeise nehme ich … , aber mein Freund Bernd nimmt … und Steffi …**

1 **Vervollständige den Text über einen Einkaufsbummel!** (◄◄ S. 24–25)

Beispiel: **Zuerst gehe ich in die Bäckerei und kaufe Brot …**

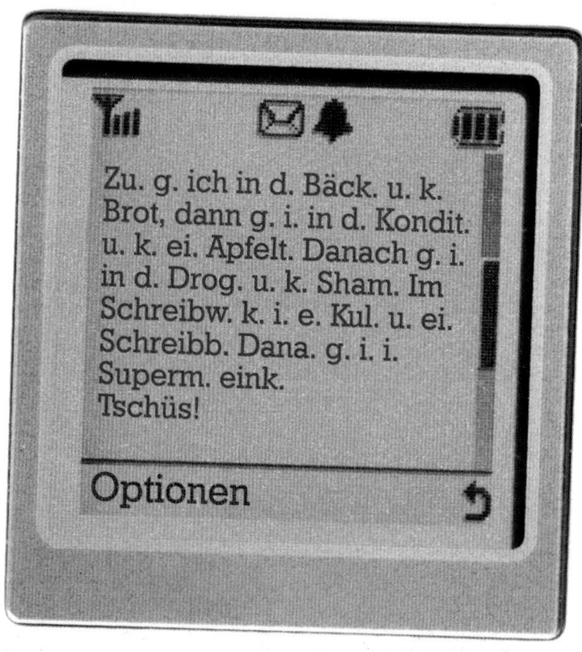

Zu. g. ich in d. Bäck. u. k. Brot, dann g. i. in d. Kondit. u. k. ei. Apfelt. Danach g. i. in d. Drog. u. k. Sham. Im Schreibw. k. i. e. Kul. u. ei. Schreibb. Dana. g. i. i. Superm. eink. Tschüs!

Optionen

2 **Schreib eine E-Mail für Philipp an seine Freunde!** (◄◄ S. 26–27)

Beispiel: **Bernd, ich hole dich um 15.00 Uhr an der Bushaltestelle ab.**

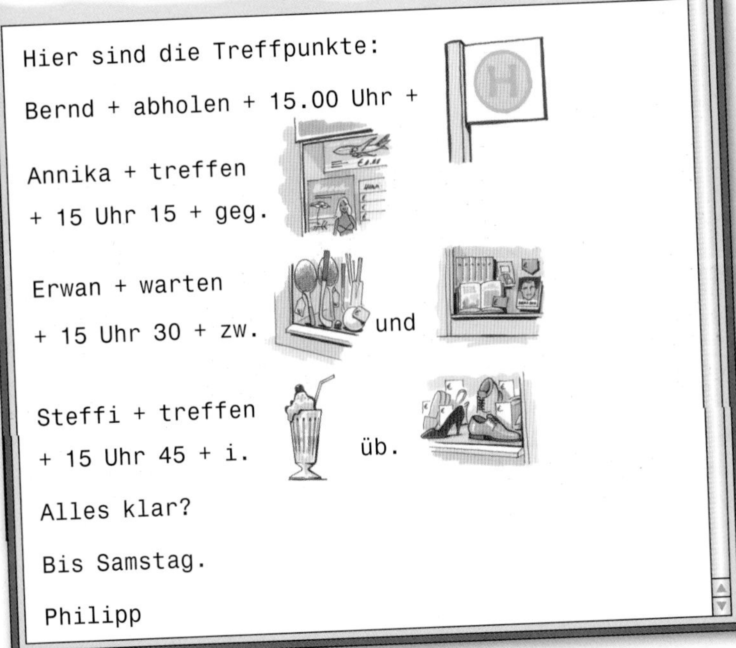

Hier sind die Treffpunkte:

Bernd + abholen + 15.00 Uhr +

Annika + treffen + 15 Uhr 15 + geg.

Erwan + warten + 15 Uhr 30 + zw. und

Steffi + treffen + 15 Uhr 45 + i. üb.

Alles klar?

Bis Samstag.

Philipp

3 **Lies den Brief! Wähl die richtigen Antworten!** (◄◄ S. 28–30)

Beispiel: **1 Lisa had a birthday last week.**

1. Lisa was 14 last week / had a birthday last week / is 14 next week.
2. She liked the idea of / was opposed to / requested a birthday meal cooked by her friends.
3. She can't stand soup / loves peas / hates pea soup.
4. She didn't like the trout because it was cold / she has a fish allergy / she prefers noodles.
5. The dessert was disgusting / tasted good / made her feel ill.

Letzte Woche hatte ich am 14. Geburtstag. Am Samstagabend haben mir meine Freunde ein Geburtstagsessen gekocht. Das war so lieb von ihnen, aber eigentlich war es furchtbar!

Als Vorspeise haben wir Erbsensuppe gegessen. Suppe mag ich gern, aber bitte keine Erbsen! Das kann ich nicht ausstehen. Als Hauptgericht haben wir Forelle mit Nudeln gegessen. Leider bin ich allergisch gegen Fisch und die Nudeln waren kalt. Als Nachtisch haben wir Milchreis mit Vanillesoße und Jogurt gegessen. Mir ist fast übel geworden.

Lisa, Bremen

1 a **Finde vier Filmtypen und ergänze die Antwort!** (◄◄ S. 32–33)

Antwort: Was läuft? Eine ____________, ein ____________, ein ____________, oder ein ____________?

1 b **Finde jetzt die Frage mit den übrigen Worten!**
Use the words which are left over to find the question. (◄◄ S. 32–33)

Frage: Kommst ____________ ____________ ____________ ____________?

2 **Sieh dir die Bilder an, wähl die passenden Formen von *dieser/diese/dieses* und füll die Lücken aus!** (◄◄ S. 32–35)

Beispiel: **1 Ich kann *diese Jacke* nicht leiden.**

1 Ich kann  ____________ ____________ nicht leiden.

4  ____________ ____________ sind cool.

2 Hast du  ____________ ____________ schon gesehen?

5 Ich finde  ____________ ____________ total blöd.

3  ____________ ____________ gefällt mir gut.

3 **Was sind die Fragen? Füll die Lücken aus!** (◄◄ S. 36–37)

Beispiel: **1 *Wo* ist Fritz Lang geboren?**

1 ____________ ist Fritz Lang geboren? Fritz Lang ist in Wien geboren.
2 ____________ für Filme hat er gemacht? Er hat Stummfilme gemacht.
3 ____________ hat seine Filme verboten? Die Nazis haben seine Filme verboten.
4 ____________ hat er 22 Filme gemacht? Er hat 22 Filme in Hollywood gemacht.
5 ____________ und ____________ ist er gestorben? Er ist am 2. August 1976 in Los Angeles gestorben.

1 **Was passt zusammen? Sieh dir die Texte und die Bilder 1–5 und A–E an, und schreib die passenden Zahlen und Buchstaben auf!** (◄◄ S. 32–33)

Beispiel: **Suna – 1 D**

A B C D E

Suna: Ich kann mir den Horrorfilm nicht ansehen. Ich muss meine Hausaufgaben machen.

Philipp: Ich kann mir den Martial-Arts-Film nicht ansehen. Ich muss meinen Eltern helfen.

Laetitia: Den Kriegsfilm möchte ich mir nicht ansehen. Kriegsfilme mag ich nicht.

Jakob: Ich kann mir den Zeichentrickfilm nicht ansehen. Ich muss zu Hause bleiben.

Käthe: Ich muss Staub saugen. Ich kann mir die Komödie nicht ansehen.

2 **Wie ist die richtige Reihenfolge? Schreib den Text richtig auf!** (◄◄ S. 34–35)

Beispiel: **Letzte Woche habe ich „Toy Story 2" gesehen. Ich fand …**

war ein toller Film.
waren lustig. Das
„Toy Story 2" gesehen. Ich fand
Letzte Woche habe ich
aber die Zeichentrickfiguren
die Handlung ganz blöd,

3 a **Gedächtnisquiz. Wer ist das? Lies die Texte und schreib den richtigen Namen auf!** (◄◄ S. 36–37)

A Dieser Mann ist nicht in Deutschland, sondern in Österreich geboren. Er ist aber nicht in seinem Heimatland geblieben, weil er Probleme mit den Nazis hatte. Er hat einen der ersten Science-Fiction-Filme gemacht.

B Dieser Mann ist ziemlich jung gestorben. Sein Geburtsort war Salzburg in Österreich. Er war ein echtes Wunderkind, weil er schon mit 5 Jahren sein erstes Konzert gegeben hat.

C Dieser schweizerische Maler ist am 18. Dezember 1879 geboren. Viele Leute haben seine Bilder ganz verwirrend gefunden.

Wolfgang Amadeus Mozart

Paul Klee

Michael Ende

Fritz Lang

3 b **Schreib einen kurzen Text über die vierte berühmte Person! Benutze folgende Informationen!** (◄◄ S. 36–37)

Beispiel: **Dieser Mann heißt … und ist am … in … geboren. Er hat …**

Geboren am: 12. November 1929	ist am … geboren
Geburtsort: Garmisch-Partenkirchen, Deutschland	ist in … geboren
Beruf: Autor von Kinderbüchern	hat … geschrieben
Gestorben: 28. August 1995 in Stuttgart	ist am/in … gestorben

1 Lies die Sätze und wähl die passenden Wörter! (◄◄ S. 42)

Beispiel: 1 In Verl gibt es *ein* Kino.

1 In Verl gibt es ein / eine / keine Kino.
2 Es gibt auch viele / kein / eine Kegelbahn.
3 In der Stadtmitte gibt es kein / viele / einen Geschäfte.
4 Es gibt aber einen / keinen / kein Hallenbad.

2 Was hast du vor? Sieh dir die Bilder an und schreib Sätze! (◄◄ S. 42–43)

Beispiel: 1 Ich fahre morgen mit dem Bus ins Sportzentrum.

1 morgen + +

2 heute + +

3 am Samstag + +

4 dieses Wochenende + +

3 Lies Claudias E-Mail! Richtig (R), falsch (F) oder nicht im Text (NT)? (◄◄ S. 44–45)

1 Am Donnerstag ist Claudia mit Freunden ausgegangen.
2 Der Ausflug am Wochenende war nicht interessant.
3 Sie sind mit der Straßenbahn gefahren.
4 Claudia ist nicht einkaufen gegangen.
5 Sie ist mit ihren Freunden ins Eiscafé gegangen.

An: Karlotta Bühler
Von: Claudia Göppert
Betr.: Letztes Wochenende

Hallo!

Was hast du letztes Wochenende gemacht? Ich habe einen Ausflug mit Freunden gemacht, aber meiner Meinung nach war das langweilig. Am Samstagvormittag sind wir mit der U-Bahn nach Hamburg gefahren. Wir haben uns dann den Dom angesehen und sind einkaufen gegangen. Ich habe aber nichts gekauft. Danach sind wir ins Eiscafé gegangen.

Und du? Wohin bist du gegangen und mit wem? Hat es Spaß gemacht?

Schreib bald wieder!

Claudia

1 **Sieh dir die Bilder an und mach Vorschläge! Vervollständige die Sätze!** (◀◀ S. 42–43)

Beispiel: **1 Willst du ins Kino gehen?**

1 … du ➔ 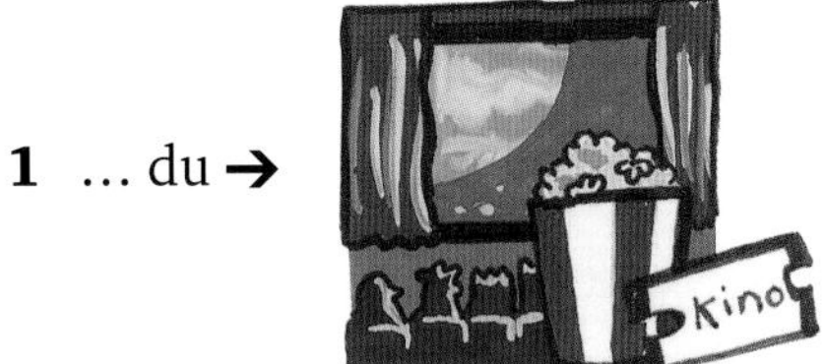

3 … wir ➔ 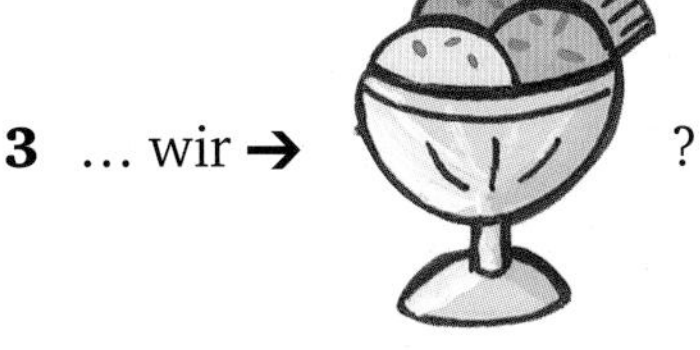 ?

2 Willst … ➔  ?

4 … ihr ➔  ?

2 **Lies den folgenden Text und beantworte die Fragen auf Englisch!** (◀◀ S. 46–47)

1. Where was Amelie going, with whom and why?
2. What two things does she say about the first train journey to Hanover?
3. How worried were they at the time?
4. Why did they miss their connection and how long did they have to wait?
5. What caused their next delay?
6. Why was their journey a complete waste of time?

Keine feine Reise!

Letztes Wochenende bin ich mit meinen Freunden mit dem Zug nach Düsseldorf gefahren, um einkaufen zu gehen. Tolle Idee! Der Zug ist pünktlich um 11 Uhr 30 abgefahren, aber er ist mit ein bisschen Verspätung in Hannover angekommen. „Kein Problem!" haben wir gesagt. Leider sind wir zum falschen Gleis gegangen und haben den Zug verpasst! Eine halbe Stunde später ist der nächste Zug nach Düsseldorf abgefahren. Wisst ihr was? Wir sind erst um 5 Uhr 30 in Düsseldorf angekommen, weil der Zug eine Panne gehabt hat. Sechs Stunden unterwegs! Wir haben auch nichts gekauft, weil alle Geschäfte schon geschlossen waren! Toller Ausflug, was?

Amelie, Hamburg

3 **Schreib einen kurzen Absatz über den vergangenen Freitagabend und deine Pläne für nächsten Freitagabend! Benutze die Fragen in den Sprechblasen!** (◀◀ S. 44–47)

Beispiel: **Meistens bleibe ich am Freitagabend zu Hause und … , weil ich … . Dieses Wochenende möchte ich aber …**

Was machst du normalerweise am Freitagabend?

Warum?

Deiner Meinung nach, wie ist es?

Was machst du diesen Freitagabend?

Wie fährst du dahin?

1 Wie ist das Wetter? Sieh dir die Bilder an und schreib Sätze! (◄◄ S. 50–51)

Beispiel: **a Es ist heiß.**

2 a Bist du umweltfreundlich oder umweltfeindlich? Lies die Fragen! Wie viele Punkte hast du? Sieh dir dann die Tabelle an und finde deine Ergebnisse heraus! (◄◄ S. 52–53)

Fragen	Punkte: Ja	Nein
1 Bringst du Flaschen zum Altglascontainer?	1	0
2 Badest du oft/Duschst du selten?	0	2
3 Benutzt du Plastiktüten vom Supermarkt?	0	2
4 Trennst du deinen Müll?	3	0
5 Fährst du oft mit dem Rad?	2	0

8–10 Punkte	Toll! Du bist sehr umweltfreundlich.
5–7 Punkte	Nicht schlecht, aber du kannst noch mehr machen.
0–4 Punkte	Schade! Du bist umweltfeindlich.

2 b Schreib einen kurzen Absatz! (◄◄ S. 52–53)

Beispiel: **Ich habe acht Punkte. Ich bin sehr umweltfreundlich, weil ich Flaschen zum Altglascontainer bringe und ...**

3 Lies folgende Meinungen von Tobias und wähl die richtigen Antworten! (◄◄ S. 54–55)

Beispiel: **1 auf dem Land**

1 Tobias wohnt in der Stadtmitte / am Stadtrand / auf dem Land.
2 Er findet das Landleben toll / interessant / langweilig.
3 Er findet das Leben in der Stadt langweilig / praktisch / ruhig.
4 In der Stadt ist es schmutziger / ruhiger / langweiliger als auf dem Land.
5 In der Stadt kann man keine / nicht viele / mehr Freunde kennen lernen.
6 Am liebsten möchte Tobias am Stadtrand / in der Stadt / auf dem Land wohnen.

Das Landleben gefällt mir überhaupt nicht, auch wenn es in der Stadt schmutziger, lauter und gefährlicher ist. Auf dem Land gibt es keine Geschäfte, keine Schulen und keine Busse. Man kann auch nicht viele neue Freunde kennen lernen.

Was mich betrifft, so finde ich das Stadtleben viel interessanter und viel praktischer. Ich möchte nicht auf dem Land wohnen, sondern in der Stadtmitte.

Tobias, Neudorf

1 Lies den Text! Richtig (R), falsch (F) oder nicht im Text (NT)?

(◄◄ S. 50–51)

Beispiel: **1 R**

1. Es gefällt Käthe nicht, wenn es schneit.
2. Sie fährt nicht gern Ski.
3. Sie bleibt am liebsten zu Hause.
4. Es gefällt ihr auch nicht, wenn es regnet.
5. Sie will nicht ausgehen, wenn es windig ist.
6. Drachensteigen ist ihr Hobby.

Es nervt mich, wenn es schneit, weil mir das zu kalt und zu gefährlich ist. Wenn es regnet, ist es auch nicht gut, weil ich zu Hause bleiben muss. Für mich ist das Wetter am besten, wenn es windig ist. Dann kann ich meinen Drachen steigen lassen. Das ist supertoll!

Käthe

2 Sieh dir den Umweltfreund und den Umweltfeind an! Was sagen sie über das Recyceln?

(◄◄ S. 52–53)

Beispiel: **(Der Umweltfreund) Ich bringe Flaschen zum Altglascontainer.**
(Der Umweltfeind) Ich bringe keine Flaschen …

3 Lies den folgenden Text! Ersetze die unterstrichenen Wörter mit anderen Informationen!

(◄◄ S. 54–55)

Beispiel: **Ich bin *13* Jahre alt und habe schon einmal *in der Stadt* gewohnt. Das …**

Ich bin 14 Jahre alt und habe schon einmal auf einem Dorf gewohnt. Das Landleben war zwar manchmal zu ruhig und oft ganz langweilig, aber es hat mir meistens gut gefallen. Jetzt wohne ich aber direkt in der Stadtmitte. Das finde ich unheimlich laut, gefährlich und schmutzig. Ich glaube, ich werde später wieder auf das Land ziehen. Dann wird mein Leben ganz ruhig sein und es wird gar nicht so viel Lärm und Umweltverschmutzung geben.

1 Was passt zusammen? (<< S. 60–61)

Beispiel: **1 d**

a Sie hat Magenschmerzen.

b Hat sie Halsschmerzen?

c Der Fuß tut mir weh.

d Ich habe Rückenschmerzen.

e Der linke Arm tut ihm weh.

2 Lies den Text und füll die Lücken aus! (<< S. 62–63)

Beispiel: **1 gesund**

Um fit zu bleiben, muss man (**1**) __________ essen und trinken, das heißt, man muss viel (**2**) __________ trinken und so viel (**3**) __________ essen, wie man mag. Man darf auch ein bisschen (**4**) __________ essen. Natürlich darf man keinen (**5**) __________ trinken und keine (**6**) __________ essen.

Obst | Süßigkeiten | Wasser | Alkohol | Käse | gesund

3 Lies die Texte und wähl die richtigen Antworten! (<< S. 64–65)

Beispiel: **1 Philipp ist kein Sportler.**

1. Philipp ist kein Sportler / treibt gern Sport / ist lustig.
2. Er möchte nichts essen / gesünder leben / dicker werden.
3. Am liebsten isst er Hähnchen / Fast-Food / Fisch.
4. Wann und wohin muss er joggen? Am Montag bis zum Restaurant / Am Wochenende vom Restaurant bis zur Stadtmitte / Am Wochenende in die Stadtmitte.
5. Er darf / muss / will nicht Hamburger mit Pommes und Cola dazu bestellen.
6. Er muss zu Fuß / mit dem Bus / mit dem Rad nach Hause kommen.

Ich möchte gern fit werden und gesund essen, aber ich treibe nicht gern Sport und mein Lieblingsessen ist Hamburger mit Pommes und dazu ein Liter Cola. Ich will nicht auf alles verzichten! Hilfe!

Ich sage dir, was du machen musst. Jedes Wochenende musst du die drei Kilometer von zuhause bis zum Hamburger-Restaurant in der Stadtmitte joggen. Dann darfst du dein Lieblingsgericht ohne Pommes aber mit Tomaten und grünem Salat essen.

Dazu musst du ein Liter Mineralwasser trinken. Danach musst du wieder nach Hause joggen – im Bus, natürlich!

Philipp

Florian

1 Lies den Entschuldigungszettel! Schreib dann deinen eigenen Zettel als E-Mail an deine Schule! Benutze das Bild, wenn du willst! (◄◄ S. 60–61)

Beispiel: **Es geht (Name) nicht gut und … . Am … hat er … und … .**

Entschuldigungszettel

Heute kann Thomas leider nicht zur Schule kommen, weil es ihm nicht gut geht. Gestern Abend haben wir Fisch mit Reis gegessen und heute hat er starke Magenschmerzen und Kopfschmerzen. Er hat auch Fieber.

2 Isst sich Hannah gesund? Schreib, was sie (A) normalerweise isst und trinkt, und was sie (B) gestern gegessen und getrunken hat! (◄◄ S. 62–63)

Beispiel: **Normalerweise isst Hannah zum Frühstück … . Zu Mittag …**

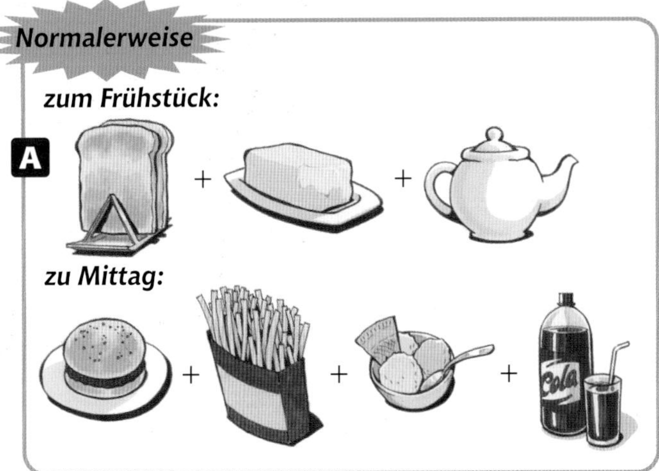

3 a Lies den Text und beantworte die Fragen auf Englisch! (◄◄ S. 64–65)

Beispiel: **1 Not at all fit.**

1. How fit or unfit is Tina?
2. What sort of fitness does she want to achieve? (*2 points*)
3. What decision has this prompted?
4. What two daily activities does she do and how long has she been doing them?
5. When does she plan to go walking frequently?
6. Where does she travel to every day and how?
7. Why has her concentration apparently improved?

Tina ist überhaupt nicht fit, sie möchte aber körperlich und geistig fit werden. Darum hat sie beschlossen, gesünder zu leben und mehr Sport zu treiben. Letzte Woche hat sie angefangen, jeden Tag zu joggen und schwimmen zu gehen. Im Sommer möchte sie auch viel Tennis spielen und am Wochenende wird sie so oft wie möglich spazieren gehen. Im Moment fährt sie jeden Tag mit dem Rad in die Stadt. Seit einer Woche isst sie gesund und sie findet, dass sie sich viel besser konzentrieren kann, weil sie kein Fast-Food gegessen hat.

3 b Jetzt bist du dran. Stell dir vor, du bist Tina! Schreib den Text um! (◄◄ S. 64–65)

Beispiel: ***Ich bin* überhaupt nicht fit, *ich* möchte aber körperlich …**

1 **Lies den Text! Bring dann die Bilder in die richtige Reihenfolge!** (◄◄ S. 68–69)

Beispiel: **c, …**

Das Flugzeug ist um 13 Uhr abgeflogen. Es ist um 15 Uhr 30 in Hamburg angekommen. Dann bin ich um 16 Uhr 15 mit dem Zug weitergefahren. Ich war eine Stunde unterwegs. Ich bin erst um 17 Uhr 15 in Pinneberg angekommen und habe meine Eltern angerufen. Ich war um 18 Uhr bei meinem Austauschpartner.

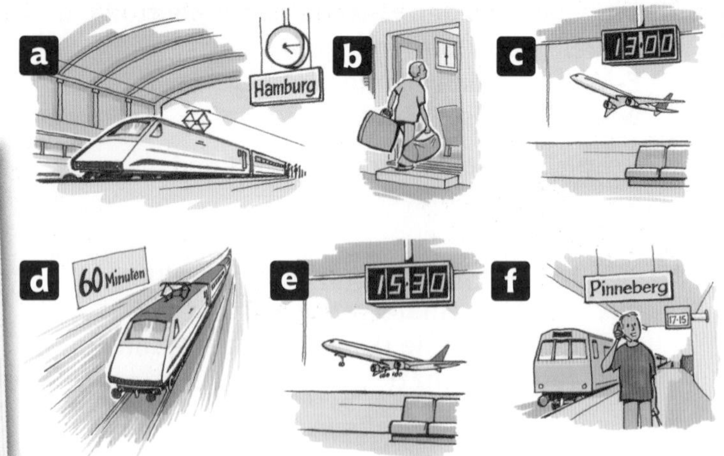

2 **Vervollständige diese E-Mail an deinen Freund/deine Freundin und beschreib, was du gestern Abend bei deiner Gastfamilie gegessen hast!** (◄◄ S. 70–71)

Beispiel: **Hallo!**
Gestern Abend habe ich bei meiner Gastfamilie …

Abendessen bei meiner Gastfamilie
Hallo!
Gestern Abend habe ich bei …
Als Vorspeise …
Als Hauptgericht …
Als Nachtisch …
Das war …

3 **Lies den Text! Was meint Martia und was hält ihre Familie wirklich von den Geschenken? Sieh dir das Bild an und vervollständige die Antworten auf Englisch!** (◄◄ S. 72–73)

Beispiel: **Martia thinks her mother's gift is lovely/a great gift. But her mother thinks …**

wirklich – *really, honestly*
auf der Erde – *on Earth*

Weißt du was? Ich war letzte Woche auf der Erde und habe tolle Geschenke für die ganze Familie gekauft. Für Mutti habe ich eine schöne Flasche Kölnischwasser gekauft. Sie denkt ganz sicher, dass das ein tolles Geschenk ist. Dann habe ich für Vati einen großen Bierkrug gekauft. Das ist ein supertolles Geschenk für ihn, meine ich. Omas Basketballmütze ist auch fantastisch! Und für meinen Bruder habe ich jede Menge tolle Plüschtiere gekauft. Toll, was?
Martia

1 Sieh dir die Bilder an und beschreib deine Reise! (◄◄ S. 68–69)

Beispiel: **Der Zug ist um 11 Uhr abgefahren.**

2 Sieh dir die Tabelle an und schreib, was du gestern bei deiner Gastfamilie gegessen hast und was du heute essen wirst! Hat es geschmeckt oder nicht? (◄◄ S. 70–71)

Wann?	Vorspeise	Hauptgericht	Nachtisch
gestern	Zwiebelsuppe	Bohneneintopf	Quark mit Apfelmus
heute	Tomatensuppe	Schweinekoteletten	Obst mit Eis

Beispiel: **Gestern haben wir als Vorspeise Zwiebelsuppe … . Heute essen wir …**

3 a Lies den folgenden Text! Was heißt das auf Deutsch? (◄◄ S. 72–73)

Beispiel: **1 bei meiner Austauschpartnerin**

1. at my exchange partner's home
2. It was so much fun.
3. I bought great presents.
4. that went wrong
5. they all think
6. for myself
7. nothing at all

Letztes Jahr habe ich zehn Tage bei meiner Austauschpartnerin in Luzern verbracht. Das hat so viel Spaß gemacht, dass ich nicht wieder nach Hause wollte! Ich habe tolle Geschenke für meine Freunde gekauft, aber das ist dann doch schief gelaufen. Alle finden, dass meine Geschenke – Schokolade, T-Shirts und Bücher – doofe Geschenke sind.

Jetzt bin ich wieder bei meiner Austauschpartnerin und werde heute noch einmal Geschenke kaufen – eine Tafel Schokolade, ein paar T-Shirts und Bücher über die Gegend. Das sind doch tolle Geschenke … für mich selber! Und für meine Freunde, was kaufe ich da? Gar nichts!

Katja

3 b Lies den Text noch einmal und beantworte folgende Fragen! (◄◄ S. 72–73)

Beispiel: **1 (Sie ist) nach Luzern (gefahren).**

1. Wohin ist Katja letztes Jahr gefahren?
2. Wie lange ist sie dort geblieben?
3. Woher weiß man, dass es ihr gut gefallen hat?
4. Was halten ihre Freunde von den Geschenken?
5. Was hält Katja davon?
6. Wo ist sie im Moment?
7. Was wird sie dieses Mal für ihre Freunde kaufen?

1 a Schau dir die Wortschlange an! Kannst du acht Adjektive finden? (◄◄ S. 78–79)

Beispiel: **1 ehrlich**

WieehrlichfaulistgeduldiggeizigdeinsympathischschüchternBruderselbstbewusstselbstsüchtig

1 b **Finde jetzt die Frage heraus!** ***Use the left-over words in the wordsnake to find the question!*** (◄◄ S. 78–79)

Frage: __________ __________ __________ __________ ?

1 c **Beschreib vier Leute! Benutze die acht Adjektive aus Übung 1a!** (◄◄ S. 78–79)

Beispiel: **1 Mein Bruder ist ehrlich, aber faul.**

Mein Bruder …
Meine Schwester …
Mein Opa …
Meine Oma …
Mein bester Freund …
Meine beste Freundin …

2 **Lies die Texte in den Sprechblasen und finde die vier richtigen Sätze! Schreib die Buchstaben auf!** (◄◄ S. 80–81)

1 Andreas Eltern sind überhaupt nicht streng.
2 Sie darf ab und zu spät nach Hause kommen.
3 Sie darf nicht spät nach Hause kommen.
4 Am Samstag und am Sonntag muss sie ihren Eltern helfen.
5 Gudrun hat sympathische Eltern.
6 Sie kommt mit ihrer Stiefmutter nicht gut aus.
7 Sie darf spät nach Hause kommen.
8 Sie muss die ganze Hausarbeit machen.

Ich finde, dass meine Eltern ein bisschen zu streng sind. Ich muss jeden Tag um 9 Uhr ins Bett gehen und darf nie spät nach Hause kommen. Ich darf in meinem Schlafzimmer fernsehen, aber ich muss am Wochenende bei der Hausarbeit helfen. Das finde ich nicht fair.

Andrea

Gudrun

Du hast Pech! Mein Vater ist überhaupt nicht streng und meine Stiefmutter ist eine sehr nette Frau. Ich darf manchmal spät nach Hause kommen und am Wochenende darf ich spätabends in die Disko gehen, aber dafür habe ich kein Interesse. Ich muss aber mein Zimmer aufräumen.

3 **Schreib einen Brief an Tante Claudia! Benutze folgende Bilder!** (◄◄ S. 82–83)

Beispiel: **Liebe Tante Claudia, du musst mir helfen! Meine Eltern sind so streng. Ich muss …**

1 Sieh dir das Bild an und beschreib deine Familienmitglieder!
(◄◄ S. 78–79)

Beispiel: **Meine Oma ist eine nette und freigiebige Frau, aber mein Opa ist ein launischer und fauler Mann.**

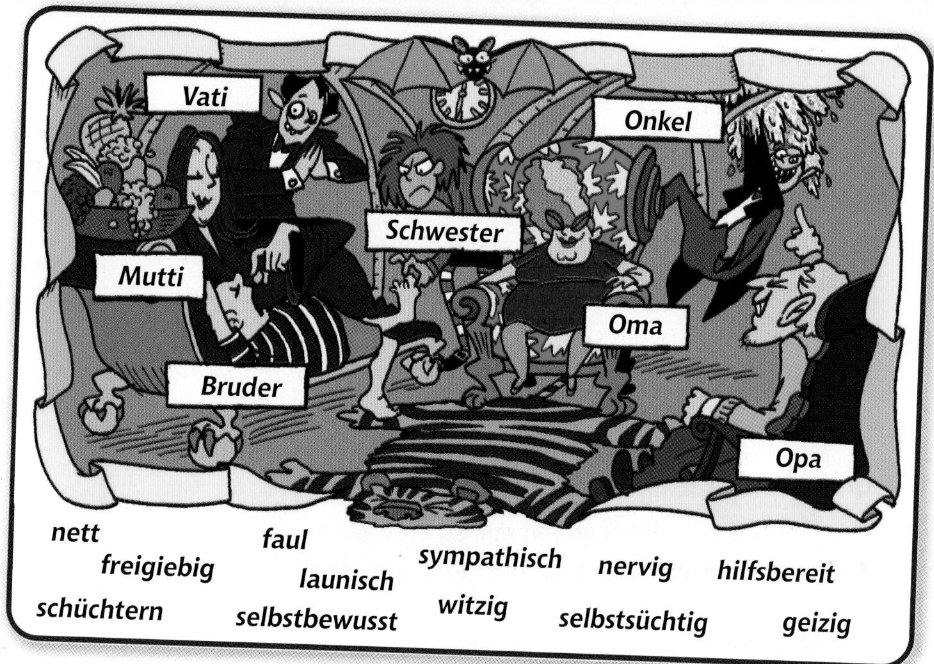

nett *freigiebig* *schüchtern* *faul* *launisch* *selbstbewusst* *sympathisch* *witzig* *nervig* *selbstsüchtig* *hilfsbereit* *geizig*

2 Lies den Text und sieh dir die Bilder an! Wie ist die richtige Reihenfolge? Schreib die richtigen Buchstaben auf!
(◄◄ S. 80–81)

Beispiel: **1 c**

Ein schlechter Schultag

Im Moment habe ich große Probleme mit der Schule. Am Montag bin ich spät aufgestanden und bin erst um halb zehn in der Schule angekommen. Wie ihr wisst, muss man doch pünktlich sein, aber was konnte ich tun? Man muss auch sein Handy draußen lassen, aber ich wollte meine Eltern anrufen, um ihnen meine Verspätung zu erklären, also habe ich es ins Klassenzimmer mitgebracht. Herr Müller war sehr böse mit mir, als es geklingelt hat! Ich musste auch dringend etwas essen – wenn man so spät aufsteht, hat man keine Zeit zu frühstücken. Ich wusste ja, dass man im Klassenzimmer nicht essen darf, aber ich hatte Hunger wie ein Bär! Und jetzt habe ich Stubenarrest – ich darf vor Samstag nicht ausgehen.

Christl

dringend – *urgently*

3 Wähl einen Titel aus Tante Claudias „Meckerecke" und schreib einen kurzen Absatz darüber! (◄◄ S. 82–83)

Meckerecke – *moaner's corner*

Beispiel: **Mein Freund hat eine Andere**
Liebe Tante Claudia,
hilf mir bitte! Ich bin total verliebt in meinen Freund, aber er hat eine Andere. Er hat mit meiner Freundin geflirtet und jetzt bin ich total deprimiert. Ich bin so einsam ohne ihn! Was kann ich tun?

- Mein Freund hat eine Andere
- Meine Freundin hat Angst vor Prüfungen
- Meine Eltern sind zu streng
- Ich rauche und weiß nicht, wie ich aufhören kann
- Ich esse zu viel Fast-Food

1 a **Was passt zusammen?** (◄◄ S. 86–87)

Beispiel: **1 c**

1	Meine Eltern	**a**	ihm 8 Euro die Woche.
2	Mein Geld reicht	**b**	dein Taschengeld?
3	Wie viel Taschengeld	**c**	geben mir 10 Euro die Woche.
4	Sein Vater gibt	**d**	mir nicht.
5	Reicht dir	**e**	Taschengeld.
6	Sie bekommt kein	**f**	bekommst du?

1 b **Wähl einen Satz aus Übung 1a und schreib zwei bis drei Sätze!** (◄◄ S. 86–87)

Beispiel: **Meine Eltern geben mir 10 Euro die Woche. Meine Oma gibt mir auch Taschengeld, 5 Euro die Woche. Mein Geld reicht mir gut.**

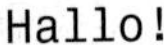

2 **Sieh dir die Bilder an! Wähl zwei Nebenjobs und schreib eine kurze E-Mail darüber!** (◄◄ S. 88–89)

```
Hallo!
Im Moment habe ich zwei Nebenjobs. Ich … . Das
gefällt … (nicht), weil … . Ich … auch …
```

3 **Bring die folgenden Satzteile in die richtige Reihenfolge! Schreib den ganzen Text auf!** (◄◄ S. 90–91)

Beispiel: **Wenn ich erwachsen bin, habe ich die Absicht, …**

Meine Zukunft
vor, eine interessante
ich vielleicht
Lehrer oder Arzt zu
Leuten helfen kann. Wenn
Wenn ich erwachsen
werden. Meine
Mutter ist Ärztin, und ich habe
das nicht möglich ist, werde
bin, habe ich die Absicht,
Stelle zu suchen, wo ich
im Freien arbeiten.

1 **Welche vier Bilder passen zum Text? Schreib die richtigen Buchstaben auf!** (◄◄ S. 86–87)

Beispiel: **b, …**

Im Großen und Ganzen reicht mir mein Geld. Meine Eltern geben mir 12 Euro pro Woche und mein Opa gibt mir noch 3 Euro Taschengeld dazu. Wenn ich erwachsen bin, werde ich nicht viel Geld brauchen, weil ich kein Haus und kein teures Auto kaufen will – dafür habe ich kein Interesse. Hoffentlich werde ich anderen Leuten helfen können.

2 **Lies Tante Claudias Text! Schreib dann einen Brief an sie! Stell dir vor, du hast Nebenjobs. Benutze ihre Fragen!** (◄◄ S. 88–89)

Beispiel: **Liebe Tante Claudia,**
ich mache drei- oder viermal in der Woche Babysitting. Das ist ein toller Nebenjob, weil ich … , aber …

Nebenjobs

Tante Claudia fragt dich:

Hast du einen Nebenjob oder viele Nebenjobs? Was hältst du davon? Ist der Lohn gut oder schlecht? Wie viele Stunden musst du arbeiten? Machst du das gern oder nur, weil du musst? Welche Nebenjobs hast du schon gemacht? Hat das Spaß gemacht, oder war es total langweilig?

Schreib mir jetzt bitte.

Tschüs!

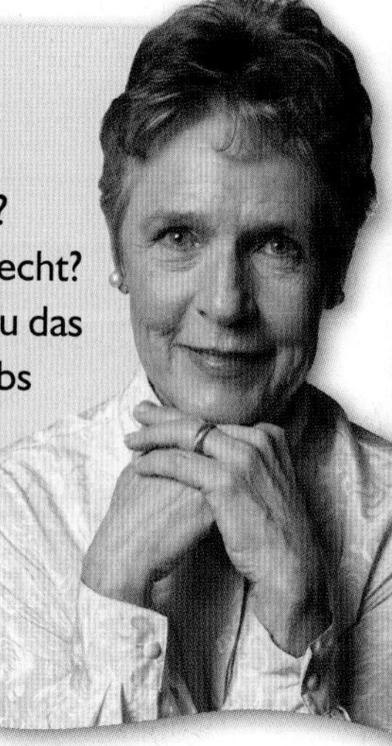

3 **Lies Brunos E-Mail und beantworte folgende Fragen auf Englisch!** (◄◄ S. 90–91)

1. What has made Bruno start thinking about the future?
2. What job has he decided to do in the future?
3. Why is it important for him to have an interesting job?
4. Where has he already worked as a part-time job?
5. How did he find it? (*give at least 3 details*)
6. Where would he like to go to find a job?
7. What does he think people should do in life?

An: Gerd Auer
Von: Bruno Lorenz
Betr.: Meine Zukunftspläne

He, du da!

Wie geht's? Mir geht's im Moment ganz gut.

Auf der Schule reden wir über die Zukunft, das heißt, was wir später machen möchten! Hast du schon einen Beruf gewählt? Ich weiß noch nicht, was ich als Beruf machen möchte, aber ich glaube, dass mir mein Beruf nicht nur Spaß machen muss, sondern dass er auch interessant sein muss. Und du, was für eine Stelle willst du suchen? Hast du die Absicht, in einem Büro oder im Freien zu arbeiten? Als Nebenjob habe ich schon in einem Büro gearbeitet. Das war total langweilig, in einem dunklen Raum mit verstaubten Akten und muffigen Leuten zusammen zu sein.

Ich habe auch vielleicht vor, ins Ausland zu fahren, um einen Job zu suchen. Vielleicht werde ich Leuten helfen. Meiner Meinung nach sollte man versuchen, seine Träume zu verwirklichen. Was meinst du?

Schreib bald wieder.

Tschüs!

Bruno

1 **Was würden sie gerne machen? Sieh dir die Bilder an und vervollständige die Sätze!** (◄◄ S. 96–97)

Beispiel: **1 a Ich *könnte* in den Schweizer Alpen *wandern*, das *wäre* schön.**

1 Ich k________ in den Schweizer Alpen ________, das w________ schön.
2 Ich möchte ni________ in einen Frei________ gehen, das w________ langweilig.
3 Wir k________ zum Strand g________, weil ich Vo________ spielen könnte.
4 Du k________ nach Wien f________, das w________ interessant.

a

b

c

d

2 **Hotel oder Jugendherberge? Lies den Dialog und beantworte die Fragen auf Englisch!** (◄◄ S. 98–99)

Beispiel: **1 better**

1 Does Meike think that hotels are cheaper, dearer or simply better than youth hostels?
2 Name four things that Meike says are readily available when you stay in an hotel in the town centre.
3 What does she say about the food in hotel restaurants?
4 What does Hakan say about hotel prices?
5 Why does he dislike being in an hotel at night time?
6 Name two advantages of staying in a youth hostel, according to him.

Meiner Meinung nach sollte man im Urlaub immer in einem Hotel in der Stadtmitte wohnen. Dann kann man sicher sein, dass alles ganz in der Nähe ist – Sehenswürdigkeiten, Stadtrundfahrten, Restaurants, Shows, tolle Geschäfte. Und die meisten Hotels bieten einen guten Service und leckeres Essen.

Meike

Hakan

Das stimmt nicht! Oft isst man schlecht im Hotel, aber es kostet immer so viel. Die Zimmer sind auch nicht billig! Normalerweise ist es im Hotel nicht gut – zu viele Gäste, zu viel Lärm nachts im Hotel und zu viel Verkehr in der Stadtmitte. Lieber in einer Jugendherberge übernachten. Das kostet nicht viel, da kann man neue Leute kennen lernen und vor allem kann man das schöne Wetter und die frische Luft auf dem Land genießen.

3 **Sieh dir die Bilder an und schreib eine E-Mail ans Hotel Diehl!** (◄◄ S. 101–102)

Beispiel: **Sehr geehrter Herr Diehl,**
ich muss mich beschweren! Ich habe zehn Tage …
…
Ihr …

sich beschweren – *to complain*

Hotel Diehl – 10 Tage

1 Lies den Text über Urlaubsmöglichkeiten, sieh dir die Bilder an und schreib den ganzen Text auf! (◄◄ S. 96–97)

Urlaubsmöglichkeiten – *holiday possibilities*

Beispiel: **1 Geschichte**

Wenn man sich für (**1**) __________ interessiert, könnte man wohl nach Wien (**2**) __________ . Es (**3**) __________ auch schöne (**4**) __________ und fantastische (**5**) __________ in der Stadtmitte. Wenn man aber aktiver sein (**6**) __________ , (**7**) __________ es schön, (**8**) __________ __________ __________ zu (**9**) __________ . Sonst (**10**) __________ man freiwillige (**11**) __________ unternehmen oder Spaß (**12**) __________ __________ __________ haben. Schöne Ferien!

2 Schreib einen Text für eine Jugendzeitschrift: Warum ich lieber im Hotel/in einer Jugendherberge übernachten möchte. Schreib im Perfekt, im Präsens und im Konditional! (◄◄ S. 99, 101–102)

Beispiel: **Warum möchte ich lieber im Hotel/in einer Jugendherberge übernachten? Also, ich erkläre das alles.**
Letztes Jahr bin ich mit ... nach ... gefahren. Wir haben ... reserviert. Normalerweise ... , aber in diesem Hotel/dieser Jugendherberge ...

3 Lies den Beschwerdebrief und korrigiere die 20 Fehler! Schreib den ganzen Brief auf! (◄◄ S. 101–102)

Beispiel: **1 Harald Diehl (*Direktor*)**

Harald Diehl (Direktorin)
Hotel Diehl
Domstraße 13
25462 Rellingen

Hamburg, 32. Juli

Sehr geehrte Frau Diehl,

ich muss mich unbedingt beschweren, und zwar weil die Bedienung in Ihrem Hotel fantastisch ist. Wir haben nämlich nächste Woche drei Stunden in Ihrem Hotel verbracht und haben keine Probleme gehabt. Als wir am ersten Tag abgefahren sind, hat das Telefon gut funktioniert, aber niemand hat sie repariert. Ich fand das ideal. Am Abend haben wir im Restaurant geschlafen. Leider waren die Bedienung und das Essen besonders gut. Die Zwiebelsuppe war heiß und das Eis war kalt. Ich bin Vegetarier, aber es waren viele vegetarische Gerichte auf der Speisekarte.

Ich hoffe, Sie haben die Absicht, Ihr Hotel nicht zu verbessern. Wenn die Bedienung so schlecht ist, werden wir wieder das Hotel Diehl besuchen.

Wir hoffen auf eine verspätete Antwort und keine Entschuldigung.

Ihr Franz Fehlermann

1 a **Hier sind die Antworten. Wie heißen die Fragen?** (◄◄ S. 104–105)

Beispiel: **1** Wohin fahrt ihr auf Urlaub?

	Fragen	Antworten
1		Wir fahren nach Sylt.
2		Wir fahren mit dem Schiff nach Sylt.
3		Wir fahren im August nach Sylt.
4		Wir gehen schwimmen, fahren mit dem Rad und segeln auf Sylt.

1 b **Schreib alle Informationen in einem Satz auf!** (◄◄ S. 104–105)

Beispiel: **Wir fahren im ... mit ... Sylt, wo wir ...**

1 c **Schreib jetzt alle Informationen in einem Satz im Futur auf!** (◄◄ S. 104–105)

Beispiel: **Wir werden im ... mit ... Sylt fahren, wo wir ...**

2 **Sieh dir die Bilder an und schreib einen kurzen Bericht über deinen Besuch in Lübeck!** (◄◄ S. 104–107)

Beispiel: **Ich bin/Wir sind im ... mit ... nach ... in Norddeutschland ...**

das Holstentor besucht, toll

Stadtrundfahrt Lübeck gemacht, interessant

Bei Niederegger: Marzipan gegessen, lecker

3 **Lies den Bericht über Johannas Urlaubserlebnisse und finde die vier richtigen Sätze!** (◄◄ S. 108–109)

Beispiel: **1, ...**

1 Johanna ist oft unglücklich, wenn sie auf Urlaub ist.
2 Sie hat in Paris ein Portmonee gekauft.
3 Die Polizei hat ihr Portmonee in der U-Bahn gefunden.
4 Ihr Fotoapparat war zu Hause.
5 Sie konnte nichts fotografieren.
6 Das Hotel in Paris hat ihr gut gefallen.
7 Die Bedienung im schweizerischen Hotel war besonders gut.
8 Johanna wollte nicht Ski fahren.

Johanna hat immer Pech im Urlaub gehabt. Letzten Sommer zum Beispiel ist sie nach Paris gefahren. Am ersten Tag hat sie ihr Portmonee in der U-Bahn verloren, aber die Polizei konnte ihr nicht helfen. Leider hat sie auch ihren Fotoapparat nicht mitgebracht und hatte nicht genug Geld, einen Neuen zu kaufen, um Fotos zu machen. Ihr Hotelzimmer war gar nicht billig, aber das Hotel war schmutzig und laut und die Bedienung war furchtbar. Im Winter ist sie noch auf Urlaub in die Schweiz gefahren. Das Hotel war fantastisch und das Wetter auch, aber Johanna musste leider ins Krankenhaus, weil sie einen Skiunfall hatte.

1 **Sieh dir die Bilder an! Du hast vor, nach Sylt auf Urlaub zu fahren. Wann und wie wirst du dorthin fahren? Was wirst du machen und warum?** (◄◄ S. 104–105)

Beispiel: **Ich habe vor, im Juli … mit dem/der … nach … zu … . Ich werde …**

2 **Lies den folgenden Text über einen Urlaub in Lübeck! Beantworte dann die Fragen auf Englisch!** (◄◄ S. 104–107)

Beispiel: **1 They spent the summer holidays there.**

1. Which holidays did Melissa and her friends spend in North Germany?
2. What did they do in Hanover, Hamburg and Kiel?
3. What kind of place is Sylt and what activities does it offer?
4. Why were they still able to swim and sail, even though they did not go to Sylt?
5. What is the speciality of both Niederegger and the town of Lübeck?
6. Why do Melissa's friends not want to go with her to Sylt next year?

das Holstentor

der Dom

Melissa und ihre Freunde haben ihre Sommerferien in Norddeutschland verbracht. Sie haben Hannover, Hamburg und Kiel besucht und viele Sehenswürdigkeiten besichtigt. Sie wollten auch auf die Insel Sylt fahren, um dort segeln, schwimmen, reiten und windsurfen zu gehen, aber sobald sie an der Nordküste angekommen sind, haben sie beschlossen, Lübeck zu besuchen, wo sie den Rest des Urlaubs verbracht haben. Dort konnten sie sicher schwimmen gehen und segeln, weil Lübeck dicht an der Küste liegt, aber am besten waren die schönen alten Gebäude wie das Holstentor, der Dom, der Marktplatz vor dem Dom und das Niederegger-Café. Bei Niederegger kann man das feinste Marzipan essen, weil Lübeck auch die Marzipanstadt heißt!

Wie sind ihre Urlaubspläne für nächstes Jahr? Melissa möchte nach Sylt fahren, aber ihre Freunde, die Marzipanliebhaber sind, würden lieber wieder nach Lübeck fahren. Das werden wir mal sehen, oder?

das Niederegger-Café

der Market vor dem Rathaus

3 **„Letztes Jahr, dieses Jahr, nächstes Jahr". Schreib einen Bericht über Urlaubserlebnisse in der Vergangenheit, heute und in der Zukunft!** (◄◄ S. 108–109)

Beispiel:

Ich habe katastrophale und tolle Urlaubserlebnisse gehabt, und ich hoffe auf gute Erlebnisse dieses Jahr und nächstes Jahr. Wieso? Lies mal weiter …

Normalerweise … ich …
Letztes Jahr war alles katastrophal/toll …
Nächstes Jahr werde/hoffe/möchte ich …

Grammatik

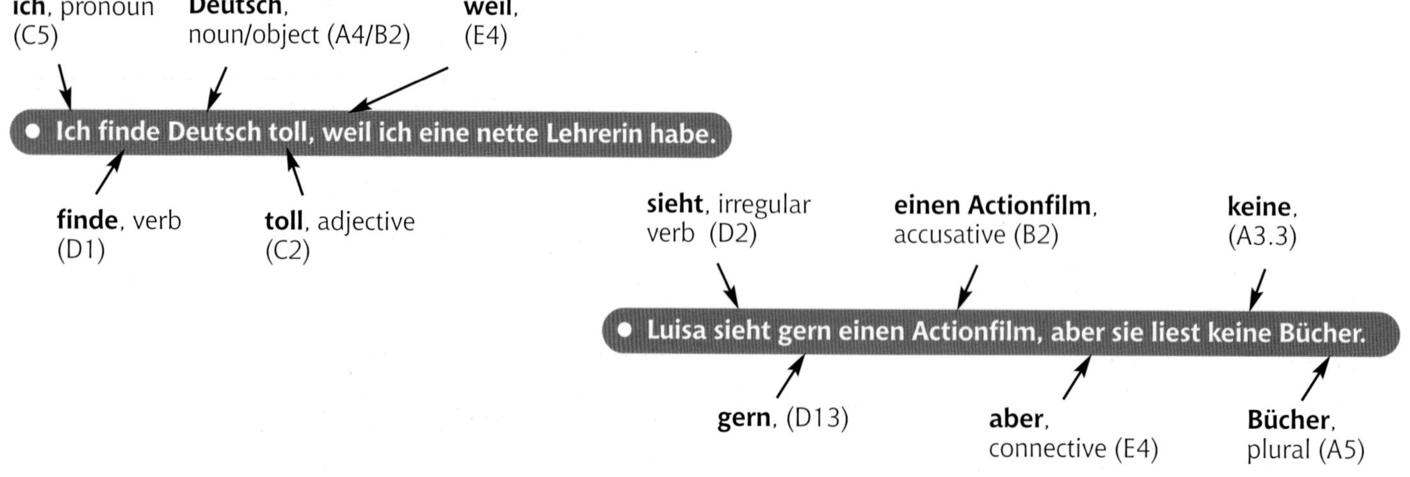

ich, pronoun (C5)
Deutsch, noun/object (A4/B2)
weil, (E4)
Ich finde Deutsch toll, weil ich eine nette Lehrerin habe.
finde, verb (D1)
toll, adjective (C2)
sieht, irregular verb (D2)
einen Actionfilm, accusative (B2)
keine, (A3.3)
Luisa sieht gern einen Actionfilm, aber sie liest keine Bücher.
gern, (D13)
aber, connective (E4)
Bücher, plural (A5)

Glossary of terms

- ***Adjectives*** **die Adjektive**
  ... are words that describe somebody or something:
  groß *big* **blau** *blue*

- ***Articles (definite and indefinite)***
  ... are the words 'the' and 'a':
  der, die, das *the*
  ein, eine, ein *a*

- ***Cases***
  – The nominative case is used for the subject of the sentence:
  Der Junge spielt Klavier.
  The boy plays the piano.
  – The accusative case is used for the object of the sentence:
  Amelie kauft einen Kuli.
  Amelie buys a pen.
  – The dative case is used after some prepositions:
  Ich wohne in der Stadt.
  I live in the town.
  Tom wohnt auf dem Land.
  Tom lives in the country.
  Die Katze ist neben der Lampe.
  The cat is next to the lamp.

- ***Infinitive*** **der Infinitiv**
  ... is the 'name' of the verb as listed in the dictionary:
  spielen *to play* **gehen** *to go*
  haben *to have* **sein** *to be*

- ***Nouns*** **die Nomen**
  ... are words for somebody or something:
  das Haus *house* **die Tür** *door*
  der Bruder *brother*

- ***Object*** **das Objekt**
  ... is a person or thing affected by the verb:
  Ich esse einen Apfel. *I eat an apple.*
  Ich spiele Tennis. *I play tennis.*

- ***Prepositions*** **die Präpositionen**
  ... are words used with nouns to give information about where, when, how, with whom, etc.:
  mit *with* **aus** *from* **nach** *to*
  zu *to* **in** *in*

- ***Pronouns*** **die Pronomen**
  ... are short words used instead of a noun or name:
  ich *I* **du** *you*
  er *he, it* **sie** *she, it* **es** *it*

- ***Singular and plural*** **Singular und Plural**
  – 'singular' refers to just one thing or person:
  Hund *dog*
  Bruder *brother*
  – 'plural' refers to more than one thing or person:
  Hunde *dogs*
  Brüder *brothers*

- ***Subject*** **das Subjekt**
  ... is a person or thing 'doing' the verb:
  Martina lernt Deutsch. *Martina is learning German.*
  Ich gehe ins Kino. *I am going to the cinema.*

- ***Verbs*** **die Verben**
  ... express an action or a state:
  ich wohne *I live* **ich habe** *I have*
  ich bin *I am* **ich mag** *I like*

Masculine/feminine/neuter, singular/plural

A1 Number

Many words in German change according to whether they are **singular** or **plural**.

You use the singular when there is **only one** of something or someone.

You use the plural when there **is more than one** of something or someone:

das Auto *the* ***car*** die Autos *the* ***cars***
ich wohne ***I*** *live* wir wohnen ***we*** *live*

A2 Gender

Many words in German also change according to whether they are **masculine**, **feminine** or **neuter**.

This is called **grammatical gender**. It does not exist in English, but it does in most other languages.

The grammatical gender of something has nothing to do with its sex or gender in real life.

For instance, in German 'table' is masculine but 'girl' is neuter!

A3 Articles

Articles are words like 'the' and 'a', and are usually used with nouns.

There are **three** kinds of article in German: definite ('the'), indefinite ('a') and negative ('not a').

The **gender** of an article must match the **gender** of the **word(s) it is with.**

Its **number** must match the **number** of the **word(s) it is with.**

In the **plural**, all genders have the same article.

A3.1 The definite article: *der, die, das, die*

The **definite article** means 'the':

masculine	feminine	neuter	plural
der	**die**	das	**die**

Das ist **der** Tisch. *That is* ***the*** *table.*

A3.2 The indefinite article: *ein, eine, ein*

The **indefinite article** means 'a'. There is **no plural** because **a** has no plural!

masculine	feminine	neuter
ein	**eine**	ein

Das ist **ein** Tisch. *That is* ***a*** *table.*

A3.3 The negative article: *kein, keine, kein, keine*

The **negative article** means 'not a' or 'not any' or 'no'.

masculine	feminine	neuter	plural
kein	**keine**	kein	**keine**

Das ist kein Tisch. *That is **not a** table* or *That **isn't a** table.*

A4 Nouns

A noun is a word used to **name something**.

Nouns are **objects** or **things**, but not all nouns are things that can be touched (e.g. 'laughter').

A good test of a noun is whether or not you can put 'the' in front of it (e.g. **the** book ✔; **the** have ✗).

All German nouns are either **masculine**, **feminine** or **neuter**, and either **singular** or **plural**.

When you see a noun, you can often work out its **gender** or **number** from its **article**:

masculine	feminine	neuter	plural
der Tisch	**die Tasche**	das Heft	**die Hefte**

A5 Plurals of nouns

There are different ways of making nouns plural in German, just as in English.

Unfortunately, there isn't really a quick rule – you just have to get the feel of them!

You haven't met all the different ways of forming plurals in *Na klar! 2*, but here are a few important ones:

- Feminine nouns: usually you just **add -n**:
  eine Katze – zwei Katze**n**
- Some nouns **stay the same** in the plural:
  ein Hamster – drei **Hamster**
- Some nouns **add -e**: ein Hund – drei Hund**e**
- Some nouns just add **-s**, as in English:
  ein Auto – zwei Auto**s**
- Some nouns add **-e**, but also take an umlaut (¨) on the first vowel: eine Maus – hundert M**ä**us**e**

A6 Possessive adjectives

Possessive adjectives are words like 'my', 'your', 'his' and 'her'.

Their **gender** and **number** must match (or 'agree') and their endings change (just like *der*, *ein*, etc.).

Here are the endings they use:

	masculine	feminine	neuter	plural
my	mein	**meine**	mein	**meine**
your	dein	**deine**	dein	**deine**
his/its	sein	**seine**	sein	**seine**
her/its	ihr	**ihre**	ihr	**ihre**
our	unser	**unsere**	unser	**unsere**
your	euer	**eure**	euer	**eure**
their	ihr	**ihre**	ihr	**ihre**
your	Ihr	**Ihre**	Ihr	**Ihre**

mein Bruder *my brother*
deine Schwester *your sister*
sein Vater *his father*
ihre Schwestern *her sisters*

A7 *Dieser, diese, dieses, diese*

Dieser, etc. means 'this'. It follows the same pattern of endings as the definite article.

masculine	feminine	neuter	plural
dieser	**diese**	dieses	**diese**

Dieser Film ist eine Komödie. *This film is a comedy.*
Dieses Buch handelt von einem Hund. *This book is about a dog.*

B Case

Besides **number** and **gender**, German nouns and the words that go with them have a **case**.

The way cases work is quite complex, but they tell you certain simple things about the noun.

B1 The nominative

A word is in the nominative if it is the 'doer' of an action (and actions include words like 'is').

All the words listed so far have been in the nominative (e.g. *ein, der, kein, mein*).

Der Tisch **ist** braun. *The table is brown.*
Mein Bruder **wohnt** in London. *My brother lives in London.*
Seine Katze **ist** launisch. *His cat is moody.*

	masculine	feminine	neuter	plural
the	der	**die**	das	**die**
a	ein	**eine**	ein	**–**
not a	kein	**keine**	kein	**keine**

Dieser (this) uses the same endings in the nominative as the definite article (*der, die, das, die*).

The possessive adjectives (*mein, dein*, etc.) use the same endings as the negative article (*kein, keine, kein, keine*).

B2 The accusative

After verbs like *haben* or *es gibt*, and some prepositions, you use the accusative.

Words like *ein, mein*, etc., are different in the accusative – but only in the **masculine** form:

Ich habe **einen** Bruder. *I have a brother.*
Er hat **keinen** Stuhl. *He hasn't got a chair.*
Es gibt **einen** Supermarkt. *There's a supermarket.*

Es gibt **keinen** Park. *There isn't a park.*

	masculine	feminine	neuter	plural
the	**den**	**die**	**das**	**die**
a	**einen**	**eine**	**ein**	–
not a	**keinen**	**keine**	**kein**	**keine**

Dieser (this) uses the same endings in the accusative as the definite article (*den, die, das, die*).
The possessive adjectives (*mein, dein*, etc.) use the same endings as the negative article (*keinen, keine, kein, keine*).

B3 The dative

After some prepositions (e.g. *zu, mit, gegenüber, bei, seit*) you use the dative.
Words like *ein, mein*, etc., are different in the dative. You will have to learn them.
With *zu, der, die* and *das* change to **zum**, **zur** and **zum.**

mit **dem** Mann *with the man*
mit **meinem** Bruder *with my brother*
zum (= zu **dem**) Bahnhof *to the station*
zur (= zu **der**) Post *to the post office*

	masculine	feminine	neuter	plural
the	**dem**	**der**	**dem**	**den**
a	**einem**	**einer**	**einem**	–
not a	**keinem**	**keiner**	**keinem**	**keinen**

Dieser (this) uses the same endings in the dative as the definite article (*dem, der, dem, den*).
The possessive adjectives (*mein, dein*, etc.) use the same endings as the negative article (*keinem, keiner, keinem, keinen*).

C Other parts of a German sentence

C1 Prepositions

Pre**positions** are words that tell you **where** things are (or their 'position'), for example 'on', 'under', 'by', 'at', 'with'.

C1.1 Prepositions + dative

Five of the prepositions you have met in *Na klar! 2* are always followed by the **dative**: *mit* (with), *zu* (to), *gegenüber* (opposite), *bei* (at/at the home of) and *seit* (since).
(Don't forget that *zu dem* and *zu der* become *zum* and *zur*.)

mit **ihrem** Hund *with her dog*
zur Schule *to school*
gegenüber **der** Post *opposite the post-office*
bei **meinem** Onkel *at my uncle's (home)*
seit **einer** Woche *for (since) a week*

C1.2 Prepositions + accusative

So far you have only met one preposition that is always followed by the accusative: **für** (for):

für **meinen** Vater *for my father*

C1.3 Prepositions + dative or accusative

There is a group of prepositions which are sometimes followed by the dative and sometimes (but not as often) by the accusative. Here is a list of them with their meanings when followed by the dative:

an *at, on (vertical things)*
auf *on (horizontal things)*
hinter *behind*
in *in*
neben *near, next to*
über *above*
unter *underneath*
vor *in front of*
zwischen *between*

Es gibt Posters an **der** Wand. *There are posters on the wall.*
Wir treffen uns an **der** Bushaltestelle. *We're meeting at the bus-stop.*
Der Kuli ist auf **diesem** Tisch. *The pen is on this table.*
Das kaufst du in **einer** Bäckerei. *You buy that in a baker's shop.*
Ich warte neben **dem** Geldautomaten. *I'm waiting next to the cash machine.*

Remember that *in dem* and *an dem* usually become *im* and *am*.

Usually when there is **movement** involved (e.g. 'into' rather than 'in'), these same prepositions are followed by the **accusative**. (Don't forget that *in das* shortens to **ins**.)

Wir gehen **ins** Kino. *We're going (in)to the cinema.*
Gehst du **in den** Supermarkt? *Are you going (in)to the supermarket?*
Er läuft hinter **die** Schule. *He runs behind the school.*

C2 Adjectives

Adjectives are words that describe nouns. When adjectives come **after** the noun, they work just like English adjectives:

Die Tasche ist **blau**. *The bag ist blue.*
Das Haus ist **rot**. *The house is red.*

However, when adjectives come **before** the noun, you have to put an ending on them. The endings you use depend on whether the adjective comes after an indefinite or a definite article. They also change according to the gender, number and case of the noun they refer to.

C2.1 Adjectives after the indefinite article

Here are the adjective endings for **nominative**, **accusative** and **dative nouns**, after *ein/eine/ein* (or *kein/keine/kein, mein/meine/mein*, etc.).
They are almost, but not quite, like the endings on *der/die/das*:

	masculine	feminine	neuter	plural
nominative	**großer**	**große**	**großes**	**großen***
accusative	**großen**	**große**	**großes**	**großen***
dative	**großen**	**großen**	**großen**	**großen**

* A plural noun cannot be used with *ein* (as there is no plural of 'a'), but it can be used with *kein, mein, dein*, etc. If you use an adjective and noun without any article at all, the ending on plural adjectives in the nominative or accusative is -e.

Ich trage schwarze Schuhe. *I'm wearing black shoes.*
Ich trage meine schwarzen Schuhe. *I'm wearing my black shoes.*
Er hat einen kleinen Hund. *He has a little dog.*
Sein kleiner Hund ist zu Hause. *His little dog is at home.*
Wo ist dein weißes Hemd? *Where is your white shirt?*
Es ist mit meiner blauen Jacke. *It's with my blue jacket.*

C2.2 *Adjectives after the definite article*

Here are the adjective endings after *der, die, das* (or *dieser, diese, dieses*).

	masculine	feminine	neuter	plural
nominative	**große**	**große**	**große**	**großen**
accusative	**großen**	**große**	**große**	**großen**
dative	**großen**	**großen**	**großen**	**großen**

Das rote Oberteil ist teuer. *The red top is expensive.*
Ich finde den grauen Pulli altmodisch. *I find the grey jumper old-fashioned.*
Magst du diese gestreifte Krawatte? *Do you like this striped tie?*
Das trage ich mit den gelb**en** Socken. *I wear that with the yellow socks.*

C3 Comparatives and superlatives

You use the comparative to say 'bigger', 'louder', etc. In German, as in English, you add *-er* to the adjective. Some short adjectives also add an umlaut to the first vowel in the word.

klein → klein**er**
groß → gr**ößer**

The comparative of *gut* (good) is *besser* (better).
To say 'than', you use *als.*

Dein Haus ist größer **als** unser Haus. *Your house is bigger than our house.*

If you want to say the 'biggest', 'loudest', etc, you use the superlative. Just add *-est* or *-st* to the adjective, and then the correct adjective ending. The umlaut change in short adjectives still applies.

alt → **ältest(e)**

Das ist das **größte** Problem. *That's the biggest problem.*
Mein **ältester** Bruder heißt Karl. *My eldest brother is called Karl.*

The superlative of *gut* (good) is *best(e)* (best).

If you want to say something **is** the 'fastest', 'loudest', etc., you use *am* and add *-sten* or *-esten* to the adjective.

Das Leben in der Stadt is **am lautesten**.
Life in town is the loudest.

Man fährt **am schnellsten** mit dem Zug.
You travel fastest by train.

C4 Words for 'you'

There are **three** German words for 'you', depending on the **number** of people and your **relationship** to them:

- du informal singular – for talking to **one** young person or friend:
  Kommst **du** mit?
- ihr informal plural – for talking to **more than one** young person or friend:
  Kommt **ihr** mit?
- Sie formal singular **or** plural – for talking to **one or more than one** older person or stranger:
  Kommen **Sie** mit?

C5 Pronouns

C5.1 *Subject pronouns*

Subject pronouns are words like 'I', 'you', 'he', etc. They are usually used with a verb.

ich *I*
du *you (informal singular)*
er *he (or 'it', to refer to a masculine noun)*
sie *she (or 'it', to refer to a feminine noun)*
es *it (to refer to a neuter noun)*
man *you, we, they, people*
wir *we*
ihr *you (informal plural)*
sie *they*
Sie *you (formal singular or plural)*

The subject pronoun **man** is used when you are not talking about anyone in particular. It is used to say 'one', 'people', 'you', 'they' or 'we':

Man kann das Schloss besichtigen. *You can visit the castle.*
Man tanzt bis spät in die Nacht. *They (People) dance late into the night.*

C5.2 *Direct object pronouns*

Direct object pronouns are pronouns in the accusative case. They are words like 'me', 'him', 'her', 'us' and 'them'. They are used when the pronoun is not the **subject** of the sentence (the doer of the action), but the **object** of the sentence (on the receiving end of the action).

mich	*me*	uns	*us*
dich	*you*	euch	*you*
ihn	*him/it*	sie	*them*
sie	*her/it*	Sie	*you*
es	*it*		

Ich finde **ihn** langweilig. *I find him boring.*
Wir treffen **dich** um acht Uhr. *We'll meet you at 8 o'clock.*

Direct object pronouns are also used after prepositions that take the accusative case.

Das Buch ist für **dich**. *The book is for you.*

C5.3 Indirect object pronouns

Indirect object pronouns are pronouns in the dative case. They are used as a 'shorthand' way of saying **to** or **for** me/you/him, etc., even though we sometimes miss out the word 'to' or 'for' in English.

mir	uns
dir	euch
ihm	ihnen
ihr	Ihnen
ihm	

Gib **mir** das Buch. *Give (to) me the book.*
Seine Eltern geben **ihm** 10 Euro. *His parents give (to) him 10 euros.*

Indirect object pronouns are also used in certain expressions.

Das Bein tut **ihr** weh. *Her leg hurts.*
Wie geht es **dir**? *How are you?*

And indirect object pronouns are used after prepositions that take the dative case.

Du arbeitest mit **mir**. *You're working with me.*

D Verbs

D1 The present tense of regular verbs

Verbs are 'doing words' – they describe actions. With each verb you use a noun (e.g. *mein Bruder*) or a pronoun (*ich, du,* etc.). For each different person or pronoun you will need to use the correct verb **ending**.
In the present tense, **regular** verbs (verbs which follow the usual pattern) use the following endings:

ich wohn**e**	*I live, I'm living*
du wohn**st**	*you live, you're living*
er wohn**t**	*he lives, he's living*
sie wohn**t**	*she lives, she's living*
es wohn**t**	*it lives, it's living*
man wohn**t**	*you/we/they/people live, are living*
wir wohn**en**	*we live, we're living*
ihr wohn**t**	*you live, you're living*
sie wohn**en**	*they live, they're living*
Sie wohn**en***	*you live, you're living*

* For *du/Sie/ihr* ('you') see Section C4 on page 142.

Ich wohn**e** in Manchester. *I live in Manchester.*
Mein Onkel wohn**t** in Dresden. *My uncle lives in Dresden.*
Sie wohn**en** in Leipzig. *They're living in Leipzig.*

Other verbs that work like this are:
machen *to do*
saugen *to suck*
kommen *to come*
kochen *to cook*

D2 The present tense of irregular verbs

Irregular (or **strong**) verbs use the same endings as regular verbs, but there is a difference: the first vowel usually changes in the *du* and *er/sie/es* forms. There are three types of vowel change:

• **tragen** *to wear*	ich trage	wir tragen
	du tr**ä**gst	ihr tragt
	er/sie/es/man tr**ä**gt	sie/Sie tragen
• **helfen** *to help*	ich helfe	wir helfen
	du h**i**lfst	ihr helft
	er/sie/es/man h**i**lft	sie/Sie helfen
• **sehen** *to see*	ich sehe	wir sehen
	du s**ie**hst	ihr seht
	er/sie/es/man s**ie**ht	sie/Sie sehen

Another important irregular verb is **haben** (to have) which drops the **b** in the *du* and *er/sie/es* forms:

• **haben** *to have*	ich habe	wir haben
	du **hast**	ihr habt
	er/sie/es/man **hat**	sie/Sie haben

Note also the following parts of *arbeiten* (to work), *segeln* (to sail) and *kegeln* (to bowl), in which a letter is added or dropped to make them easier to say:

du arbeit**e**st wir/sie/Sie segeln/kegeln (not segelen/kegelen)

D3 *Sein*

The verb **sein** (to be) is totally different: you'll have to learn it off by heart!

• **sein** *to be*	ich **bin**	wir **sind**
	du **bist**	ihr **seid**
	er/sie/es/man **ist**	sie/Sie **sind**

D4 Modal verbs

These are verbs like 'will', 'must' and 'could', and they normally have to be used with another verb.
When they are used with another verb, that verb is in the **infinitive** and it goes to the **end** of the sentence.
Usually, the singular forms of modal verbs are different from others because the vowel changes.
Also, most modal verbs have no endings in the *ich* and *er/sie/es* forms.

können *to be able to ('I can', etc.)*	**dürfen** *to be allowed to ('I may/can', etc.)*
ich **kann**	ich **darf**
du **kannst**	du **darfst**
er/sie/es/man **kann**	er/sie/es/man **darf**
wir **können**	wir **dürfen**
ihr **könnt**	ihr **dürft**
sie/Sie **können**	sie/Sie **dürfen**

müssen *to have to ('I must', etc.)*
ich **muss**
du **musst**
er/sie/es/man **muss**
wir **müssen**
ihr **müsst**
sie/Sie **müssen**

mögen *to like*
ich **mag**
du **magst**
er/sie/es/man **mag**
wir **mögen**
ihr **mögt**
sie/Sie **mögen**

wollen *to want to*
ich **will**
du **willst**
er/sie/es/man **will**
wir **wollen**
ihr **wollt**
sie/Sie **wollen**

Willst du ins Kino gehen? *Do you want to go to the cinema?*
Ich **kann** nicht ausgehen. *I can't go out.*
Ich **muss** meine Hausaufgaben machen.
I must / have to do my homework.
Er **darf** keine Horrorfilme sehen.
He's not allowed to watch horror films.
Wir **mögen** Martial-Arts-Filme unheimlich gern.
We really like martial arts films.

D5 Separable verbs

Some verbs are in **two parts**. They consist of the **normal verb** and a **separable prefix**.
The normal verb goes in the usual place (second idea), but the prefix goes at the **end** of the sentence.
When listed in a dictionary or glossary, the separable prefix is always listed first.
Here is a separable verb in full:

einkaufen *to shop*
ich **kaufe ein**
du **kaufst ein**
er/sie/es **kauft ein**
wir **kaufen ein**
ihr **kauft ein**
sie/Sie **kaufen ein**

Ich **kaufe** am Montag **ein**. *I go shopping on Monday.*
Er **kauft** mit seiner Mutter **ein**. *He goes shopping with his mother.*
Sie **kaufen** in Berlin **ein**. *They go shopping in Berlin.*

Here are some other separable verbs you have met:

abwaschen (ich wasche ab) *to wash up*
aufräumen (ich räume auf) *to tidy up*
aufstehen (ich stehe auf) *to get up*
fernsehen (ich sehe fern) *to watch TV*

D6 Reflexive verbs

Reflexive verbs use a subject pronoun **and** an object pronoun.

Ich wasche **mich**. *I wash (myself).*
Er zieht **sich** an. *He gets dressed (dresses himself).*

D7 The perfect tense

- The perfect tense is used to talk about things that happened in the past.
  It is made up of two parts: the **auxiliary** (or 'helping') **verb** and the **past participle**.
  The auxiliary verb goes in the usual place (second): it is usually **haben**.
  The past participle goes at the **end** of the sentence.
- To form the past participle, you take the **-en** off the infinitive of the verb. Then you (usually) add **ge-** to the beginning of the word and **-t** to the end.

ich habe **gespielt**	*I played, I have played*
du hast **gemacht**	*you did, you have done*
er/sie/es hat **gekauft**	*he/she/it bought, has bought*
wir haben **gespielt**	*we played, we have played*
ihr habt **gemacht**	*you did, you have done*
sie/Sie haben **gekauft**	*they/you bought, have bought*

- Some verbs are irregular in the perfect tense. They still make their perfect tense with *haben*, but the past participle is formed differently. You (usually) change the **vowel** in the participle and keep the **-en** from the infinitive on the end.
  Here are the ones you have learnt so far:

essen → ich habe … **gegessen**	*I ate/have eaten …*
trinken → ich habe … **getrunken**	*I drank/have drunk …*
sehen → ich habe … **gesehen**	*I saw/have seen …*

- Verbs that begin with *ver-* or *be-* do not add *ge-*.

  Ich habe vergessen. *I forgot/have forgotten.*
  Er hat seine Oma besucht. *He visited/has visited his granny.*

- Another group of verbs form their perfect tense with **sein** (to be). These are usually **verbs of movement**.
  As with the other verbs, the auxiliary (*sein*) is in second place and the participle still goes at the end of the sentence.
- Some of the verbs which take *sein* are: *fahren* (to go/drive), *gehen* (to go/walk), *kommen* (to come), *fliegen* (to fly), *bleiben* (to stay) and *schwimmen* (to swim).

  Ich **bin** mit dem Bus **gefahren**. *I travelled/have travelled by bus.*
  Du **bist** ins Kino **gegangen**. *You went/have gone to the cinema.*
  Er/Sie/Es/Man **ist** zur Party **gekommen**. *He/She/It/We came to the party.*
  Wir **sind** nach London **geflogen**. *We flew to London.*

Ihr **seid** gut **geschwommen**. *You swam well.*
Sie/Sie **sind** zu Hause **geblieben**. *They/You stayed at home.*

- In the perfect tense, separable verbs have *-ge-* between the separable prefix (*auf, um, fern*, etc.) and the past participle. Some separable verbs take *haben* and some take *sein*.

  Wir haben fern**ge**sehen. *We watched/have watched TV.*
  Der Zug ist spät ab**ge**fahren. *The train left/has left late.*

- With reflexive verbs in the perfect tense, the object pronoun goes after the subject.

  Hast du **dich** schon gewaschen?
  Have you washed/Did you wash (yourself) already?

D8 The imperfect tense

The imperfect tense is another past tense. Most verbs are only used in the imperfect in writing. However, *sein* (to be), *haben* (to have) and the modal verbs are also used in the imperfect tense in speech.
Sein and *haben* are irregular:

sein	**haben**
ich **war**	ich **hatte**
du **warst**	du **hattest**
er/sie/es/man **war**	er/sie/es/man **hatte**
wir **waren**	wir **hatten**
ihr **wart**	ihr **hattet**
sie/Sie **waren**	sie/Sie **hatten**

Der Film **war** langweilig. *The film was boring.*
Die Darsteller **waren** doof. *The characters were stupid.*
Die Webseite **hatte** gute Links. *The website had good links.*
Wir **hatten** kein Geld. *We had no money.*

To form the imperfect tense of modal verbs, you take *-en* off the infinitive and add the following endings. *Müssen, dürfen, können* and *mögen* lose their umlaut.

ich	**-te**
du	**-test**
er/sie/es/man	**-te**
wir	**-ten**
ihr	**-tet**
sie/Sie	**-ten**

Ich muss**te** meine Hausaufgaben machen. *I had to do my homework.*
Sie durf**ten** nicht ausgehen. *They were not allowed to go out.*
Du soll**test** nicht rauchen. *You shouldn't smoke.*
Man konn**te** die Tür nicht öffnen. *You couldn't open the door.*
Er woll**te** mit dir sprechen. *He wanted to speak to you.*

D9 The future tense

One way of referring to the future is to use the present tense, usually with a time phrase.

Morgen gehe ich einkaufen. *I'm going shopping tomorrow.*
In den Ferien fahren wir nach Paris. *In the holidays we're going to Paris.*

To form the future tense proper, you use the correct part of the verb *werden* with the infinitive of another verb. The verb in the infinitive goes to the end.

ich **werde**	wir **werden**
du **wirst**	ihr **werdet**
er/sie/es/man **wird**	sie/Sie **werden**

Was **wirst** du am Wochenende **machen**?
What are you going to do at the weekend?
Ich **werde** nach Österreich **fahren**. *I'm going to go to Austria.*

D10 The conditional

You use the conditional to say what you **would** do. You normally form it by using *würde* plus an infinitive.

ich **würde**	wir **würden**
du **würdest**	ihr **würdet**
er/sie/es/man **würde**	sie/Sie **würden**

Wir **würden** gern nach Spanien **fahren**. *We would like to go to Spain.*
Das **würde** Spaß **machen**. *That would be fun.*

Some common verbs shorten *würde* + infinitive to just one word:

haben	ich hätte, wir hätten, etc.
sein	ich wäre, wir wären, etc.
können	ich könnte, wir könnten, etc.
mögen	ich möchte, wir möchten, etc.

Wir **könnten** Fußball spielen. *We could play football.*
Das **wäre** toll. *That would be great.*

D11 *Es gibt*

- If you want to say 'there is' or 'there are', you use *es gibt* with the **accusative** case:
  Es gibt einen Supermarkt. *There is a supermarket.*
- If you want to say 'there is no' or 'there are no', use *es gibt* + *kein(e)(n)* + accusative case:
  Es gibt kein Schwimmbad. *There is no swimming pool.*

D12 Negatives

- *Nicht* means 'not' and it usually comes after the verb:
  Ich **bin nicht** doof. *I am not stupid.*
- However, when there is an object in the sentence, *nicht* comes after the object:
  Lena mag **Englisch nicht**. *Lena doesn't like English.*

(Don't forget that you use **kein** to say 'not a'. See Section A3.3 on page 140.)

- Other useful negatives are *nichts* (nothing), *nie* (never) and *niemand* (nobody, no one).

  Am Wochenende hat er **nichts** gemacht.
  At the weekend he did nothing/didn't do anything.
  Ich trage **nie** eine Krawatte. *I never wear a tie.*
  Niemand wird zur Party kommen.
  Nobody's coming to the party.

- A different kind of negative expression is *weder … noch …* (neither … nor …).

  Sie isst **weder** Fleisch **noch** Fisch.
  She eats neither meat nor fish. (She doesn't eat meat or fish.)

D13 *Gern, lieber* and *am liebsten*

To say what you like, don't like, prefer or like doing best of all, you use *gern, nicht gern, lieber* or *am liebsten*. These expressions go after the verb.

Ich spiele **gern** Fußball. *I like playing football.*
Du gehst **nicht gern** einkaufen. *You don't like going shopping.*
Sie hört **lieber** Musik. *She prefers listening to music.*
Wir sehen **am liebsten** fern. *We like watching TV best of all.*

D14 Giving instructions (the imperative)

When you give someone instructions (e.g. Turn right!) you use a particular form of the verb called the imperative.

- With friends and family, use the *du*-form without the **-st** ending. Some verbs also lose their umlaut. Put the verb first:

  Du **geh**st rechts. → **Geh** rechts! *Go right!*
  Du **fähr**st mit dem Bus. → **Fahr** mit dem Bus! *Go by bus!*

- With teachers or adults you don't know very well, use the *Sie*-form. Again, the verb goes first:

  Sie gehen geradeaus. → **Gehen** Sie geradeaus!
  Go straight on!

E Word order

E1 Basic word order

Here is the basic word order in a German sentence:

noun/pronoun	verb	rest of the sentence
Ich	**spiele**	**Gitarre.**
Mark	**geht**	**in die Stadt.**

E2 Verb as second idea

In German, the verb is always in second place in a sentence or clause. It's not always the second word, because you can't separate a phrase like *in meinem Zimmer*, but the verb must be the second idea or concept in the sentence:

1 2 3 4
[Ich] [**habe**] [ein Bett] [in meinem Zimmer]

1 2 3 4
[In meinem Zimmer] [**habe**] [ich] [ein Bett]

E3 Time – manner – place

When you mention **when (time)**, **how (manner)** and **where (place)** you do something, you say the time first, then the manner and then the place.

Ich fahre **am Wochenende mit dem Auto nach Paris**.
Er fährt **mit dem Zug nach Berlin**.

E4 Connectives

Connectives are words that join sentences (or clauses, which are bits of sentences) together. For example, *und* (and), *oder* (or) and *aber* (but).

- These do not affect the word order in a sentence:

  Er singt. Er spielt. → Er singt **und** er spielt.
  He sings. He plays. → *He sings and he plays.*

  Sie liest gern. Sie kocht nicht gern. → Sie liest gern, **aber** sie kocht nicht gern.
  She likes reading. She doesn't like cooking. → She likes reading but she doesn't like cooking.

- However, the connectives *weil* (because) and *wenn* (if, when, whenever) send the verb in the second part of the sentence right to the end:

  Ich mag meinen Bruder. Er ist nett. → Ich mag meinen Bruder, **weil** er nett **ist**.
  I like my brother. He is nice. → I like my brother because he is nice.

- *Wenn* is more often used at the beginning of a sentence, in which case the 'verb as second idea' rule also applies to the second part of the sentence.

  Wenn das Wetter gut ist, **gehe** ich in den Park.
  When the weather is good, I go to the park.

- The connectives *erstens* (first of all), *dann* (then), *danach* (afterwards) and *also* (so) need to be followed by the verb (verb as second idea).

  Erstens gehe ich einkaufen, **dann** mache ich meine Hausaufgaben.
  First I'm going into town, then I'm doing my homework.

E5 Relative clauses

A relative clause is joined to the main clause by a word for 'which', 'that' or 'who'. The words for 'which', 'that' or 'who' are *der* (*den* in the accusative), *die*, *das* and *die*. They agree with the gender and number of the word they refer to. You put a comma straight after the word before *der/die/das/die* and move the verb to the end of the second clause. Sometimes, we miss out the word for 'that' in English, but it must always be there in German.

First clause	Second clause
Es handelt von einem Mann,	**der** ein Paket finden muss.
(It's about a man who has to find a parcel.)	
Wo ist das Buch,	**das** ich gelesen habe?
(Where is the book (that) I read?)	
Der Hund,	**den** die alte Dame sucht, heißt Lumpi.
(The dog (that) the old lady is looking for is called Lumpi.)	

E6 Reported speech

When you want to report what someone thinks or says, you use *denken*, *meinen* or *sagen*, followed by a comma and the word *dass*. The verb in the second clause goes to the end.

Er sagt, **dass** Schokolade ein tolles Geschenk ist.
He says that chocolate is a great present.

E7 Um … zu …

To say 'in order to' (or, usually, just 'to'), you use *um* at the beginning of a clause and *zu*, with an infinitive, at the end.

Wir gehen auf den Markt, **um** Obst **zu** kaufen.
We're going to the market, (in order) to buy fruit.
Um fit **zu** bleiben, esse ich gesund.
(In order) to stay fit, I eat healthily.

E8 *Zu* plus infinitive

Some verbs or expressions need the word *zu* when you use them with the infinitive of another verb.

Lust haben	*to want to*
hoffen	*to hope to*
versuchen	*to try to*
vergessen	*to forget to*
vorhaben	*to intend to*
die Absicht haben	*to intend to*

Zu goes in front of the infinitive. If the second verb is separable it goes between the separable prefix and the infinitive:

Ich habe Lust **zu** schwimmen. *I want to swim.*
Er versucht fit **zu** werden. *He's trying to get fit.*
Wir haben vor, nach Amerika **zu** fliegen.
We're intending to fly to America.
Er hat vergessen seine Badehose mit**zu**bringen.
He forgot to bring his swimming costume with him.

F Asking questions

F1 Verb first

You can ask questions by putting the verb first in the sentence:

Du **hörst** Musik.	→	**Hörst** du Musik?
You are listening to music.	→	*Are you listening to music?*
Birgit **ist** sportlich.	→	**Ist** Birgit sportlich?
Birgit is sporty.	→	*Is Birgit sporty?*

F2 Question words

You can ask a question by starting with a question word. (Remember that the verb comes next.) Most German question words start with **w**:

wer	*who*
wo	*where*
wohin	*where (to)*
woher	*where from*
wann	*when*
was	*what*
wie	*how*
warum	*why*
wie viel(e)	*how much/many*

Wo wohnst du? *Where do you live?*
Wann kommt sie? *When is she coming?*
Wer ist das? *Who is that?*
Wohin gehst du? *Where are you going (to)?*
Woher kommst du? *Where do you come from?*

G Alphabet, numbers, time

G1 The alphabet

The German alphabet is like the English one but with four extra letters: **ä ö ß ü**

G2 Numbers

G2.1 Cardinal numbers

1 eins	6 sechs	11 elf	16 sechzehn
2 zwei	7 sieben	12 zwölf	17 siebzehn
3 drei	8 acht	13 dreizehn	18 achtzehn
4 vier	9 neun	14 vierzehn	19 neunzehn
5 fünf	10 zehn	15 fünfzehn	20 zwanzig

21 einundzwanzig	24 vierundzwanzig
22 zweiundzwanzig	25 fünfundzwanzig
23 dreiundzwanzig	

10 zehn	15 fünfzehn	11 elf
20 zwanzig	25 fünfundzwanzig	21 einundzwanzig
30 dreißig	35 fünfunddreißig	37 siebenunddreißig
40 vierzig	45 fünfundvierzig	43 dreiundvierzig
50 fünfzig	55 fünfundfünfzig	56 sechsundfünfzig
60 sechzig	65 fünfundsechzig	62 zweiundsechzig
70 siebzig	75 fünfundsiebzig	78 achtundsiebzig
80 achtzig	85 fünfundachtzig	84 vierundachtzig
90 neunzig	95 fünfundneunzig	99 neunundneunzig
100 hundert		

G2.2 Ordinal numbers

- To make the ordinal numbers (first, second, etc.) up to 19th you add **-ten** to the cardinal number.
  There are a few exceptions: first (*ersten*), third (*dritten*), seventh (*siebten*) and eighth (*achten*).
- To make the ordinal numbers from 20th upwards you add **-sten** to the cardinal number.

1st	ersten	11th	elften
2nd	zweiten	12th	zwölften
3rd	dritten	13th	dreizehnten
4th	vierten	14th	vierzehnten
5th	fünften	15th	fünfzehnten
6th	sechsten	16th	sechzehnten
7th	siebten	17th	siebzehnten
8th	achten	18th	achtzehnten
9th	neunten	19th	neunzehnten
10th	zehnten	20th	zwanzigsten

When giving dates, use **am** before the number:
Ich habe **am zwölften** Dezember Geburtstag.
My birthday is on the twelfth of December.

G3 The time

To tell the time, you say **es ist** followed by:

The 24-hour clock is used for things like travel information. You simply add 12 to the normal hour and follow it with a number between 1 and 59.

Der Zug nach Berlin fährt um dreizehn Uhr fünf ab.
The train to Berlin leaves at 1.05 p.m.
Der Flug aus London kommt um zwanzig Uhr dreißig an.
The flight from London arrives at 8.30 p.m.

Wortschatz: Deutsch–Englisch

Strategie! ***Using the glossary***

Words are listed in alphabetical order. To find a word, look up its first letter, then find it according to the alphabetical order of its second and third letters:

e.g. **Deutschland** comes before **Dialog** because **de-** comes before **di-**.

The letter(s) in brackets after each noun show you how to form its plural:

e.g. **eine Aktivität → zwei Aktivitäten**
ein Apfel → drei Äpfel
ein Auge → zwei Augen

A

ab *from*
der **Abend (-e)** *m* *evening*
am Abend *in the evening*
das **Abendessen** *n* *evening meal*
abends *in the evening(s)*
der **Abenteuerfilm** *m* *adventure film*
abholen *to pick up*
die **Abitur** *f* *school leaving exam and university entrance qualification*
abfahren (ich bin abgefahren) *to leave, to depart*
abreißen (ich habe abgerissen) *to tear off*
die **Absicht** *f* *intention*
die Absicht haben, *to intend to …*
abspülen *to wash up (dishes, etc.)*
abwaschen *to wash up*
die **Achterbahn** *f* *rollercoaster*
die **Achtung** *f* *attention*
der **Actionfilm** *m* *action film*
die **Adresse (-n)** *f* *address*
ähnlich *similar, the same*
die **Aktivität (-en)** *f* *activity*
aktuell *up to date*
der **Alkohol** *m* *alcohol*
alles *everything*
also *so, therefore*
alt *old*
altmodisch *old-fashioned*
die **Altstadt** *f* *old town*
amüsant *amusing*
amüsieren: sich amüsieren *to have fun*
an 1 *on*
an der Wand *on the wall*
am Samstag *on Saturday*
2 *at*
am Wochenende *at the weekend*
die **Ananas (- or -se)** *f* *pineapple*
das **Andenken (-)** *n* *souvenir*
andere(r, s) *other*
ändern *to change*
der **Anfang (Anfänge)** *m* *beginning*
am Anfang *at the beginning*
anfangen *to begin*
das **Angebot** *n* *offer*
angenehm *pleasant*
die **Angst (Ängste)** *f* *fear*
ich habe Angst vor (+dat) *I'm scared of*
ankommen (ich bin angekommen) *to arrive*
die **Ankunft (Ankünfte)** *f* *arrival*
der **Anorak (-s)** *m* *anorak*
anrufen *to telephone, to call*
anschauen *to look at*
anstrengend *tiring*
die **Antwort (-en)** *f* *answer*
antworten *to answer, reply*
anziehen *to put on*
sich anziehen *to get dressed*
der **Apfel (Äpfel)** *m* *apple*
der **Apfelsaft** *m* *apple juice*
die **Apotheke (-n)** *f* *chemist's, pharmacy*
die **Aprikose (-n)** *f* *apricot*
die **Arbeit** *f* *work*
arbeiten *to work*
der **Arbeitsplatz** *m* *position, job*
der **Arm (-e)** *m* *arm*
arrogant *arrogant*
der **Arzt (Ärzte)** *m* *(male) doctor*
die **Ärztin (-nen)** *f* *(female) doctor*
asiatisch *Asian*
die **Atomkraft** *f* *nuclear energy*
attraktiv *attractive*
auch *also*
auf 1 *on*
auf meinem Bett *on my bed*
2 *in*
auf Deutsch *in German*
3 auf Wiederhören *goodbye (on the phone)*
die **Aufgabe (-n)** *f* *(school) exercise*
aufräumen *to tidy up*
der **Aufschnitt** *m* *sliced cold meat*
der **Aufzug (Aufzüge)** *m* *lift, elevator*
der **Aufschnitt** *m* *(plate of) cold meats*
aufstehen (ich bin aufgestanden) *to get up*
das **Auge (-n)** *n* *eye*
der **Ausblick (-e)** *m* *view*
der **Ausdruck (Ausdrücke)** *m* *expression*
der **Ausflug (Ausflüge)** *m* *trip, outing*
ausprobieren *to try, to try out*
ausräumen *to clear out*
die Spülmaschine ausräumen *to empty the dishwasher*
die **Ausrede (-n)** *f* *excuse*
ausschalten *to switch off*
aussehen *to look*
er sieht gut aus *he looks good*
außerdem *besides*
der **Austausch (-e)** *m* *exchange*
ausziehen (ich bin ausgezogen) *to move out*
das **Auto (-s)** *n* *car*

B

das **Babysitting** *n* *babysitting*
die **Bäckerei (-en)** *f* *baker's*
das **Bad (Bäder)** *n* *bath*
die **Badehose (-n)** *f* *swimming trunks*
baden *to have a bath*
die **Badewanne (-n)** *f* *bath tub*
das **Badezimmer (-)** *n* *bathroom*
die **Bahn (-en)** *f* *railway*
mit der Bahn fahren *to go by rail*
der **Bahnhof (Bahnhöfe)** *m* *station*
der **Bahnsteig (-e)** *m* *platform*
bald *soon*
der **Balkon (-s or -e)** *m* *balcony*
das **Ballet** *n* *ballet*
die **Banane (-n)** *f* *banana*
die **Bank (-en)** *f* *bank*
die **Baseballmütze (-n)** *f* *baseball cap*
der **Basketball** *m* *basketball*
der **Bauernhof (Bauernhöfe)** *m* *farm*
beantworten *to answer*
beginnen (ich habe begonnen) *to begin*
bei 1 *with*
bei den Mitschülern *with fellow pupils*
2 *at*
bei Pizzaman *at Pizzaman*
beide *both*
das **Bein (-e)** *n* *leg*
das **Beispiel (-e)** *n* *example*
beißen *to bite*
bekommen *to get*
Belgien *Belgium*
benehmen: sich benehmen *to behave*
benutzen *to use*
benutzerfreundlich *user-friendly*
der **Berg (-e)** *m* *mountain*
der **Beruf (-e)** *m* *job, profession*
berufstätig: berufstätig sein *to have a job*
berühmt *famous*
beschließen (ich habe beschlossen) *to decide*
beschreiben (ich habe beschrieben) *to describe*
die **Beschreibung (-en)** *f* *description*
besonders *especially*
besser *better*
besser als *better than*
besichtigen *to visit (a place)*
der/die **Besucher(in)** *m/f* *visitor*
betreffen: was mich betrifft *as far as I'm concerned*
das **Bett (-en)** *n* *bed*
ins Bett gehen *to go to bed*
bewerben (ich habe beworben) *to apply*
das **Bier** *n* *beer*
das **Bild (-er)** *n* *picture*
die **Biologie** *f* *biology*
die **Birne (-n)** *f* *pear*
bis *until, up to*
bisschen: ein bisschen *a bit, a little*
bissig *vicious*
bissiger Hund! *beware of the dog!*

bitte *please*
bitte schön 1 *here you are*
2 *you're welcome*
blau *blue*
bleiben (ich bin geblieben) *to stay*
der **Bleistift (-e)** *m* *pencil*
blind *blind*
die **Blockflöte (-n)** *f* *recorder*
blöd *stupid*
die **Bluse (-n)** *f* *blouse*
der **Boden (Böden)** *m* *floor*
die **Bohne (-n)** *f* *bean*
das **Bonbon (-s)** *n* *sweet*
böse *angry*
brandaktuell *up-to-date, the latest*
der **Brauch (Bräuche)** *m* *custom, tradition*
brauchen *to need*
braun *brown*
brav *good, well-behaved*
der **Brief (-e)** *m* *letter*
der/die **Brieffreund(in)** *m/f* *penfriend*
die **Briefmarke (-n)** *f* *(postage) stamp*
der **Briefträger (-)** *m* *postman*
die **Brille (-n)** *f* *(pair of) glasses, spectacles*
bringen (ich habe gebracht) *to bring*
die **Broschüre (-n)** *f* *brochure*
das **Brot** *n* *bread*
das **Brötchen (-)** *n* *bread roll*
Brotwürfel *mpl* *croutons, cubes of bread*
die **Brücke (-n)** *f* *bridge*
der **Bruder (Brüder)** *m* *brother*
das **Buch (Bücher)** *n* *book*
die **Buchhandlung (-en)** *f* *bookshop*
das **Bücherregal (-e)** *n* *bookcase*
der **Buchstabe (-n)** *m* *letter (of the alphabet)*
der **Bungalow (-s)** *m* *bungalow*
bunt *bright(ly coloured)*
die **Bürger** *mpl* *townspeople*
der **Bürgermeister** *m* *mayor*
das **Büro (-s)** *n* *office*
der **Bus (-se)** *m* *bus*
die **Bushaltestelle (-n)** *f* *bus stop*
die **Butter** *f* *butter*
das **Butterbrot (-e)** *n* *sandwich*

C

das **Café (-s)** *n* *café*
der **Campingplatz** *m* *campsite*
die **CD (-s)** *f* *CD*
der **CD-Spieler (-)** *m* *CD player*
der **Charakter (-e)** *m* *character*
der **Chatroom (-s)** *m* *chatroom*
die **Chemie** *f* *chemistry*
die **Chips** *mpl* *crisps*
die **Cola** *f* *cola*
der **Computer (-s)** *m* *computer*
das **Computerspiel (-e)** *n* *computer game*
cool *cool*
der **Cousin (-s)** *m* *(male) cousin*
die **Cousine (-n)** *f* *(female) cousin*

D

das **Dachboden** *n* *attic, loft*
die **Dame (-n)** *f* *lady*
danach *after that*
danke *thank you*
danke schön *thank you very much*
dann *then*
der **Darsteller (-)** *m* *character, actor*
dauern *to last*
dauernd *constantly, all the time*
dazu: dazu nehme ich … *with that I'll have …*
die **Decke (-n)** *f* *ceiling*
decken: den Tisch decken *to lay the table*
denken (ich habe gedacht) *to think*
deprimierend *depressing*
deprimiert *depressed*
das **Design** *n* *design*
designt *designed*
deswegen *therefore*
deutsch *German*
Deutschland *Germany*
deutschsprachig *German-speaking*
Dezember (-) *m* *December*
der **Dialog (-e)** *m* *conversation*
dicht: bist du noch ganz dicht? *are you crazy?*
dick *fat*
Dienstag *Tuesday*
diese/r/s *this*
die **Disko (-s)** *f* *disco*
die **Diskothek (-en)** *f* *discotheque*
doch *yes (in answer to a negative question)*
der **Dom (-e)** *m* *cathedral*
doof *stupid, silly*
Donnerstag *Thursday*
das **Doppelhaus** *n* *semi-detached house*
die **Doppelstunde** *f* *double lesson, double period*
das **Doppelzimmer (-)** *n* *double room*
das **Dorf (Dörfer)** *n* *village*
dort *there*
dran: ich bin dran *it's my turn*
draußen *outside*
das **Dreibettzimmer (-)** *n* *triple room, three-bedded room*
die **Drogerie (-n)** *f* *chemist's shop, drugstore*
dumm *stupid*
dunkel *dark*
dunkelblau *dark blue*
durch *with, through*
das **Durcheinander** *n* *mess*
so ein Durcheinander! *what a mess!*
dürfen *to be allowed to*
ich darf nicht … *I'm not allowed to …*
die **Dusche (-n)** *f* *shower*
duschen *to shower*
die **DVD (-s)** *f* *DVD*

E

die **Ecke (-n)** *f* *corner*
egal: das ist mir egal *I'm not bothered*
eher *rather, sooner*
der **Ehrgeiz** *m* *ambition*
ehrlich *honest*
das **Ei (-er)** *n* *egg*
eigen *own*
eigentlich *really*
einfach *single*
das **Einfamilienhaus** *n* *detached house*
der **Eingang (Eingänge)** *m* *entrance*
einige *some*
Einkäufe: Einkäufe machen *to go shopping*
einkaufen gehen *to go shopping*
der **Einkaufsbummel** *m* *shopping spree*
das **Einkaufszentrum (Einkaufszentren)** *n* *shopping centre*
das **Einkommen** *n* *income*
die **Einladung (-en)** *f* *invitation*
einmal *once*
einmal nach … *a single to …*
einordnen *to (put in) order*
einsam *lonely*
der/die **Einwohner(in)** *m/f* *inhabitant*
das **Einzelzimmer (-)** *n* *single room*
das **Eis** *n* *ice-cream*
das **Eiscafé (-s)** *n* *ice-cream parlour*
das **Eishockey** *n* *ice hockey*
die **Eltern** *pl* *parents*
die **E-Mail** *f* *e-mail*
empfehlen *to recommend*
das **Ende (-n)** *n* *end*
am Ende *at the end*
eng *narrow*
England *England*
englisch *English*
das **Englisch** *n* *(language or subject) English*
auf English *in English*
entdecken *to discover*
entscheiden *to decide*
die **Entscheidung (-en)** *f* *decision*
entschuldigen Sie *excuse me*
Entschuldigung! *sorry!*
die **Erbse (-n)** *f* *pea*
die **Erdbeere (-n)** *f* *strawberry*
die **Erdkunde** *f* *geography*
die **Erde** *f* *earth*
erfinderisch *inventive, imaginative*
der **Erfolg (-e)** *m* *success*
ergänzen *to complete*
erkennen *to recognize*
erleben *to experience*
ersetzen *to replace*
erste/r/s *first*
erstens *first of all*
ertrinken *to drown*
erwachsen *grown up*
Erwachsene *pl* *adults*
erzählen *to tell*
essen (ich habe gegessen) *to eat*
das **Esszimmer (-)** *n* *dining room*

F

das **Fach (Fächer)** *n* *subject*
die **Familie (-n)** *f* *family*
die **Fähre (-n)** *f* *ferry*
fahren (ich bin gefahren) *to go (by car, etc.); to drive*
Rad fahren *to ride a bike, to go cycling*
Ski fahren *to go skiing*
die **Fahrkarte (-n)** *f* *ticket*
die **Fahrt (-en)** *f* *trip*
falsch *wrong*
fantastisch *fantastic*
der **Fantasyfilm** *m* *fantasy film*
die **Farbe (-n)** *f* *colour*
farbenfroh *colourful*
die **Fasnacht** *f* *carnival time*
faul *lazy*
Februar *February*
der **Fehler (-)** *m* *mistake*
feiern *to celebrate*
der **Feiertag** *m* *holiday*
der **Fels (-en)** *m* *cliff*
das **Fenster (-)** *n* *window*
Ferien pl *holidays*
das **Fernsehen** *n* *TV, television*
im Fernsehen *on TV*
fernsehen *to watch TV*
ich habe ferngesehen *I watched TV*
der **Fernseher (-)** *m* *TV (set)*
fertig *finished, ready*
fertig machen *to get (something) ready*
das **Fest (-e)** *n* *celebration, festival*
fett *fat*
fett gedruckt *in bold (print)*

Feuerwerke *npl* *fireworks*
Fieber: ich habe Fieber *I've got a temperature*
der **Film (-e)** *m* *film*
der **Filzstift (-e)** *m* *felt-tip (pen)*
finden (ich habe gefunden) *to find*
der **Finger (-)** *m* *finger*
der **Fisch (-e)** *m* *fish*
das **Fischstäbchen (-)** *n* *fish finger*
das **Fitnesszentrum (Fitnesszentren)** *n* *gym*
die **Flasche (-n)** *f* *bottle*
das **Fleisch** *n* *meat*
fleißig *hard-working*
fliegen (ich bin geflogen) *to fly*
der **Flughafen (Flughäfen)** *m* *airport*
das **Flugzeug (-e)** *n* *plane*
der **Fluss (Flüsse)** *m* *river*
folgen *to follow*
die **Forelle (-n)** *f* *trout*
der/die **Forscher(in)** *m/f* *researcher*
das **Foto (-s)** *n* *photo*
die **Frage (-n)** *f* *question*
die **Frau (-en)** *f* *1 woman*
2 wife
Frau … *Mrs …*
Frankreich *France*
französisch *French*
das **Französisch** *n* *(language or subject) French*
das **Freibad** *n* *open-air pool*
freigiebig *generous*
Freitag *Friday*
freiwillig *voluntary*
die **Freizeit** *f* *free time*
die **Freizeithose (-n)** *f* *jogging bottoms*
der **Freizeitpark (-s)** *m* *amusement park*
der **Freund (-e)** *m* *(male) friend, boyfriend*
die **Freundin (-nen)** *f* *(female) friend, girlfriend*
freundlich *friendly*
die **Freundschaft (-en)** *f* *friendship*
frieren: es friert *it's freezing*
frisch *fresh*
froh *happy*
der **Frosch (Frösche)** *m* *frog*
der **Früchtetee** *m* *fruit tea*
früh *early*
der **Frühling** *m* *spring*
das **Frühstück** *n* *breakfast*
frühstücken *to have breakfast*
fühlen *to feel*
sich … fühlen *to feel …*
funktionieren: es funktioniert nicht *it's not working*
für *for*
furchtbar *terrible*
der **Fuß (Füße)** *m* *foot*
der **Fußball** *m* *football*
der **Fußballfan (-s)** *m* *football fan*
die **Fußballmannschaft (-en)** *f* *football team*
der **Fußballverein (-e)** *m* *football club*
der/die **Fußgänger(in)** *m/f* *pedestrian*
die **Fußgängerzone (-n)** *f* *pedestrian zone*

G

ganz *quite*
gar: gar nichts *nothing at all*
die **Garage (-n)** *f* *garage*
der **Garten (Gärten)** *m* *garden*
die **Gartenarbeit** *f* *gardening*
der **Gast (Gäste)** *m* *guest*
geben *to give*
es gibt … *there is/are …*
was gibt es …? *what is there …?*
geboren *born*
er ist geboren *he was born*
der **Geburtstag** *m* *birthday*
das **Gedicht (-e)** *n* *poem*
geduldig *patient*
gefährlich *dangerous*
gefallen *to please someone, to like*
das **Gefühl (-e)** *n* *feeling*
gegen: gegen 19 Uhr *around 7 p.m.*
die **Gegend (-en)** *f* *region, area*
das **Gegenteil** *n* *opposite*
im Gegenteil *on the other hand*
gegenüber *opposite*
gehen (ich bin gegangen) *to go*
es geht mir nicht gut *I'm not well*
die **Geige (-n)** *f* *violin*
geistlos *stupid, dull*
geizig *mean*
gelaunt: gut gelaunt *pleasant, good-natured*
gelb *yellow*
das **Geld** *n* *money*
der **Geldautomat (-en)** *m* *cash machine*
gemein *mean*
gemischt *mixed*
Gemüse *npl* *vegetables*
ein Gemüse *n* *a vegetable*
genervt: genervt sein *to be worked up, to be irritated*
genug *enough*
geradeaus *straight on*
gerecht *fair*
gern: ich spiele gern Fußball *I like playing football*
ich hätte gern … *I'd like …*
ich würde gern … *I'd like to …*
die **Gesamtschule (-n)** *f* *comprehensive (school)*
der **Gesang** *m* *singing*
das **Geschäft (-e)** *n* *shop*
das **Geschenk (-e)** *n* *present, gift*
die **Geschichte** *f* *history*
Geschwister *pl* *brothers and sisters*
gestern *yesterday*
gestreift *striped*
gesund *healthy*
die **Gesundheit** *f* *health*
gewinnen *to win*
die **Gitarre (-n)** *f* *guitar*
das **Glas (Gläser)** *n* *glass*
glatt *smooth*
glatte Haare *straight hair*
gleich *just*
das **Gleis (-e)** *n* *platform*
glücklich *happy*
glücklicherweise *luckily, fortunately*
der **Goldfisch (-e)** *m* *goldfish*
grau *grey*
grausam *awful*
groß *big, large*
im Großen und Ganzen *on the whole, in the main*
Großeltern *pl* *grandparents*
grün *green*
der **Grund (Gründe)** *m* *reason*
die **Grundschule (-n)** *f* *primary school*
die **Gruppe (-n)** *f* *group*
grüßen *to greet*
grüß dich! *hello!*
gucken *to look*
guck mal! *look!*
das **Gulasch** *n* *goulash*
gut *good, well*
gute Nacht *goodnight*
die **Gymnastik** *f* *gym, PE*

H

das **Haar (-e)** *n* *hair*
sich die Haare waschen *to wash one's hair*
der **Haartrockner (-e)** *m* *hair dryer*
haben *to have*
halb *half*
um halb elf *at half past ten*
das **Hallenbad** *n* *indoor pool*
der **Hals (Hälse)** *m* *neck*
halten *to hold*
etwas für wichtig halten *to consider something important*
die **Haltestelle (-n)** *f* *stop*
der **Hamburger (-)** *m* *hamburger*
der **Hamster (-)** *m* *hamster*
die **Hand (Hände)** *f* *hand*
handeln: es handelt von … *it's about …*
die **Handlung (-en)** *f* *1 shop*
2 plot, action
das **Handtuch (Handtücher)** *n* *towel*
das **Handy (-s)** *n* *mobile (phone)*
hassen *to hate*
hässlich *ugly*
häufig *often*
das **Hauptgericht** *n* *main course*
die **Hauptstadt** *f* *capital city*
die **Hauptstraße** *f* *main street*
das **Haus (Häuser)** *n* *house*
nach Hause kommen *to come home*
zu Hause *at home*
die **Hausarbeit** *f* *housework*
Hausaufgaben *fpl* *homework*
die **Hausfrau** *f* *housewife*
der **Haushalt (-e)** *m* *household*
das **Haustier (-e)** *n* *pet*
das **Heft (-e)** *n* *exercise book*
heiß *hot*
heiraten *to marry*
heißen *to be called*
heiter *fair (of weather)*
helfen *to help*
hellblau *light blue*
das **Hemd (-en)** *n* *shirt*
der **Herbst** *m* *autumn*
der **Herr (-en)** *m* *man*
Herr … *Mr …*
herunterkommen *to come down*
herunterladen *to download*
heute *today*
heute Abend *this evening*
hier *here*
hilfsbereit *helpful*
die **Himbeere (-n)** *f* *raspberry*
der **Himmel** *m* *sky*
der **Himmelskörper (-)** *m* *heavenly body*
hin *there*
hin und zurück *return*
hinter *behind*
historisch *historic*
das **Hobby (-s)** *n* *hobby*
hoch *high*
das **Hochhaus** *n* *high-rise (building)*
höchstens *at (the) most*
hoffen *to hope*
wir hoffen es *we hope so*
Holland *Holland*
hör zu! *listen*
hören *to hear, to listen to*
der **Horrorfilm** *m* *horror film*
die **Hose (-n)** *f* *(pair of) trousers*
hübsch *pretty*
der **Hund (-e)** *m* *dog*

I

die **Idee (-n) f** *idea*
die **Imbissstube (-n) f** *snack bar*
immer *always*
in 1 *in*
2 *to*
ins Kino *to the cinema*
der **Inhalt m** *contents*
die **Informatik f** *computing, ICT*
innerhalb *inside*
die **Insel (-n) f** *island*
insgesamt *altogether*
intelligent *intelligent*
interessant *interesting*
interessieren: sich interessieren für ... *to be interested in ...*
Irland *Ireland*
Italien *Italy*
italienisch *Italian*

J

die **Jacke (-n) f** *jacket*
der **Jäger (-) m** *hunter*
das **Jahr (-e) n** *year*
jährlich *annual(ly)*
die **Jeans f** *(pair of) jeans*
jede/r/s *each, every*
jedes Wochenende *every weekend*
jemand *someone*
jetzt *now*
jeweils *each time*
joggen *to jog*
die **Johannisbeere (-n) f** *blackcurrant*
die **Jugendherberge (-n) f** *youth hostel*
der **Jugendklub m** *youth club*
Jugendliche pl *young people*
das **Jugendzentrum (Jugendzentren) n** *youth centre*
der **Junge (-n) m** *boy*
Juli *July*
jung *young*
Juni *June*

K

der **Kaffee (-s) m** *coffee*
kalt *cold*
das **Kaninchen (-) n** *rabbit*
die **Kapelle (-n) f** *chapel*
kaputt *broken*
etwas kaputt machen *to break something*
kariert *checked*
die **Karotte (-n) f** *carrot*
die **Karriere (-n) f** *career*
die **Karte (-n) f** *card*
Karten spielen *to play cards*
die **Kartoffel (-n) f** *potato*
der **Kartoffelsalat m** *potato salad*
das **Karussell (-s) n** *carousel, merry-go-round*
der **Käse m** *cheese*
der **Kasten (Kästen) m** *box*
die **Kathedrale (-n) f** *cathedral*
die **Katze (-n) f** *cat*
das **Katzenklo n** *litter tray*
kaufen *to buy*
das **Kaufhaus n** *department store*
die **Kegelbahn (-en) f** *bowling alley*
kegeln *to bowl, to go bowling*
kein *no, not any*
der **Keks (-e) m** *biscuit*
das **Keller (-) n** *cellar*
das **Kind (-er) n** *child*
der **Kinderspielplatz m** *playground, play area*
das **Kino (-s) n** *cinema*
die **Kirche (-n) f** *church*
die **Kirmes f** *fair*
die **Kirsche (-n) f** *cherry*
Klamotten pl *clothes*
die **Klarinette (-n) f** *clarinet*
die **Klasse (-n) f** *class*
klasse *great*
die **Klassenarbeit (-en) f** *test*
das **Klassenzimmer (-) n** *classroom*
das **Klavier (-e) n** *piano*
kleben *to stick*
das **Kleid (-er) n** *dress*
Kleider pl *clothes*
der **Kleiderschrank (Kleiderschränke) m** *wardrobe*
die **Kleidung f** *clothing*
klein *small*
das **Klo (-s) n** *toilet, loo*
der **Klub (-s) m** *club*
knapp *almost*
ein knappes Jahr *almost a year*
der **Koch (Köche) m** *(male) cook*
kochen *to cook*
die **Köchin (-nen) f** *(female) cook*
der **Koffer (-) m** *(suit)case*
das **Kölnischwasser n** *eau de cologne*
kommen (ich bin gekommen) *to come*
die **Komödie (-n) f** *comedy*
die **Konditorei (-en) f** *cake shop*
können *to be able to*
ich kann *I can*
das **Konzert (-e) n** *concert*
der **Kopf (Köpfe) m** *head*
Kopfschmerzen: ich habe Kopfschmerzen *I have a headache*
kopieren *to copy*
kosten *to cost*
köstlich *delicious*
Krach: es gibt Krach *there's trouble/a row*
krank *sick, ill*
das **Krankenhaus n** *hospital*
der **Kräutertee m** *herbal tea*
die **Krawatte (-n) f** *tie*
der **Kriegsfilm m** *war film*
die **Küche (-n) f** *kitchen*
der **Kuchen (-) m** *cake*
der **Kuli (-s) m** *(ballpoint) pen*
die **Kunst f** *art*
der/die **Künstler(in) m/f** *artist*
kurz *short*
küssen *to kiss*

L

lachen *to laugh*
der **Laden (Läden) m** *shop*
die **Ladezeit (-en) f** *loading time*
die **Lampe (-n) f** *lamp*
das **Land (Länder) n** *country*
auf dem Land *in the country*
die **Landstraße (-n) f** *road*
lang *long*
langsam *slow, slowly*
langsamer *slower, more slowly*
langweilig *boring*
der **Lärm m** *noise*
lassen (ich habe gelassen) *to leave*
launisch *moody*
laut *loud*
lauter *nothing but*
das **Leben (-) n** *life*
das **Lebensmittel n** *food*
lecker *delicious*
das **Leder (-) n** *leather*
die **Lederjacke (-n) f** *leather jacket*
der **Lehrer (-) m** *(male) teacher*
die **Lehrerin (-nen) f** *(female) teacher*
Leid: es tut mir Leid *I'm sorry*
leiden: ich kann ... nicht leiden *I can't stand ...*
leider *unfortunately*
leisten *to achieve*
lernen *to learn*
lesen *to read*
letzte/r/s *last*
Leute pl *people*
das **Licht (-er) n** *light*
die **Liebe f** *love*
liebe/r/s *dear*
lieber: ich sehe lieber fern *I prefer watching TV*
ich würde lieber ... *I prefer to ...*
Lieblings ... *favourite ...*
mein Lieblingsfilm *my favourite film*
liebsten: ich lese am liebsten *I like reading best of all*
liegen *to lie*
lies ... mit! *read along*
lila *lilac*
die **Limo(nade) f** *lemonade*
das **Lineal (-e) n** *ruler*
links *left*
das **Loch (Löcher) n** *hole*
lockig: lockige Haare *curly hair*
der **Lohn (Löhne) m** *wage(s), pay*
los: was ist los? *what's wrong?*
hier ist nichts los *there's nothing happening here*
die **Lücke (-n) f** *gap*
lügen *to lie*
Lust: hast du Lust ...? *do you want to ...?*
lustig *cheerful, full of fun*
sich lustig über etwas machen *to make fun of something*

M

machen *to do, to make*
ich mache meine Hausaufgaben *I do my homework*
mach's gut *take care*
Ausreden machen *to make excuses*
das **Mädchen (-) n** *girl*
mag: ich mag *I like*
der **Magen m** *stomach*
Magenschmerzen: ich habe Magenschmerzen *I have stomach-ache*
die **Mahlzeit (-en) f** *meal*
Mai *May*
das **Mal (-e) n** *time*
jedes Mal *each time*
man *one, you*
manchmal *sometimes*
der **Mann (Männer) m** 1 *man*
2 *husband*
die **Mannschaft (-en) f** *team*
der **Mantel (Mäntel) m** *coat*
der **Markt (Märkte) m** *market*
der **Marktplatz (Marktplätze) m** *market place*
die **Marmelade f** *jam*
der **Martial-Arts-Film m** *martial arts film*
die **Maske (-n) f** *mask*
die **Mathe f** *maths*
die **Maus (Mäuse) f** *mouse*
das **Meerschweinchen (-) n** *guinea pig*
mehr *more*
mehr als *more than*
die **Meinung (-en) f** *opinion*
meisten: die meisten *most (of them)*
meistens *usually*
melden *to announce*
meld' dich mal *stay in touch*

die **Menge (-n) f** *crowd*
eine Menge ... *lots of ...*
der **Mensch (-en) m** *person*
merkwürdig *strange, curious*
die **Metzgerei (-en) f** *butcher's (shop)*
mieten *to rent*
die **Milch f** *milk*
mindestens *at least*
das **Mineralwasser n** *mineral water*
der **Mist m** *rubbish, nonsense*
mit *with*
mitbringen *to bring along*
das **Mitglied (-er) n** *member*
mitkommen *to come along*
die **Mitschüler pl** *fellow pupils*
der **Mittag m** *midday*
das **Mittagessen n** *lunch, midday meal*
die **Mitte (-n) f** *middle*
mittelalterlich *medieval*
mittelgroß *average-sized, medium-sized*
das **Mittelmeer n** *Mediterranean*
Mittwoch *Wednesday*
die **Mode (-n) f** *fashion*
das **Modegeschäft n** *boutique, fashion store*
mögen *to like*
ich möchte *I'd like*
die **Möhre (-n) f** *carrot*
der **Monat (-e) m** *month*
einmal pro Monat *once a month*
der **Mond (-e) m** *moon*
Montag *Monday*
morgen *tomorrow*
der **Morgen m** *morning*
am Morgen *in the morning*
guten Morgen *hello, good morning*
müde *tired*
muffig *grumpy*
mühsam *arduous, laborious*
der **Müll m** *rubbish*
der **Mund (Münder) m** *mouth*
das **Museum (Museen) n** *museum*
die **Musik f** *music*
müssen: ich muss *I must, I have to*
die **Mutter (Mütter) f** *mother*
Mutti f *Mum*
die **Mütze (-n) f** *cap*

N

nach 1 *after*
nach der Schule *after school*
2 *past*
Viertel nach (drei) *quarter past (three)*
3 *to*
nach England *to England*
der/die **Nachbar(in) m/f** *neighbour*
der **Nachmittag m** *afternoon*
am Nachmittag *in the afternoon*
nachmittags *in the afternoon*
die **Nachricht (-en) f** *message*
nächste/r/s *next*
die **Nacht (Nächte) f** *night*
der **Nachtisch (-) m** *dessert*
Nähe: in der Nähe *nearby*
nämlich *namely*
der **Name (-n) m** *name*
die **Nase (-n) f** *nose*
natürlich *of course, naturally*
Naturwissenschaften pl *science*
das **Navigationsmenü n** *navigation bar/menu*
neben *next to, near*
der **Nebenjob (-s) m** *part-time job*
neblig *foggy*
nehmen (ich habe genommen) *to take*
nervig *irritating*
nennen *to name*
nett *nice*
neu *new*
nicht *not*
Nichtraucher *non-smoking*
nichts *nothing*
nie *never*
das **Nilpferd (-e) n** *hippo(potamus)*
niemand *no-one, nobody*
noch 1 *still, yet*
noch ein bisschen *a bit more*
2 was noch? *what else?*
noch einmal *once again*
der **Norden m** *north*
normalerweise *normally, usually*
November *November*
die **Note (-n) f** *(school) mark*
null *zero*
die **Nummer (-n) f** *number*
die **Nuss (Nüsse) f** *nut*

O

ob *whether*
das **Oberteil (-e) n** *top*
oder *or*
oft *often*
ohne *without*
das **Ohr (-en) n** *ear*
Ohrenschmerzen: ich habe Ohrenschmerzen *I have earache*
Oktober *October*
die **Oma (-s) f** *granny*
der **Onkel (-) m** *uncle*
der **Opa (-s) m** *grandpa*
das **Opfer (-) n** *victim*
die **Orange (-n) f** *orange*
orange *orange*
ordentlich *tidy*
Ordnung: in Ordnung *OK*
originell *original*
der **Ort (-e) m** *place*
der **Osten m** *east*
Ostern n *Easter*
Österreich *Austria*
österreichisch *Austrian*

P

das **Papier n** *paper*
paragliden *to paraglide*
das **Parfüm (-e) n** *perfume*
der **Park (-s) m** *park*
das **Parkhaus n** *multi-storey carpark*
die **Party (-s) f** *party*
passen zu *to match*
die **Pause (-n) f** *break*
die **Person (-en) f** *person*
persönlich *personal*
die **Pfeife (-n) f** *pipe*
das **Pferd (-e) n** *horse*
das **Picknick (-s) n** *picnic*
die **Pizza (-s) f** *pizza*
die **Physik** *physics*
die **Plage (-n) f** *plague*
der **Planet (-en) m** *planet*
die **Plastiktüte (-n) f** *plastic bag*
Plateauschuhe mpl *platform shoes*
der **Platz (Plätze) m** 1 *place*
2 *(town) square*
3 *site*
das **Plüschtier n** *soft toy*
die **Polizei f** *police*
der/die **Polizist(in) m/f** *police officer*
das **Poloshirt n** *polo shirt*
Pommes frites pl *chips*
das **Portmonee (-s) n** *purse*
die **Post f** 1 *post office*
2 *post, mail*
das **Poster (-s) n** *poster*
die **Postkarte (-n) f** *postcard*
praktisch *practical*
prima *great*
pro *per*
pro Woche *per week*
das **Problem (-e) n** *problem*
die **Prüfung (-en) f** *exam*
der **Pulli (-s) m** *jumper*
pünktlich *punctual*
die **Puppe (-n) f** *doll*
putzen *to clean, to polish*

Q

das **Quiz (-) n** *quiz*

R

das **Rad (Räder) n** *bicycle*
Rad fahren *to cycle*
radeln *to cycle*
das **Radiergummi (-s) n** *rubber, eraser*
das **Radio (-s) n** *radio*
das **Rathaus n** *town hall*
die **Ratte (-n) f** *rat*
der **Rattenfänger m** *rat catcher*
rauchen *to smoke*
Raucher *smoker*
das **Recht (-e) n** *right*
rechts *right*
reden *to speak*
das **Regal (-e) n** *shelves*
die **Regel (-n) f** *rule*
regelmaßig *regular(ly)*
der **Regen m** *rain*
regnen: es regnet *it's raining*
reichen 1 *to pass*
2 *to be enough*
das reicht *that's enough*
die **Reihenfolge (-n) f** *order*
das **Reihenhaus n** *terraced house*
reimen: sich reimen *to rhyme*
der **Reis m** *rice*
die **Reise (-n) f** *journey, trip*
das **Reisebüro n** *travel agent's*
reisen *to travel*
die **Religion f** *(school) RE, religious studies*
rennen *to run*
reservieren *to reserve*
die **Reservierung (-en) f** *reservation*
das **Restaurant (-s) n** *restaurant*
richtig *right, correct*
das **Riesenrad n** *ferris wheel*
riesig *huge*
das **Rindfleisch n** *beef*
der **Ring (-e) m** *ring*
der **Rock (Röcke) m** *skirt*
die **Rolle (-n) f** *role, part*
Rollschuh: Rollschuh fahren *to go roller-skating*
die **Rolltreppe (-n) f** *escalator*
rosa *pink*
die **Rose (-n) f** *rose*
rot *red*
der **Rotwein m** *red wine*
der **Rücken (-) m** *back*
ruhig *quiet*
rühren *to stir*
ruiniert *ruined*

S

die **Sache (-n) f** *thing*
der **Saft (Säfte) m** *fruit juice*
sagen *to say*
die **Sahne f** *cream*
der **Salat (-e) m** *salad*
salzig *salty*

sammeln *to collect*
der **Sammler (-) m** *collector*
die **Sammlung (-en) f** *collection*
Samstag *Saturday*
der/die **Sänger(in) m/f** *singer*
der **Satz (Sätze) m** *sentence*
saugen *to suck*
schade! *(what a) pity!*
schauen *to look*
der/die **Schauspieler(in) m/f** *actor*
schicken *to send*
die **Schießhalle f** *shooting gallery*
der **Schinken m** *ham*
schlafen *to sleep*
das **Schlafzimmer (-) n** *bedroom*
die **Schlaghose f** *flares*
die **Schlange (-n) f** *snake*
schlank *slim*
schlecht *bad*
schliessen *to close*
schlimm *bad*
das **Schloss (Schlösser) n** *castle*
der **Schluss (Schlüsse) m** *end*
zum Schluss *in the end*
der **Schlüssel (-) m** *key*
das **Schlüsselloch n** *keyhole*
der **Schlüsselring m** *key ring*
schmecken: das hat geschmeckt! *that was good!, that tasted good!*
schmelzen *to melt*
der **Schmerz (-en) m** *pain*
schmutzig *dirty*
der **Schnaps m** *schnapps (clear spirits)*
schneien: es schneit *it's snowing*
schnell *fast, quickly*
schneller *faster*
der **Schnitz (-e) m** *piece, segment*
die **Schokolade f** *chocolate*
schon *already*
schön *beautiful, nice, lovely*
Schottland *Scotland*
schreiben (ich habe geschrieben) *to write*
der **Schreibwarenladen m** *stationer's*
schüchtern *shy*
der **Schuh (-e) m** *shoe*
das **Schuhgeschäft n** *shoe shop*
die **Schule (-n) f** *school*
der **Schüler (-) m** *schoolboy, (male) pupil*
die **Schülerin (-nen) f** *schoolgirl, (female) pupil*
das **Schulfach n** *school subject*
die **Schultasche (-n) f** *schoolbag*
die **Schulter (-n) f** *shoulder*
die **Schuluniform (-en) f** *school uniform*
schwarz *black*
die **Schwarzwälder Kirschtorte f** *Black Forest cherry cake/gateau*
das **Schwein (-e) n** *pig*
das **Schweinefleisch n** *pork*
die **Schweiz f** *Switzerland*
schwer *difficult*
die **Schwester (-) f** *sister*
das **Schwimmbad n** *swimming pool*
der/die **Schwimmer(in) m/f** *swimmer*
schwimmen *to swim*
der **Science-Fiction-Film m** *science fiction film*
der **Seehund m** *seal*
segeln *to sail, to go sailing*
sehen *to see*
die **Sehenswürdigkeiten fpl** *sights*
sehr *very*
seit *since*
die **Seite (-n) f** *1 page*
2 web page/site
selbstbewusst *self-confident*
selbstsüchtig *selfish*
selten *seldom*
September *September*
servieren *to serve*
die **Shorts pl** *(pair of) shorts*
sicher *certainly*
die **Sicherheit f** *safety*
sieh dir ... an! *look at the ...*
die **Silhouette (-n) f** *silhouette, outline*
sitzen *to sit*
sitzen bleiben *to repeat a year (at school)*
Skateboard: Skateboard fahren *to skateboard*
der **Skilift (-e or -s) m** *ski lift*
der **Skipass (Skipässe) m** *ski pass*
die **Socke (-n) f** *sock*
sofort *immediately, at once*
sogar *even*
so genannt *so-called*
sollen: du sollst nicht ... *you shouldn't ...*
der **Sommer m** *summer*
die **Sonne (-n) f** *sun*
die **Sonnenblume (-n) f** *sunflower*
die **Sonnenbrille (-n) f** *(pair of) sunglasses*
Sonntag *Sunday*
die **Soße (-n) f** *sauce*
die **Sorge (-n) f** *worry*
ich mache mir Sorgen *I'm worried*
die **Sozialkunde f** *PSHE*
Spanien *Spain*
spanisch *Spanish*
spannend *exciting*
der **Spaß m** *fun*
das hat viel Spaß *gemacht* *it was a lot of fun*
spät *late*
der **Spaziergang m** *walk*
einen Spaziergang *machen* *to go for a walk*
die **Speisekarte (-n) f** *menu*
spenden *to donate, to give*
das **Spiel (-e) n** *game*
spielen *to play*
die **Spinne (-n) f** *spider*
der **Spitzname (-n) m** *nickname*
Sportschuhe mpl *trainers*
sportlich *sporty*
das **Sportgeschäft n** *sports shop*
das **Sportzentrum n** *sports centre*
sprechen *to speak*
sprich nach! *repeat*
springen *to jump*
die **Spülmaschine (-n) f** *dishwasher*
das **Stadion (Stadien) n** *stadium*
die **Stadt (Städte) f** *town, city*
die **Stadtmitte (-n) f** *town centre, city centre*
der **Stadtrand m: am Stadtrand** *in the suburbs, on the outskirts of (the) town*
das **Stadtzentrum (-zentren) npl** *town centre*
der **Starrkopf m** *stubborn person, numskull*
stattfinden *to take place*
der **Staub m** *dust*
Staub saugen *to vacuum, hoover*
steigen *1 to climb*
2 to get in
die **Stelle (-n) f** *place*
sterben (ich bin gestorben) *to die*
die **Stiefmutter f** *stepmother*
der **Stiefvater m** *stepfather*
der **Stift (-e) m** *pencil*
der **Stil (-e) m** *style*
stimmt: das stimmt *that's right*
stinken: hier stinkt es *it stinks here*
stinkfaul *bone idle*
der **Stock (-) m** *floor, storey*
die **Stofftüte (-n) f** *cloth bag*
der **Strand (Strände) m** *beach*
die **Straße (-n) f** *street*
die **Straßenbahn (-en) f** *tram*
streben: streben nach *to strive for, try*
streng *strict*
die **Struktur f** *structure*
die **Strumpfhose (-n) f** *(pair of) tights*
das **Stück (-e) n** *piece*
das **Stückchen (-) n** *small piece*
der/die **Student(in) m/f** *student*
der **Stuhl (Stühle) m** *chair*
stumm *mute*
der **Stummfilm m** *silent movie*
die **Stunde (-n) f** *1 lesson*
2 hour
der **Stundenplan m** *timetable*
suchen *to look for*
der **Süden m** *south*
super *super, great*
der **Supermarkt (Supermärkte) m** *supermarket*
süß *sweet*
das **Sweatshirt (-s) n** *sweatshirt*
sympathisch *nice, pleasant*

T

die **Tabelle (-n) f** *table (of figures, etc.)*
die **Tafel (-n) f** *blackboard*
der **Tag (-e) m** *day*
jeden Tag *every day*
das **Tagebuch n** *diary*
die **Tagesroutine f** *daily routine*
die **Tankstelle (-n) f** *petrol station*
die **Tante (-n) f** *aunt*
tanzen *to dance*
der/die **Tänzer(in) m/f** *dancer*
die **Tasche (-n) f** *bag*
das **Taschengeld n** *money*
tauschen *to swap*
tausend *thousand*
die **Technik f** *technology*
der **Tee (-s) m** *tea*
die **Telefonzelle (-n) f** *telephone kiosk*
die **Terrasse (-n) f** *terrace*
teuer *expensive, dear*
der **Text m** *text*
das **Theater (-) n** *theatre*
das **Tier (-e) n** *animal*
der **Tierarzt m** *(male) vet*
die **Tierärztin f** *(female) vet*
der **Tisch (-e) m** *table*
das **Tischtennis n** *table tennis*
der **Titel (-) m** *title*
das **Titelblatt n** *cover (of magazine)*
die **Toilette (-n) f** *toilet*
toll *brilliant, great*
die **Tomate (-n) f** *tomato*
die **Tomatensuppe f** *tomato soup*
total *absolutely*
töten *to kill*
das **Tourismus n** *tourism*
tragen *to wear*
der **Trainingsanzug m** *tracksuit*
der **Traum (Träume) m** *dream*
träumen *to dream*
traurig *sad*
treffen *to meet*
wir treffen uns *we are meeting, we meet*
treiben: Sport treiben *to do sports*
trennbar *separable*
trennen *to separate*
die **Treppe (-n) f** *staircase, stairs*
trinken (ich habe getrunken) *to drink*

die **Trompete (-n)** *f* *trumpet*
tropfen *to drip*
trotzdem *nevertheless*
tschüs *bye*
das **T-Shirt (-s)** *n* *T-shirt*
die **Tür (-en)** *f* *door*
türkis *turquoise*
die **Tüte (-n)** *f* *bag*

U

die **U-Bahn** *f* *underground*
über 1 *above*
2 *about*
überall *everywhere*
überhaupt: überhaupt nicht *not at all*
übernachten *to stay, spend the night*
überprüfen *to check*
die **Überraschung (-en)** *f* *surprise*
überzeugend *convincing*
überzeugt *convinced*
ich bin davon überzeugt, dass … *I am convinced that …*
die **Übung (-en)** *f* *exercise*
die **Uhr (-en)** *f*
1 *hour*
um neun Uhr *at nine o'clock*
um wieviel Uhr? *at what time?*
2 *clock*
die **Uhrzeit** *f* *time*
um 1 *at*
um neun Uhr *at nine o'clock*
2 um … zu … *in order to …*
die **Umfrage (-n)** *f* *survey*
die **Umgangssprache (-n)** *f* *colloquialism*
die **Umgebung** *f* *surroundings*
umsteigen *to change (train, bus, etc.)*
die **Umwelt** *f* *environment*
umweltfeindlich *harmful to the environment*
umweltfreundlich *environmentally friendly*
die **Umweltverschmutzung** *f* *pollution*
der **Umzug (Umzüge)** *m* *procession*
uncool *not cool*
und *and*
unfair *unfair*
der **Unfall (Unfälle)** *m* *accident*
ungefähr *about, approximately*
ungesund *unhealthy*
unglaubhaft *unbelievable, unbelievably*
unheimlich *incredible, incredibly*
ich mag … unheimlich gern *I really like …*
die **Uniform (-en)** *f* *uniform*
unmodern *not modern*
unordentlich *untidy*
der **Unsinn** *m* *nonsense, rubbish*
unter *under*
unterhalten: sich unterhalten *to talk*
usw. (= und so weiter) *etc.*

V

der **Vater (Väter)** *m* *father*
der **Vati (-s)** *m* *dad*
veraltet *out-of-date*
vorbereiten *to get ready*
verbessern *to improve*
verbinden *to join*
verbittert *bitter(ly)*
verboten *forbidden*
verbringen *to spend (time)*
verdienen *to earn*
vergessen *to forget*
der **Vergleich (-e)** *m* *comparison*
der **Verkehr** *m* *traffic*
verlangen *to demand*
verlassen *to leave*
verlieren (ich habe verloren) *to lose*
versammeln: sich versammeln *to gather*
verschieden *different*
verschwinden *to disappear*
die **Verspätung (-en)** *f* *delay*
versprechen *to promise*
verstehen *to understand*
vertreiben *to chase away*
vervollständigen *to complete*
verwirklichen *to realise, to put into practice*
vorstellen: stell dir vor *imagine*
viel *a lot*
vielleicht *perhaps, maybe*
die **Viertelstunde (-n)** *f* *quarter of an hour*
violett *violet*
Vitamine *pl* *vitamins*
Vokabeln *pl* *vocabulary*
voll *full*
voll besetzt *fully booked*
Vollkornprodukte *pl* *wholemeal foods*
von *from*
von mir aus *it's all the same to me*
vor 1 *in front of*
2 *to*
Viertel vor (vier) *quarter to (four)*
das **Vorbild** *n* *example*
vorhaben *to plan (to)*
hast du was vor? *have you got any plans?*
der **Vorort** *m* *suburb*
der **Vorschlag (Vorschläge)** *m* *suggestion*
die **Vorspeise (-n)** *f* *starter*

W

wählen *to choose*
Wales *Wales*
die **Wand (Wände)** *f* *wall*
wann *when*
das **Wappen (-)** *n* *badge*
warm *warm*
warten *to wait*
was *what*
was ist …? *what is …?*
das **Waschbecken (-)** *n* *basin*
waschen: (sich) waschen *to wash (oneself)*
das **Wasser** *n* *water*
weder … noch *neither … nor*
weggehen *to go away*
weh: es tut (mir) weh *it hurts*
Weihnachten *pl* *Christmas*
Weihnachtsferien *pl* *Christmas holidays*
weil *because*
der **Wein** *m* *wine*
Weintrauben *pl* *grapes*
weiß *white*
weit *far*
welche/r/s *which*
der **Wellensittich (-e)** *m* *budgie*
die **Welt** *f* *world*
der **Weltraum** *m* *(outer) space*
wenig *little, not much*
wenigstens *at least*
wenn *if, when*
wer *who*
der **Westen** *m* *west*
das **Wetter** *n* *weather*
wichtig *important*
wie 1 *how*
wie geht's? *how are you?*
wie lange *how long*
wie oft *how often*
wie viel(e) *how much, how many*
2 *what*
wie spät ist es? *what time is it?*
3 wie bitte? *pardon?*
wiederholen *to repeat*
Wien *Vienna*
willkommen *welcome*
windig *windy*
der **Winter** *m* *winter*
der **Winzling (-e)** *m* *tiny person, mite*
wirklich *really*
wissen *to know*
weißt du was? *do you know what?*
witzig *fun, jolly*
wo *where*
die **Woche (-n)** *f* *week*
das **Wochenende (-n)** *n* *weekend*
am Wochenende *at the weekend*
woher *where from*
wohin *where (to)*
wohnen *to live*
das **Wohnmobil (-e)** *n* *motor-home*
der **Wohnort** *m* *place of residence*
die **Wohnung (-en)** *f* *flat, apartment*
der **Wohnwagen (-)** *m* *caravan*
das **Wohnzimmer (-)** *n* *living room*
wolkig *cloudy*
wollen *to want*
das **Wort (Wörter)** *n* *word*
das **Wörterbuch** *n* *dictionary*
der **Wunsch (Wünsche)** *m* *wish*
der **Würfel (-)** *m* *cube, dice*
würfeln *to throw (dice, etc.)*
die **Wurst (Würste)** *f* *sausage*

Z

die **Zahl (-en)** *f* *number*
die **Zahn (Zähne)** *f* *tooth*
Zahnschmerzen: ich habe Zahnschmerzen *I have toothache*
die **Zeichentrickfigur (-en)** *f* *cartoon character*
der **Zeichentrickfilm** *m* *cartoon film*
zeichnen *to draw*
zeigen *to show*
die **Zeit** *f* *time*
die **Zeitschrift (-en)** *f* *magazine*
die **Zeitung (-en)** *f* *newspaper*
Zeitungen austragen *to do a paper round*
das **Zelt (-e)** *n* *tent*
das **Zeugnis (-se)** *n* *report*
das **Ziel (-e)** *n* *goal*
ziemlich *quite*
das **Zimmer (-)** *n* *room*
der **Zoo (-s)** *m* *zoo*
zu 1 *to*
zur Schule *to school*
2 *too*
zu viel *too much*
3 *for*
zu Frühstück *for breakfast*
4 zu Fuß *on foot*
zuerst *first*
der **Zug (Züge)** *m* *train*
die **Zukunft** *f* *future*
zusammen *together*
die **Zusammenfassung (-en)** *f* *summary*
zusammenpassen *to match (up)*
der **Zweck (-e)** *m* *purpose*
zweimal *twice*
zweite/r/s *second*
die **Zwiebel (-n)** *f* *onion*
zwischen *between*

Wortschatz: Englisch–Deutsch

Strategie! *Using the glossary*

Some words will need to be changed when you use them in a sentence, e.g.

- nouns: – are they singular or plural?
  – do you need the word for 'a' (***ein*** m, ***eine*** f, ***ein*** n) instead of 'the' (***der*** m, ***die*** f, ***das*** n)?
  – do the words for 'a' and 'the' need to change (***ein*** m → ***einen***, ***der*** m → ***den***, ***der*** m/***das*** n → ***dem***)?
  (And remember that *kein/mein*, etc. take the same endings as *ein*.)
- adjectives: do they need an ending?
- verbs: check the grammar section for the endings you need.

A

a, an **ein m, eine f, ein n**
able: to be able to ***können***
adults **Erwachsene pl**
afternoon ***der Nachmittag*** m
in the afternoon **am Nachmittag**
allowed: I'm not allowed to ... ***ich darf nicht ...***
and ***und***
arm ***der Arm (Ärme)*** m
armchair ***der Sessel (-)*** m
arrive ***ankommen***
art ***die Kunst*** f
ask ***fragen***
at: 1 at the window **am Fenster**
2 at 6 o'clock **um 6 Uhr**
3 at Christmas **zu Weihnachten**
Austria **Österreich**
average-sized ***mittelgroß***
awful ***furchtbar***

B

back ***der Rücken (-)*** m
bad ***schlecht, schlimm***
baker's ***die Bäckerei (-en)*** f
bath: to have a bath ***baden***
bath(tub) ***die Badewanne (-n)*** f
ballpoint (pen) ***der Kuli (-s)*** m
beautiful ***schön***
below ***unter***
between ***zwischen***
big ***groß***
bike ***das Rad (Räder)*** n
biology ***die Biologie*** f
black ***schwarz***
blond ***blond***
blue ***blau***
book ***das Buch (Bücher)*** n
boring ***langweilig***
bread ***das Brot*** n
bread roll ***das Brötchen (-)*** n
breakfast ***das Frühstück (-e)*** n
bright(ly coloured) ***bunt***
brother ***der Bruder (Brüder)*** m
brown ***braun***
budgie ***der Wellensittich (-e)*** m
bus ***der Bus (-se)*** m
but ***aber***
butcher's ***die Metzgerei (-en)*** f

C

cake shop ***die Konditorei (-en)*** f
campsite ***der Campingplatz*** m
can: I can ***ich kann***
car ***das Auto (-s)*** n
caravan ***der Wohnwagen (-)*** m
cat ***die Katze (-n)*** f
CD ***die CD (-s)*** f
CD-player ***der CD-Spieler (-)*** m
ceiling ***die Decke (-n)*** f
club ***der Verein (-e)*** m
chair ***der Stuhl (Stühle)*** m
cheese ***der Käse*** m
chemist's ***die Apotheke (-n)*** f
child ***das Kind (-er)*** n
chocolate ***die Schokolade*** f
Christmas **Weihnachten pl**
Christmas holidays **Weihnachtsferien pl**
cinema ***das Kino (-s)*** n
citizens ***die Bürger*** mpl
clothes **Klamotten pl**
coat ***der Mantel (Mäntel)*** m
cold ***kalt***
come ***kommen (ich bin gekommen)***
computer ***der Computer (-)*** m
computer game ***das Computerspiel (-e)*** n
cream ***die Sahne*** f
crisps ***die Chips*** mpl
curly ***lockig***
curly hair ***lockige Haare***
cycling: to go cycling **Rad fahren**

D

dance ***tanzen***
dancing ***das Tanzen*** n
dangerous ***gefährlich***
dead ***tot***
Denmark ***Dänemark***
department store ***das Kaufhaus*** n
difficult ***schwer***
dinner: to have dinner ***zu Abend essen***
disappear ***verschwinden***
dog ***der Hund (-e)*** m
download ***herunterladen***
dress ***das Kleid (-er)*** n
drink ***trinken (ich habe getrunken)***
drown ***ertrinken***

E

ear ***das Ohr (-en)*** n
earache: I have earache ***ich habe Ohrenschmerzen***
Easter ***Ostern*** n
easy ***einfach***
eat ***essen***
enormous ***riesig***
evening ***der Abend (-e)*** m
in the evening **am Abend**
every ***jede/r/s***
everything ***alles***
exercise book ***das Heft (-e)*** n
expensive ***teuer***
eye ***das Auge (-n)*** n

F

factory ***die Fabrik (-en)*** f
fair (of weather) ***heiter***
farm ***der Bauernhof (Bauernhöfe)*** m
fast ***schnell***
favourite **Lieblings-**
my favourite subject **mein Lieblingsfach**
felt-tip (pen) ***der Filzstift (-e)*** m
ferry ***die Fähre (-n)*** f
finger ***der Finger (-)*** m
floor ***der Boden*** m
fly ***fliegen (ich bin geflogen)***
foggy ***neblig***
follow ***folgen***
food ***das Essen*** n
foot ***der Fuß (Füße)*** m
on foot ***zu Fuß***
football ***der Fußball*** m
forget ***vergessen***
Friday ***Freitag***
France ***Frankreich***
freezing: it's freezing ***es friert***
friend ***der Freund (-e)*** m, ***die Freundin (-nen)*** f
fruit ***das Obst*** n
fruit juice ***der Saft (Säfte)*** m
fun ***der Spaß***
it would be fun **das würde Spaß machen**

G

gardening ***die Gartenarbeit*** f
generous ***freigiebig***
geography ***die Erdkunde*** f
Germany ***Deutschland***
get up ***aufstehen (ich bin aufgestanden)***
girl ***das Mädchen (-)*** n
go 1 (on foot) ***gehen (ich bin gegangen)***
I go to bed ***ich gehe ins Bett***
2 (by car, bike, etc) ***fahren (ich bin gefahren)***
goldfish ***der Goldfisch (-e)*** m
good ***gut***
good morning! ***guten Morgen!***
grey ***grau***
guitar ***die Gitarre (-n)*** f

H

hair **Haare pl**
curly hair ***lockige Haare***
straight hair ***glatte Haare***
half: half past six **halb sieben**
hamster ***der Hamster (-)*** m
hand ***die Hand (Hände)*** f
hard-working ***fleißig***
hat ***der Hut (Hüte)*** m
have ***haben (ich habe gehabt)***
head ***der Kopf (Köpfe)*** m
healthy ***gesund***
helpful ***hilfsbereit***

history **die Geschichte f**
holiday **der Feiertag (-e) m**
on holiday **auf Urlaub**
holidays **Ferien pl**
home: at home **zu Hause**
homework **die Hausaufgaben fpl**
honest **ehrlich**
horse **das Pferd (-e) n**
hot **heiß**
hotel **das Hotel (-s) n**
house **das Haus (Häuser) n**
hungry: I'm hungry **ich habe Hunger**

I

ice-cream **das Eis n**
ICT **die Informatik f**
irritating **nervig**
Italy **Italien**

J

jacket **die Jacke (-n) f**
jumper **der Pulli (-s) m**

K

kill **töten**
kiss **küssen (ich habe geküsst)**

L

last **letzte/r/s**
lazy **faul**
leave 1 (a place) **verlassen**
2 (depart) **abfahren**
left **links**
leg **das Bein (-e) n**
like: I like … **ich mag …**
listen to **hören**
litter tray **das Katzenklo n**
live **wohnen**
long **lang**
lose **verlieren (ich habe verloren)**
loud **laut**
lunch **das Mittagessen n**
to have lunch **zu Mittag essen**

M

magazine **die Zeitschrift (-en) f**
mail **die Post f**
mask **die Maske (-n) f**
maths **die Mathe f**
mayor **der Bürgermeister (-) m**
mean **geizig**
milk **die Milch f**
mobile (phone) **das Handy (-s) n**
Monday **Montag**
money **das Geld n**
moody **launisch**
morning **der Morgen m**
mouse **die Maus (Mäuse) f**
mouth **der Mund (Münder) m**
music **die Musik f**
must: I must **ich muss**

N

name **die Name (-n) f**
nerve: it gets on my nerves **es geht mir auf die Nerven**
never **nie**
new **neu**
next **nächste/r/s**
next time **das nächste Mal**
next to **neben**
nice **sympathisch**
no **nein**
nobody **niemand**
noise **der Lärm m**
normally **normalerweise**
nose **die Nase (-n) f**
nothing **nichts**

O

often **oft**
old **alt**
on **auf**
opposite **gegenüber**
over **über**

P

paper **das Papier n**
party **die Party (-s) f**
patient **geduldig**
peas **Erbsen fpl**
pencil **der Bleistift (-e) m**
pet **das Haustier (-e) n**
petrol station **die Tankstelle (-n) f**
piece **das Stück (-e) n**
plane **das Flugzeug (-e) n**
play **spielen**
Portugal **Portugal**
post **die Post f**
potatoes **Kartoffeln fpl**
promise **versprechen**

Q

quiet **ruhig**

R

rail: by rail **mit der Bahn**
rain: it's raining **es regnet**
read **lesen**
red **rot**
ride: to ride a bike **Rad fahren**
right **rechts**
room **das Zimmer (-) n**
rubbish **der Müll m**

S

sad **traurig**
sadness **die Traurigkeit f**
sandwich **das Butterbrot (-e) n**
Saturday **Samstag**
sausage **die Wurst (Würste) f**
school **die Schule (-n) f**
schoolbag **die Schultasche (-n) f**
science **Naturwissenschaften pl**
Scotland **Schottland**
seldom **selten**
self-confident **selbstbewusst**
selfish **selbstsüchtig**
shirt **das Hemd (-en) n**
shoe **der Schuh (-e) m**
shopping: to go shopping **einkaufen gehen**
short **kurz**
shorts **die Shorts pl**
shoulder **die Schulter (-n) f**
shower: to have a shower **duschen**
shy **schüchtern**
sick: I was sick **ich habe gekotzt**
singing **das Singen n**
sister **die Schwester (-n) f**
slim **schlank**
small **klein**
snake **die Schlange (-n) f**
snow: it's snowing **es schneit**
socks **Socken fpl**
sofa **das Sofa (-s) n**
somebody **jemand**
sometimes **manchmal**
spend (time) **verbringen (ich habe verbracht)**
sport **der Sport m**
start **anfangen**
stay **bleiben (ich bin geblieben)**
stomach **der Magen m**
straight: straight hair **glatte Haare**
straight on **geradeaus**
strict **streng**
striped **gestreift**
stupid, silly **doof**
subject **das Fach (Fächer) n**
summer **der Sommer m**
summer holidays **Sommerferien pl**
supermarket **der Supermarkt m**
Sunday **Sonntag**
sunny **sonnig**
sweets **Bonbons npl**
swim **schwimmen (ich habe geschwommen)**
Switzerland **die Schweiz f**

T

table tennis **das Tischtennis n**
tall **groß**
teacher (male) **der Lehrer (-)**
(female) **die Lehrerin (-nen)**
technology **die Technologie f**
textbook **das Schulbuch n**
tennis **das Tennis n**
then **dann**
there is/there are **es gibt**
Thursday **Donnerstag**
tights **die Strumpfhose (-n) f**
to: to Paris **nach Paris**
too **zu**
too much **zu viel**
tooth **die Zahn (Zähne) f**
toothache: I have toothache **ich habe Zahnschmerzen**
tracksuit **der Trainingsanzug m**
traffic **der Verkehr m**
trainers **Sportschuhe mpl**
trip **der Ausflug (Ausflüge) m**
Tuesday **Dienstag**
TV **das Fernsehen n**
TV (set) **der Fernseher (-) m**

U

ugly **hässlich**
under **unter**
underground **die U-Bahn f**
up-to-date **aktuell**
usually **normalerweise**

V

vegetables **Gemüse npl**

W

Wales **Wales**
wall **die Wand (Wände) f**
want to **wollen**
wash (oneself) **(sich) waschen**
watch television **fernsehen**
weather **das Wetter n**
Wednesday **Mittwoch**
week **die Woche (-n) f**
weekend **das Wochenende n**
at the weekend **am Wochenende**
well **gut**
what **was**
where **wo**
where from? **woher?**
where to? **wohin?**
white **weiß**
window **das Fenster (-) n**
windy **windig**
work **arbeiten**
world **die Welt f**

Y

year **das Jahr (-e) n**
yellow **gelb**
yes 1 **ja**
2 (in answer to negative question) **doch**
yesterday **gestern**

Common instructions in *Na klar!*

Im Schulbuch

Ändere die fett gedruckten Wörter!	*Change the words in bold.*
auf Deutsch/Englisch	*in German/English*
Beantworte die Fragen!	*Answer the questions.*
Benutze die Bilder unten!	*Use the pictures below.*
Bring die Sätze in die richtige Reihenfolge!	*Put the sentences in the right order.*
Erfindet Dialoge!	*Make up dialogues.*
Ergänze/Vervollständige die Sätze!	*Complete the sentences.*
Füll die Lücken aus!	*Fill in the gaps.*
Gruppenarbeit.	*Group work.*
Hast du Recht?	*Are you right?*
Hör (noch einmal) zu!	*Listen (again).*
Hör zu und sprich nach!	*Listen and repeat.*
Kopiere die Tabelle und füll sie aus!	*Copy the table and fill it in.*
Lies den Text!	*Read the text.*
Lies mit!	*Read along.*
Mach eine Liste!	*Make a list.*
Mach Notizen!	*Make notes.*
Macht Dialoge!	*Make up conversations.*
Nehmt die Dialoge auf Kassette auf!	*Record the dialogues.*
Ordne den Dialog richtig ein!	*Put the dialogue in the right order.*
Richtig oder falsch?	*True or false?*
Richtig, falsch oder nicht im Text?	*True, false or not in the text?*
Schlag/Such im Wörterbuch nach!	*Look in a dictionary.*
Schreib die Resultate auf!	*Write up the results.*
Schreib einen kurzen Bericht!	*Write a short description.*
Schreib etwa 60 Wörter!	*Write around 60 words.*
Schreib Sätze!	*Write sentences.*
Sieh dir die Bilder an!	*Look at the pictures.*
Stellt Fragen!	*Ask questions.*
Tauscht Rollen!	*Swap roles.*
Übt die Dialoge zusammen!	*Practise the dialogues together.*
Überprüfe!	*Check.*
Wähl die richtige Antwort!	*Choose the correct answer.*
Was ist das?	*What's that?*
Was heißt das auf Deutsch?	*What's that in German?*
Was passt zusammen?	*What matches up?*
Welche Antwort passt?	*Which answer matches up?*
Welche Farbe?	*What colour?*
Welches Bild ist das?	*Which picture is it?*
Wer ist das?	*Who is it?*
Wer spricht?	*Who is speaking?*
Wie heißen sie?	*What are they called?*
Wie ist die richtige Reihenfolge?	*What's the correct order?*
Wie viel(e)?	*How much/many?*

Im Klassenzimmer

Wie bitte?	*Pardon?*
Das verstehe ich nicht.	*I don't understand.*
Langsamer bitte.	*Slower, please.*
Was heißt „Kuli" auf Englisch?	*What is 'Kuli' in English?*
Wie sagt man „*book*" auf Deutsch?	*How do you say 'book' in German?*
Wie schreibt man das?	*How do you spell that?*

die Aktivität	*activity*
die Tabelle	*the table*
alles	*everything*
die Antwort	*answer*
das Beispiel	*example*
die Beschreibung	*description*
das Bild	*picture*
dann	*then*
der Dialog	*conversation*
falsch	*false*
für	*for*
die Klassenarbeit	*test*
die Klassenumfrage	*class survey*
langsam	*slow, slowly*
mit	*with*
nicht	*not*
noch einmal	*once again*
oder	*or*
oft	*often*
Partnerarbeit.	*Pairwork.*
richtig	*right, correct*
der Satz	*sentence*
sehr	*very*
die Vokabeln	*vocabulary*
welche	*which*
wie	*how*
wiederholen	*to repeat*
wo	*where*
die Zusammenfassung	*summary*

Acknowledgements

The authors and publisher would like to thank the following people, without whose support they could not have created *Na klar! 2*:

Elaine Armstrong and Steve King for detailed advice throughout the writing;
Frances Reynolds for editing the materials;
Klaus Martin Höfer (text A, p23); Raumfahrtlexicon des Chemnitzer Schulmodells, www.schulmodell.de/astronomie/raumfahrt/tourismus (text, p 113); www.jetzt.de "JETZT Deutsch lernen", http://www.goethe.de/jetzt/; www.juma.de

Front cover photograph: Michael Schumacher, U.S. Grand Prix 2004, by Michael Kim/Corbis.

David SimsonB-6940Septon(DASPHOTOGB@aol.com) pp 6 (top, bottom), 7, 9, 10-11, 18-19, 25 (e,f,g), 28-29, 30 (left), 37 (2nd from bottom), 47, 51 (bottom), 52 (b-e,h,i), 54 (people, g), 56 (background), 59 (insets, background bottom), 61, 63, 64-65, 66, 69, 70 (a-c, i-p), 77 (bottom), 78, 83, 90, 91 (top, bottom), 96 (d), 99, 104 (people), 106 (top), 110 (bottom), 116, 117, 119, 123, 124, 126, 129, 130, 134; Alamy: Bernd Mellmann p 3 (background), Dynamic Graphics Group / IT Stock Free p 14, archivberlin Fotoagentur GmbH p 24 (b) & p 104 (2nd from top), Comstock Images p 30 (right), POPPERFOTO p 36 (bottom) & p 121 (a), Agence Images p 37 (bottom), David Lyons p 42, Dynamic Graphics Group / Creatas p 44, foybles p 54 (top right), Michael Klinec p 54 bottom left), mediacolor's p 70 (d), Aflo Foto Agency p 77 (middle top), POPPERFOTO p 81, Image Source p 86, Simon Wilkinson p 91 (middle), David R. Frazier Photolibrary, Inc. p 104 (2nd from bottom), Andre Jenny p 110 (a), Cephas Picture Library p 110 (b), ImageGap p 110 (c), p 113 as p 110, Hideo Kurihara p 137 (top left), Bildarchiv Monheim GmbH p 137 (top right); Bananastock E (NT) p 23 (top); Bilderbox.com pp 20, 24 (c,d,h), 29, 46, 52 (a,g), 54 (far left), 70 (h), 95 (inset), 96 (c), 104 (bottom), 107 (top left, bottom right); Bridgeman Art Library/DACS p 37 (top: Paul Klee, Fire, Full Moon, 1933); Martyn Chillmaid p 16; Corbis pp 23 (bottom), 36 (2nd from top), 37 (2nd from top), 41 (right), 48, 53 (f,j), 56 (inset), 96 (a), 105, 106 (middle), 113 (top right), 121 (d), 137 (bottom left, bottom right); Corel 495 (NT) p 70 (f); Corel 550 (NT) p 96 (e); Corel 590 (NT) p 70 (e); Digital Vision EP (NT) p 59 (background top), 104 (top); Getty pp 3 (bottom left, bottom right), 33, 36 (top), 41 (left), 77 (left, bottom right), 113 (top left), 121 (b); www.heidepark.de p 96 (e); Ingram ILV2CD5 (NT) p 70 (g); IPS (International Publishing Services AB) p 68; Isolde Ohlbaum, ohlbaum.de p 36 (2nd from bottom), 121 (c); Photodisc 14B (NT) p 77 (top right); Photodisc 16 (NT) p 82, 133; Photodisc 54B (NT) p 51 (top); Photodisc 71 (NT) p 84; Michael Spencer p 24; travel-ink.co.uk p 107 (top right); Archiv, Verkehrshaus der Schweiz p 106 (bottom); Vital/Jahreszeiten Verlag, Hamburg p 62; Zoo Salzburg p 107 (bottom left).

Recorded by Nordqvist Productions.